The Mystery of the Eucharist and the Economy of Salvation

An Appraisal of Dom Anscar Vonier's Insight into the Eucharist

The Mystery of the Eucharist and the Economy of Salvation

An Appraisal of Dom Anscar Vonier's Insight into the Eucharist

Sudhir Kumar Kujur

2021

The Mystery of the Eucharist and the Economy of Salvation: *An Appraisal of Dom Anscar Vonier's Insight into the Eucharist* - Published by the Indian Society for Promoting Christian Knowledge (ISPCK), Post Box 1585, Kashmere Gate, Delhi-110006.

Online order: http://ispck.org.in/book.php

Also available on amazon.com

ISBN: 978-93-90569-25-0

Laser typeset by

ISPCK, Post Box 1585, 1654, Madarsa Road, Kashmere Gate, Delhi-110006 • *Tel:* 23866323

e-mail: ashish@ispck.org.in • ella@ispck.org.in
website: www.ispck.org.in

Contents

PART I
A Brief Sketch of the Historico-Theological Background of Dom Anscar Vonier's Understanding of the Eucharist

CHAPTER - 1

The Place of the Eucharist in the
Writings of Dom Anscar Vonier

PART II
A Chronological Exposition of Dom Anscar Vonier's Eucharist Theology

CHAPTER - 2

The Early Period: The Traditional Teaching
on Eucharistic Sacrifice in Sacramental Terms

Preface

The study of the mystery of the Eucharist can be approached in various ways from different perspectives with specific motives and goals. For, in every person, born in a Christian family, there is a childhood experience of frequently participating in the celebration of the Mass purely based on an inherited faith of the parents. It does not or hardly make any sense then to the child as his reason is not developed; however, it remains in his subconscious level; at a later stage in life, he recalls something of the past events. Moreover, frequent Catechism classes and instructions in the school acquaint him with the basics of the Catholic faith on sacraments, which the student learns by heart. By now, he knows or expected to learn that the Eucharist is a sacrament, nay one of the seven sacraments of the Catholic Church; that the bread and wine which the priest gives to the faithful during the celebration of the Mass is the Body and Blood of Christ.

Another approach to acquire the knowledge of the Eucharist and grow in one's faith is through the consistent reading of and familiarity with the Scriptures such as the institution narratives of the Synoptic Gospels (Mt.26: 26-29;

Mk.14: 22-25; Lk. 22: 17-19), Pauline notion of the Eucharist (1Cor.10: 16; 1Cor.11: 23-26), John's narration of the discourse on the multiplication of loaves (Ch.6) washing of the disciples' feet (Ch.13) and the Acts of the Apostles (2: 42-46; 20: 7-11). Frequent reading, reflection and meditation on these biblical passages will acquaint one with its proper setting, Jesus' desire and motive for instituting the sacrament of the Eucharist as well as its salvific effect for all mankind.

Yet, another reliable source to grow in the knowledge and wisdom of the Eucharistic mystery is to familiarize oneself with the practices of celebrating the memory of the Lord during the Apostolic period, in the Early Christian traditions, writings of the Fathers of the Church, Apologetics and Doctors of the Church, Papal documents, Catechism of the Catholic Church, historico-theological researches and devotional practices as well as literary outputs of various mystics and authors at different epochs of history to the recent periods.

The present literary work is the result of an in-depth research on the Abbot's insights into the theology of the sacrament of the Eucharist, which are dispersed in his various books and numerous articles. The attempt all through has been to comprehend the author's profound theological and spiritual insights into the sublime mystery of the Eucharist, its existential, Christological, pneumatological, soteriological, ecclesiological and eschatological dimensions and nuances and organize them into a systematic doctrine, and present them in a manner and language within the reach of a common reader with some theological background. Firmly rooted in the Benedictine spirituality and well versed in Scriptures and *Summa Theologiae* of St. Thomas, Dom Vonier perceives the eminent place of the Eucharist in the complexity of the seven sacraments and locates it in the economy of supernatural life. In this process, while re-reading and appreciating his writings in the literary form, a supplementary view point is proposed so as to enhance the Abbot's foresights of the urgent need of a sound Catholic doctrine in the climate of the Church-state and inter-denominational conflict prevalent chifely in the Western world.

Biographical Data of
Dom Anscar Vonier, OSB

[A concise biographical data and some of the determining events of Dom Anscar Vonier's life would provide the reader an initial glimpse of his spiritual and intellectual vitality. It also complements the reader's appreciation for the Abbot's distinctive contribution to the theology of the sacrament of the Eucharist.]

Martin Vonier was born of Catholic German parents at Ringschnait in Württemberg, South Germany, on November 11, 1875. Because of the tense atmosphere caused by anti-Catholic sentiment during the *Kulturkampf,* many German monasteries were closed, and the monks fled abroad. In September 1888, when not yet thirteen years of age, Martin left his home with the intention of joining exiled German monks at Buckfast in Southwest England. He was directed first to go to Beauvais in France to begin classical studies at the academy of the Fathers of the Holy Ghost. In the summer of the following year, Martin arrived at Buckfast where, as a lay student, he continued his studies of the humanities.[1] He deepened his knowledge of Greek and Latin and began to read the Scriptures and the works of St. Thomas in their original form. He also became more aware of the need for sound Catholic apologetics as he reflected on the climate of Church-State conflict in his native land. In effect, his socio-ecclesial background contributed to the spiritual and intellectual growth of Martin Vonier; he acquired a depth of faith, zeal for the Kingdom of God, and fidelity to the magisterium of the Church.

After four years of study, Martin Vonier entered the novitiate on May 28, 1893 and received the religious name Anscar. The period of formation centred on knowledge of Benedictine spirituality and of its basis in Scripture. After pronouncing simple vows on July 2, 1894, Br. Anscar dedicated himself to philosophical and theological studies in which he soon distinguished himself as a forceful exponent of the underlying principles of the sacred sciences.[2] The *Summa Theologiae* of St. Thomas Aquinas and the writings of St. Paul provided him the firm ground on which he was later to base his theology of the Eucharist.

Shortly after his ordination to the priesthood on December 17, 1898, Father Anscar was sent to the Benedictine athenaeum, Sant' Anselmo, in Rome where he attained a doctoral degree in philosophy within a lapse of one year. His thesis *De Infinito*[3] was "characteristic of the temper of his penetrating mind; treating of the Infinite in a long essay filling about a hundred foolscap pages, he subjected to a most critical examination the abstruse problems arising from a consideration of the illimitable and immeasurable".[4] On his return to Buckfast Abbey, Fr. Anscar Vonier was appointed master of the lay students and procurator of the community, offices which he held until 1905. The same year, he was called back to Sant' Anselmo to teach philosophy to Benedictines from diverse continents. In the summer of 1906, his own Abbot, Boniface Natter, requested that Fr. Anscar accompany him on the canonical visitation of a newly established monastery in Argentina. The two of them embarked in Barcelona, but on August 4, the vessel sank after it crashed on submerged rocks. Among those who lost their lives was Abbot Boniface.

Shortly thereafter, Dom Anscar Vonier was elected the second Abbot of Buckfast on September 14, 1906 and remained the head of the large community until his death on December 26, 1938. He dedicated his thirty-two years of abbatial leadership not only to the rebuilding of the Abbey Church, but also to the steady production of numerous theological writings. His successor, Bruno Fehrenbacher, remarks that "the material Church in its splendid simplicity and massive strength is the embodiment of the spiritual building exhibited in the admirable writings of the Abbot; if so, his admitted success as a builder in stone will be a striking proof of the reality and actuality of the Christian faith built up, a more lasting because spiritual edifice, in his books". [5]

Endnotes

[1] "The Abbot's Jubilee," (an appreciation from the community of Buckfast), *BACh*, I, No. 3 (Autumn 1931), p. 142; "Dom Anscar Vonier: A Chronological Summary of Events in his Life," *In Memoriam Abbot Vonier* (1875-1938), (Bristol: Buckfast Abbey Publications by the Burleigh Press, 1939), p. 8.

[2] "The Abbot's Jubilee, "*BACh*, I, No. 3 (Autumn 1931), pp. 142-43.

[3] Anscar Vonier, *De Infinito*, a doctoral thesis in the Faculty of Philosophy (Roma: P. U. Anselmiano, 1900), pp. 1-145; The author does not leave any bibliography; notes are inserted in the text itself.

[4] "Dom Anscar Vonier: A Chronological Summary of Events in his Life," *In Memoriam Abbot Vonier* (1875-1938), (Bristol: Buckfast Abbey Publications by the Burleigh Press, 1939), p. 9.

[5] Bruno Fehrenbacher, "The Works of Abbot Vonier: A Spiritual Edifice," *In Memoriam Abbot Vonier* (1875-1938), (Bristol: Buckfast Abbey Publications by the Burleigh Press, 1939), p. 36.

Introduction

The main interest of this work lies in the marked similarity to contemporary Eucharistic theology, which is to be found in the various writings of Dom Anscar Vonier (1875-1938). It is chiefly based on the Pauline corpus in the New Testament as well as on Thomistic insights found in the *Summa Theologiae*. A Benedictine monk of clear vision accompanied by intellectual energy, Dom Vonier was able to probe deeply into the Catholic tradition and to re-state it for his contemporaries in a forceful and appealing manner. He wrote constantly on matters pertaining to the theological underpinnings of ecclesiology, liturgy, and sacraments, but due to the occasional character of many essays, which demanded his office as the Abbot of Buckfast, was not able to present his thought as a systematic body of doctrine. Therefore, because of Vonier's intellectual and spiritual vitality and possession of a keen historical sense, this work seems to be most justified, since it sets out to arrange the Eucharistic themes dispersed in his multiple books and articles of theological character, and to present them in a chronological and ordered fashion. However, since the work centres mainly on the Eucharistic themes treated in published snd unpublished works of Dom Anscar Vonier, it is clearly beyond its scope to expose at length all of his theological suppositions. In the process of examining one aspect of his thought, however, it will frequently be necessary to refer to his understanding of philosophical anthropology, Christology, pneumatology, and ecclesiology. A constant effort has been made to subordinate the treatment of other important themes such as the many complementary facets of his explanation of the Eucharist as the centre of ecclesial life.

The first part of the work furnishes a succinct theological biography of Dom Anscar Vonier by providing an historico-theological explanation of the influences which formed his basic thought pattern. Relying on the published works of and on Dom Vonier as well as the unpublished documents and the historical data collected from the archives of Buckfast Abbey, England, and various libraries, an enquiry has been made into the place of the Eucharist in his writings. It examines first the way he resolutely considers the Eucharist as the centre of the economy of salvation, that is, as the privileged means by which the *extra nos* of the passion, death and resurrection of Jesus Christ is continually rendered present *in nobis* through the power of the Holy Spirit. Dom Vonier understands that, since the salvific acts of Jesus Christ were carried out in the power of the Holy Spirit, they are universal, and as such will be prolonged in an analogous manner in the spiritual and ethical lives of believers. In other words, God's salvific design for humanity, accomplished in His Son Jesus Christ, continues within history in and through the Church and its sacraments. This is especially evident in the Eucharist which not only symbolizes but also contains the salvific person and self-offering of God Incarnate. Thus, based on the concern of all humanity for salvation, Dom Vonier affirms the objectivity of the Eucharist as God's answer to the need of humanity to experience divine life from within.

After appreciating Dom Vonier's ability to explain the Eucharist in a mode adapted to contemporary Christians, a justification is given of the need to present his thought in a chronological and systematic manner. As it has already been briefly mentioned, although Dom Vonier wrote mostly on themes concerning faith and sacraments, he could not organize them chronologically because of their occasional character and the varying audiences to which they were addressed. Moreover, as the purpose of his publications was to instruct fellow Christians in their faith, he illumined the Eucharist by means of simple as well as profound insights drawn chiefly from St. Paul and St. Thomas. Insofar as Dom Vonier's approach to the Eucharist has been corroborated in the works of later sacramental theologians, he can be considered as one of the most distinguished pioneers of a revitalized theology of symbol.

Part Two succinctly depicts Dom Vonier's understanding of the Eucharistic mystery in three distinct phases: the early period dedicated to restating the traditional teaching on the sacrifice of the Eucharist in sacramental terms; the middle period marked by expounding the Christological and ecclesiological bases of the Eucharistic liturgy; and the late period characterized by understanding the Eucharist as oriented by the Spirit to rendering the life of the glorified

Christ both accessible to Christians and relevant to their ethical and social existence.

The initial chapter considers Dom Vonier's early attempts to interpret the traditional stances of the Church on the sacrament of the Eucharist. While Vonier made insightful observations on the validity of the Eucharistic teaching of St. Thomas Aquinas, the Council of Trent and the Post-Tridentine theologians, he realized that they had to be adapted to the needs of modern Christians. In this intellectual research, the *Summa Theologiae* of St. Thomas offered Dom Vonier a solid foundation for his sacramental theology. St. Thomas' fundamental assertions that Christians have an indispensable psychological need for sacramental signs, and that a Christian sacrament is an ecclesial sign mediating to His followers the salvation won for them by Jesus Christ, caused Dom Vonier to argue that all human persons have an inherent need to relate to the Divine through external sacred signs. Thus, by placing the specific Christian teaching on the necessity of sacraments against the wide horizon of world religions, Dom Vonier anticipated the later missiological concern to relate the Christian sacraments to the universal search for salvation.

Commenting on the Church's teaching on the unity between the unique sacrifice of Jesus Christ on the Cross and the sacramental sacrifice of the altar, Dom Vonier, on the one hand, appreciates its biblical and dynamic structure of thought, and on the other, reacts against the static way it was being articulated in his time. For, its exaggerated stress on immolation aggravated rather than alleviated the controversy between Catholics and Protestants over the Eucharist. Dom

Vonier states that, in the Decree *De Sanctissimo Missae Sacrificio*, the Council of Trent rightly gave primary place to the unique self-immolation of Jesus Christ on Calvary, of which the Eucharist is the true re-presentation. Dom Vonier regrets, however, that neither the Council Fathers nor their followers sufficiently grounded their arguments on scriptural and liturgical sources. The latter means would certainly have enabled them to situate the Eucharist in the economy of redemption obtained by Jesus Christ so as to convince Protestants that the sacrifice of the Mass is not the repetition of the once-and-for-all immolation of Christ on Calvary. The Eucharistic sacrifice is rather its symbolic re-enactment on the altar through which the Church offers the highest worship to God and extends the benefits of the Cross to the faithful.

As one follows Dom Vonier's observations on St. Thomas and the Council of Tent, one recognizes in him a theologian who was open to the then nascent ecumenical concerns. While being faithful to the Church's teaching, Dom Vonier reacted negatively to the various speculative immolation theories of Post-Tridentine theologians who sought to explain the real nature of the sacrifice of Jesus Christ taking place in the Eucharist, but who failed to emphasize its sacramental nature. Dom Vonier concluded that, while those arguments based on a merely symbolic understanding of the concept of immolation were insufficient, an exclusively real understanding of the Eucharistic sacrifice is impossible, because in heaven Christ's Body and Blood are conjoined by virtue of concomitance, and as such they are not subject to any kind of suffering or separation. Thus, Dom Vonier argued that the Eucharist is a sacrament-sacrifice; it symbolizes and re-actualizes the

Body and the Blood of Jesus Christ pierced and poured out on Calvary but does not imply that in his glorified state an actual, physical immolation takes place. Dom Vonier gradually leads one to the understanding that there is a permanent connection between the passion and the resurrection of Jesus Christ so that the Eucharist is the symbolic representation of the paschal mystery.

Dom Anscar Vonier bases his understanding of the Eucharist as the prolonged salvific encounter between Christians and the person and mission of Jesus Christ on Christology, ecclesiology, and liturgy. In assuming flesh, the Son of God initiated a new era in human history: by emptying himself of the fullness of divinity and entering fully into human nature, the Son of God won victory over sin and death in his Body and Blood and established a new and permanent covenant between God and humanity. Dom Vonier further argues that, lest this covenant lose its significance in human history, Jesus Christ instituted symbols by which it could be perpetuated. The sacrament of the Eucharist is unique, however, because it not only symbolizes the salvific act of the redemption-in-person, Jesus Christ, but contains him in the consecrated elements of bread and wine. In this way, the members of his mystical body are conjoined to their head, so that with him they form the *Totus Christus*, and enjoy anew their inheritance as children of the heavenly Father. By means of such considerations, Dom Vonier leads one to understand that, insofar as the Church is the one active celebrant of the Paschal events through its re-actualization of the self-offering of the redemption-in-person, Jesus Christ, for the faithful, it makes the Eucharist. On the other hand, insofar as the

Eucharist conjoins the individual members to Christ, and to one another in charity as one people and enables them with him to render solemn worship to the Father, it makes the Church.

Dom Vonier further understands the Eucharist as signifying and containing the *cause*, the *essence*, and the *goal* of human sanctification. Following the classical pattern, he states that the sacrificial death of Jesus on the Cross is the cause of human sanctification; the salvific grace accomplished because of this historic event is the essence of human sanctification; and the assurance of eternal life because of the redemptive grace operative in Christians is the goal of human sanctification. Therefore, the Passover of Jesus Christ is symbolized and re-actualized in the Eucharistic celebration of the Church, so that the redemptive grace won by him is presently rendered accessible to and operative in the faithful. Since the Eucharist re-presents the sacrifice of the Cross and pre-presents the future glory of the Kingdom, it is at once the commemorative, the demonstrative and the prognostic sign of human sanctification. Thus, Dom Vonier proves to be a liturgist who, in restating in a forceful modern style the traditional teaching on the Eucharist as the symbolic re-enactment of Calvary, attempts to render the Paschal mystery of Christ the basis of the ecclesial and social spirituality of his contemporaries.

The final expository chapter concentrates on Dom Vonier's insight into how the Holy Spirit assures the continued presence of Jesus Christ within history in and through the Eucharistic liturgy of the Church. With his teaching on the epiclesis, Dom Vonier states that the Spirit who at the resurrection saved the life of Jesus Christ from being merely a limited historical event, now renders his existence as the redemption-in-person a permanent historical reality which at the same time transcends time and space, and as such can become accessible to generations of Christians until he comes in glory. In other words, Dom Vonier says that, insofar as the faithful of all times are nourished by the sacramental body and blood of Christ, they are incorporated into one social and transcendent body united to Christ their head. Evidently, the Divine Spirit who at the Eucharist enables the Church to become ever more identical to oneself is the bond of profound and active love between the risen Christ and the baptized of all ages. Insofar as Dom Vonier advocates the unity of many Christians in the one Spirit of the risen Lord, he can be appreciated as a pioneer exponent of the newly discovered relevance of pneumatology in the field of sacramental theology. For example, the invocation of the Holy Spirit on the Eucharistic assembly stimulates Christians to conform their external behaviour to the ethical value of justice and brotherhood preached by Jesus. Through the symbolic re-enacting of the Paschal mystery, the Spirit inculcates in the personal and social life of Christians adherence to the theological virtues of faith, hope and charity. Dom Vonier's observations on the relationship between the Eucharist and the dedicated life of contemporary Christians in society, to prefigure the Kingdom of God, can be appreciated as harbingers of the eschatological themes presently emphasized in sacramental theology.

Part Three of the exposition is dedicated to the evaluative and prognostic synthesis of Dom Vonier's theology of the Eucharist. Thus, it has summarized both his major achievements and some of the open questions raised by his theological approach. As mentioned earlier, Dom Vonier heavily relies on the Pauline, Benedictine and Thomistic intuitions for his Eucharistic theology. His comprehension of the Pauline notion of Christians as members of the Mystical Body of Christ united to their head through the power of the Holy Spirit, symbolized in the sharing of the one bread and the one cup, induced Vonier to link Christology, pneumatology, and ecclesiology. Thus, he re-discovered for his contemporaries the inseparable connection between the sacramental grace and moral action. Furthermore, Dom Vonier considers sacramental symbols as indispensable means of relating Christians to the mysteries of Christ, so that their entire lives become living sacrifices to God, thereby extending the fruits of the Paschal mystery to all humanity until the Lord comes in glory. Dom Vonier's new awareness of the Eucharist as a real symbol is grounded on the classical Thomistic teaching on sacrament. Among many of the significant lines of thought developed by Dom Vonier, liturgical renewal was one of his principal contributions.

After a positive evaluation of Dom Vonier's understanding of sacramental theology culled from his numerous writings, some of the limitations of the author's thought system have been pointed out. For, although his various works contain dogmatically solid and pastorally relevant understanding of the theology of the Eucharist, they lacked a systematic presentation, which affected their widespread impact. Furthermore, because of his training in Thomistic thought, Dom Vonier's dependence on the latter has restricted his sacramental theology, which *"per se"* strove to be more existential and dynamic through primary reliance on Scripture. St. Augustine's notion of sacred signs in general, and of the Eucharist in particular, could have been a valuable source to expand his thought pattern on sacramental theology. Similarly, while Dom Vonier's familiarity with the Pauline corpus of the New Testament is noteworthy, the Eucharistic themes of the Synoptic and Johannine theology would have significantly enhanced his treatment of the sacrament. Likewise, although Dom Vonier comprehended the finality of the Eucharist to be the definitive union of life with God when Christ comes in glory, the *not yet* eschatological aspect of the Eucharist lacks sufficient emphasis, which is found both in the Pauline corpus and the theological writings of St. Irenaeus of Lyons. Dom Vonier has rightly accentuated the *realized* eschatology underlying the Eucharistic mystery, but the insufficient emphasis on its *to-be-realized* aspect needs to be complemented by exposing the way Irenaeus links the Eucharist to the first creation, to the Paschal mystery as the initial glorification of the flesh, to the Church as its focal point, and to the final resurrection of the body as the goal of creation.

By means of such observations, the prognostic section of the work is concluded with a genuine concern to preserve the significant contribution of Dom Anscar Vonier to the theology of the Eucharist in such a way that its inherent limitations are corrected and its lasting value for contemporary theologians is enhanced.

PART I

A Brief Sketch of the Historico-Theological Background of Dom Anscar Vonier's Understanding of the Eucharist

CHAPTER - 1

The Place of the Eucharist in the Writings of Dom Anscar Vonier

Dom Vonier subjected himself to the arduous discipline of the pen in order to meet the requests of his hearers for written transcriptions of his thoughts as well as to inspire them to find spiritual and moral sustenance for their life.[1] Since the publication of *The Human Soul* [2] in 1913, other literary works followed in rapid succession, and a new book of theological character became almost an annual feature for the next twenty-five years. Here, this section by no means intends to introduce the reader to all the insights found in Dom Vonier's writings on the Eucharist. Rather, it concentrates on exposing some of the underlying themes which the Abbot treated in different books and articles. Dom Vonier situated the Eucharist in the economy of supernatural life as its most appropriate setting. In the light of the claim of the Catholic Church that its spiritual inheritance is rooted in the past, he visualized the objectivity of the economy of the supernatural life, that is, as the divinely guided process which takes place *nos extra* and is meant to have a transformative effect *in nobis*. Dom Vonier understands God's self-revelation to human beings in the Incarnation, death and resurrection of Jesus Christ, the objective centre of salvation, as establishing his new and everlasting covenant with them. The salvific acts of Christ are universal in the truest sense because what the Holy Spirit uniquely accomplished in him are being achieved in an analogous manner in his followers. Christianity is the instrument by which the salvific and sanctifying events of the supernatural order accomplished in the past are repeatedly bequeathed to generations of believers through the words and signs of the authoritative and dynamic community called the Church. Eucharist as the primary sacrament of God is grounded in the salvific person and actions of Jesus Christ, containing in the form of a sacrificial banquet these very same realities.

Dom Vonier envisions the specific manner in which the objective economy of salvation has diverse implications for humanity, that is, how it exerts its power *in nobis*. He does this by means of a decided preference for an existential rather than objectified comprehension of symbol. Through such meaningful symbols the inherited past actions of Jesus are continually made accessible to his followers. Dom Vonier asserts that the sacramental signs of the Church, carried out in the power of the Holy Spirit, enable Christians to participate in the supernatural life they have inherited from Christ. In the light of this consideration, Dom Vonier accounts for the efficacy of symbols in bringing about the sanctifications of human persons, in particular, it deepens the soteriological setting in which he places the sacrament of the Eucharist.

The final section justifies the need of a chronological and ordered presentation of Dom Vonier's theology of the Eucharist. Such an analysis of his works would be worthwhile since, although "they deal with most of the contents of the faith, their author never attempted to develop them into a systematic body of doctrine".[3] His Eucharistic theology consistently reflects the faith of the early Church and of medieval Catholicism. In this sense, the insights of Dom Vonier are traditional; yet his ability to present them in a mode adapted to the mentality of his contemporaries provides the basis of their intellectual vitality. Therefore, Dom Vonier is considered as a theologian who integrated themes derived from the early Church, the middle Ages, and the Counter-Reformation so as to render them meaningful for the twentieth-century audience. Insofar as later Church documents such as *Mystici Corporis* (1943), *Mediator Dei* (1947), *Sacrosanctum Concilium* (1963) and *Lumen Gentium* (1964) corroborate Vonier's approach to the Eucharist, he can be appreciated as one of their most distinguished forerunners.

Finally, a preview of the three major periods of Dom Vonier's theological production is offered into which his treatment of the Eucharist will be divided in the subsequent expository parts.

1. The Economy of the Supernatural Life as the Setting for the Eucharist

In the article, "The Worth of the Supernatural,"[4] Dom Vonier reaffirms one of the most persistent claims of the Catholic

Church: its corporate sanctity consists of past deeds of the supernatural order. The doctrines of Christianity are expressions of its vital connection to the unique events of salvation history:

> Catholicism.... lives essentially on the past; every fresh moment of Catholic history is the fringe of that past; it is a remembrance of all the things that have gone before; it is a treasuring up of values which are not so much of our own making as of the making of those whose inheritors we are. Catholicism is essentially a great inheritance, and we are most fervent in our religion then when we live by the inheritance which has come to us. We are rich in the riches of Christ who died on the Cross, and whose testament was made valid in his death... We are rich through the Apostles, through the Martyrs of the past, and if there is for the Church an actual existence, this existence again is great and real because we do what was done by our Fathers, by the Apostles, by Christ himself.[5]

A careful analysis of the passage reveals the depth of Dom Vonier's insight into the relation between the past, the actual, and the future dimensions of Christianity. As early as the Apostolic Age, Christians understood the privileged place of the Son of God in the divine plan for human salvation because they were already nurtured in a monotheistic faith in God which was so powerful: "Their conversion of necessity implied a recall to the mystery of Christ, a grasp of the new and wonderful fact that God was in Christ reconciling the world to Himself".[6] Further, the acceptance of the Christian faith by the non-Jews entailed a double aspect of conversion... first, to the living and true God of Israel and then to Christ Jesus whom He raised up from the dead (1 Thess.1: 9-14). Dom Vonier states that, if the Christian faith were not a divine gift, the catechumens "should have been found incapable of sustaining the double vision of God and of Christ".[7]

The process of intellectual and moral conversion was clearly viewed by Dom Vonier in pneumatological terms: "To make Christ understood of such men was the first and the greatest achievement of the Spirit of Truth when he came down upon Jerusalem on the day of Pentecost; to understand Christ was the miracle of grace wrought in the soul of that fanatic protagonist of God, Saul of Tarsus".[8] Thus, Dom Vonier emphasizes that the spiritual tenor of apostolic Christianity was founded on the conviction that the mystery of Christ was authentically revealed to the baptized by the Holy Spirit. No doubt, then, that the first generations of Christians possessed the assurance that their participation in the person and mission of Christ was guaranteed by the Holy Spirit. When the Apostles elected seven men to perform the functions of diaconal charity among the brethren, they made the choice conditional upon the possession of certain virtues- men of good reputation, and full of the Holy Spirit and wisdom (Acts 6: 3). Dom Vonier notes the way the *Acts of the Apostles* designate the Holy Spirit as the distinctive element in the sanctity of Christians:

> The Spirit which came down at Pentecost – and of this Spirit the Acts speak uniformly – has become the adorning note of the faithful Christian, visible unto all, and that to such a point that men can be classed according to the degree in which they possess the Holy Spirit. Quite clearly the early Christians found it natural to speak of the Holy Spirit as one of the most active principles of Christian holiness.[9]

The descent of the Holy Spirit marks a new presence and activity of God in human history. Always present to the world from the beginning of its creation, the Holy Spirit was sent on the day of Pentecost by the risen Lord from the Father so as to make known the fundamental sanctity of renewed humanity. From that point on, the Holy Spirit has been active in the baptized, strengthening their faith both in the mercy of the Father and in the redemptive work of Christ.

Furthermore, possessed by the Holy Spirit, Christians behaved in an authentically moral way, which was meant to manifest that their deeds were of the supernatural character:

> The past deeds on which the spiritual structure of Christianity stands are all of them deeds of the supernatural order; they are deeds done in the Holy Ghost; they are fruits of divine grace; they are deeds truly done in God, partaking of the perfection of God; their worth is greater than any temporal worth; they are more than brave deeds which shine for one moment and then pass away; they are truly endowed with an element of everlastingness.[10]

Thus, Dom Vonier states that the reliance of Christianity on the past is to be understood in the light of a much higher truth- the worth of the supernatural, "the state into which the created and finite spiritual being is raised by a direct act of God; such an act is due to His "excessive liberality".[11] Becoming a Christian is essentially a free gift of the Father to the created beings, which is carried out in the Son through the power of the Holy Spirit. In this sense, all the past deeds of the supernatural order continue in history, and hence are unchanged and eternal.

By means of this consideration, Abbot Vonier affirms that in Christianity "there is really no relying on the past as a mere past",[12] for faith relies on Christ's merits which are of the supernatural order:

> In every one of those acts the Son of God was moved by the Holy Ghost, every one of those acts was the act, not of man only, but of God, and because the very acts of God they were supernatural, and their worth is truly inexhaustible. They are, in a way, above

time and space as far as their moral worth is concerned; they are, in the truest sense, things of eternity. The external doing is indeed a thing of time; it takes place in a definite point of history; but their spiritual worth exceeds all time. This is why the merits of Christ are applied to our souls wherever we are, however distant we may be, according to the measurements of human time, from Christ's mortal career.[13]

This passage recapitulates Dom Vonier's comprehension of the supernatural worth of Christ's salvific acts which were guided by the divine power of the Holy Spirit. All the earthly deeds of the Lord were performed entirely under the inspiration of the Third Person of the Trinity, and as such, although historically circumscribed in one sense, transcend time and space in another: "His mysteries are secrets brought down from heaven, they are supernatural in the truest sense because they come from the very heart of God and meet, not the temporal needs of man, but the everlasting needs of the human race".[14] In a similar manner, Dom Vonier attributes to all of Christ's words a supernatural character: "His preaching is of things which are unchanging; His doctrines are eternally true".[15]

As Christianity is necessarily the living inheritance of the past, its doctrines express the divine concern for the human race throughout the history of salvation. In turn, the object of the teaching of the Church is the same as that of the Incarnate Son of God. By depicting the preaching and the mission of Christianity in terms analogous to the activities of Christ, Dom Vonier locates the true setting not only of the doctrine but also of the sacramental life of the Church in the economy of divine salvation. Thus, the Church's sacramental acts, carried out here on earth, are truly "breathings of the Spirit who proceeds from the Father and the Son in the unchanging light of eternity.[16] Dom Vonier observes then that through strong faith in the economy of the supernatural order as continued in the sacramental acts of the Church, Catholicism has preserved the truth that the Kingdom of God is here on earth. In other words, by means of visualizing the sacraments against the horizon of the history of salvation, generations of Christians lived those practices of old in their daily life.

In order to clarify his reflection on this particular point, Dom Vonier culls an example from his article, "St. Martin of Tours,"[17] regarding the manner in which this fourth century bishop maintained faith in the God Incarnate, which was completely in accord with the apostolic life of the first century; for this reason, Christianity was simply uninterrupted communion with his Divine Person. Thus, Dom Vonier affirms that Christianity is the visible manifestation of living faith in Christ, to which the apostles, numerous saints and martyrs attested. Similarly, Dom Vonier observes how the content of faith were explained in the patristic era and in the Middle Ages in terms well-defined and accessible to the people so that they could understand the ultimate ground of the values they put into practice.

Similarly, Dom Vonier's aim in writing *A Key to the Doctrine of the Eucharist* (1925) was to enable the faithful of his time to discover the supernatural origin of the Eucharist by setting it within the economy of salvation. In other words, the Abbot explained how the Eucharistic mystery was to be inserted in the salvific design of God for human race, the culminating point of which is the Incarnation, death and resurrection of His Son, Jesus Christ. Indeed, the Word of God was always operative in the history from the outset of creation. But the same Word gained a new existence through the Incarnation, or the assumption of the concrete humanity of Jesus of Nazareth. The Word entered the conditions of history, that is, into the sinful situation in which humanity found itself. Thus, the Incarnation is the external manifestation of the Divine Word of God in history. For this reason, Dom Vonier states that the Son of God made flesh is "the sacrament *par excellence*, the *magnum sacramentum*, the invisible made visible".[18] The saving encounter between God and His people is made tangible and effective in and through the humanity of Jesus. In other words, the human nature of Jesus Christ is the sacramental symbol of the unique presence and activity of God among His people. In this sense, then, Christ's humanity is the sacrament of the activity of God in historical, even perceptible form.

Now, since the salvific activities of Jesus of Nazareth were performed by a divine person, they have a supernatural value which, according to the eternal design of God, means that they possess forever a sacramental dignity of the highest spiritual order. Although Christ's preaching and acting might appear, externally, quite ordinary, they are truly supernatural on account of their divine origin, and demonstrate universal divine concern for the human race. In every one of the words and events of Christ it is the divine Logos who acts, of all the supernatural acts of Jesus Christ, his death on the Cross is the greatest, because God established a new and everlasting covenant with His people in the broken Body and the poured out Blood of His Son.

Thus, Dom Vonier insists that the sacrificial death of Jesus Christ on Calvary is the supreme historical expression of God's unconditional love for the world, a visible sign of the permanent relationship God intended to form with the whole human race:

> The victory of God over evil has been achieved through this human, historic fact that the Son of God shed his Blood on the Cross: His Blood was most truly the instrument of that marvellous piece of divine power and divine wisdom. So, wherever the Blood of Christ is, there is also the covenant in all its reality and vitality. To have the Blood of Christ is to have full possession of the covenant, or, as St. Paul puts it: "Where there is death the testament is of force". Man succeeds to all the wealth of the covenant through the death of Christ, which is essentially effusion of Blood.[19]

This passage, grounded on the Pauline theology of redemption, affirms the permanence and gratuity of the new covenant established through the offering of Christ's Body and Blood. In the physical death of His Son, God's salvific plan for humanity was accomplished in "complete independence of man's merit, of time and of evolution".[20] Viewed from this perspective, the sacrificial acts of Jesus Christ, performed in time and history, are truly supernatural; they are the deeds of the human nature fully united to the Second Person of the Trinity. As such, the new covenant is unchanging and eternal; it is "not a thing for the few, but a thing for the many".[21]

Dom Vonier further states that, although salvation was accomplished once-and-for-all through the physical death of the Son of God on the Cross, Jesus Christ instituted the sacramental signs consisting of edible and potable elements expressive of the unique reality of his salvific death.[22] Jesus Christ's behaviour in the Cenacle constitutes the "institution of a most definite kind, with a material side and an external expression", such that Christians could speak of it as a gratuitous monument that has been preserved for ages.[23]

Dom Vonier, then, locates the Eucharist in the personality itself of Christ:

> Christ is essentially and personally Eucharistic, in the sense that if any mind were able to understand that most mysterious of all personalities – the Incarnate God – there would be found in him such features of life and power and reality as would make him most perfectly fitted to be the Eucharist in its double aspect of sacrifice and food. The Incarnation, the conception in a Virgin's womb, the kind of body and soul he has, the sort of life he led on earth, the manner of his death and resurrection; these all prepare him to be the ideal Eucharist of the Christian people.[24]

Through this insight into the Eucharistic dimension of Christ's personality, Dom Vonier is able to understand the mystery which occurs on the Christian altar: "Christ's passion and death are such as to be contained in reality in the bread that is broken and in the cup that is drunk at the Eucharistic banquet."[25] In other words, Christ's Eucharistic death on the Cross is re-presentable in and through the sacramental sacrifice of the altar.

Moreover, the institution of the Eucharist arose from Christ's ardent desire to eat the Pasch with his Apostles for the last time until its fulfilment in the Kingdom of God. Abbot Vonier therefore states that the Eucharistic mystery in the Church in its double aspect of sacrifice and food is this anticipated fulfilment. Thus, the Church's faith in the Eucharistic mystery is rooted in the life, death and resurrection of Christ, as these salvific events are symbolically re-enacted on the altar. Without affirming that the Christ-reality is present sacramentally on the altar, the Church cannot account for how the Apostles and martyrs lived the values of Christ in perfect accordance with his commands. Indeed, even today the Church lives them through its "sacramental" activities in the world which, by their very nature, are extensions of the mystery of Christ present in the Eucharist.

It is interesting to note here that Dom Vonier challenges two classes of thinkers; the first consists of those who tend to make the remembrance of the past reality of the Cross a mere mental act; the second is made up of those who want a Christianity whose main doctrines are grounded not in the past but in the present or the future. In the article, "The Psychological Import of the Catholic Faith in the Eucharist,"[26] Dom Vonier observes that the opposition to the fact that the Catholic faith relies on the past deeds of Christ arises from two false philosophies which are diametrically opposed to each other. Those thinkers who hold the first principle believe in the objectivity of the supernatural order, but they do not grasp its perpetual efficacy; it suffices for them that the past acts of the supernatural order are accessible through the mental act of recalling them with faith, which in turn, allows them to benefit fully from the salvation offered by God in Jesus Christ. The followers of the second principle manifest incapacity to believe in the objective worth of the supernatural. Advocates of this position say that "there is far too much of the past in our religious system; let us come to the present, let us look into the future"; they seem to want "the replacement of the old historic Christ, of the old historic Church by new forces".[27]

In opposition to these principles, Dom Vonier emphatically declares that "Christian doctrines are essentially old; nothing can be added unto them; the course of centuries cannot improve them".[28] This is true for the simple reason that they pertain to the supernatural divine order which is unchanging and eternal. On the other hand, Dom Vonier asserts that "the Church is the natural friend of the immense army of workers in the fields of all human interests"; this is especially true of "those movements which start from the assumption that much infinitely much, has to be done before mankind enters into its inheritance".[29] Viewed from this perspective, the sacraments, and in particular the Eucharist can be understood as the means by which the Church makes a past reality a present one, and thereby anticipates the future glory of humanity. Thus, while holding the objective truth of the past realities, Dom Vonier expresses his preference to accentuate their dynamic presence today so that Christians can truly speak to the world of "the living Christ" and the "living Church".[30]

2. The Preference for an Existential Understanding of Sacramental Symbols

An old theological dictum, *Sacramenta sunt propter homines* introduces one to Dom Vonier's understanding of the existential nature of sacramental symbols. This means that, in the order of supernatural grace, the sacraments exist for the glory of God and the salvation of man. Christian sacraments are divine realities put at the disposal of the Church so as to render present and effective the salvific grace of God the Father obtained through the words and actions of Jesus Christ in the power of the Holy Spirit. Relying on St. Thomas' understanding of Christian sacraments, Dom Vonier states that the latter were instituted by Jesus Christ for the explicit purpose of symbolizing the cause, essence and goal of human sanctification.[31] Evidently, in the sacramental dispensation of the Church the cause of sanctification is the death and resurrection of Jesus Christ; its essence is the grace brought about in the life of the faithful; the goal of sanctification is the attainment of eternal life.[32] This representative significance of the past, the present and the future is common to all the seven sacraments of the Church; they all belong to the divine cult, since each represents a definite aspect of the economy of salvation.

However, the Eucharist constitutes the perfect cult of God, because it symbolizes and contains the sacrificial offering of himself to God the Father by which Jesus Christ established the New Covenant:

> The Eucharist is essentially a gift to the Church, not only of Christ, but of the sacrifice of Christ, so that the Church herself has her sacrifice; nay, every Christian has his sacrifice. To participate in Christ's great sacrifice on the Cross in a merely utilitarian mode by receiving the benefit of such a sacrifice is only one half of the Christian religion. The full Christian religion is this, that the very sacrifice is put into our hands, so that we too, have a sacrifice, and we act as men have acted at all times when they walked before God in cleanness of faith and simplicity of heart; we offer to God a sacrifice of sweet odour.[33]

Thus, the Eucharist, when viewed from the perspective of its power of representation, is the sacramental re-presentation of the physical immolation of Jesus Christ on Calvary. On the basis of this understanding, Dom Vonier states that, unlike the actual death of Jesus Christ which caused the redemption of the whole world, the Eucharistic sacrifice is sacramental in nature. It is essentially the gratuitous gift from God to the Church, which makes accessible to each of its members a visible re-presentation of the sacrifice of Jesus, the greatest manner to glorify God. By employing natural signs of bread and wine, the Church attests that its symbolic acts participate in the symbolic self-immolation made in the Cenacle by Christ to the Father and in the real physical fulfilment of the signs on Golgotha.

Aware of the symbolic power of the Eucharistic elements, Dom Vonier declares that "a false, hypocritical reluctance to enter into communion with the things of the natural order, besides leading to a most disastrous spiritual pride, takes it for granted that nature is not God's creation, that there is a chasm between Christ and the natural universe".[34] However, Dom Vonier is not content merely to state that the external elements are useful to human beings' spiritual life or that there is an objective reality in which the symbols of the Church participate; rather he insists that the symbolism of external realities is already half the life of the Church and that she possesses unending power so as to give testimony to the unseen through everything nature can provide.[35] The history of Christianity, from the Apostolic age down through the centuries, can be understood only by recognizing the indispensable role of symbolism in rendering the inherited past deeds of the supernatural order meaningful and accessible to the believers:

> The supremest instances of symbolism are, as we all know, the manifestation of the Spirit Himself, of the Third Person of the Trinity, who appears either as a Dove or as a Flame. We adore the Dove and we adore the Fire in the sense that Divinity showed itself as Dove and Fire. The Lamb is also for us a divine Person, the Word Incarnate. We adore the Lamb because we adore the Son of God who most persistently is called the Lamb by every inspired author of the New Testament.[36]

Assuming the divinity of the Holy Spirit and the Word Incarnate in their objectivity, Dom Vonier accentuates the manner in which their revelation in history is understood by human beings' use of symbols in terms of Dove, Fire and Lamb. Dom Vonier concludes that there is hardly any object in the universe, which could not be made a symbol of the Godhead by Christians. In fact, Dom Vonier regards the importance of symbols as a guarantee that Christians will not forget that Jesus Christ is himself an external symbol of the Word of God.:

> It is certainly a fact that in the Catholic Church, where such symbols are most numerous and most constant, there has been preserved the full faith in Christ's Divinity, whereas where men have pretended to approach Christ directly, where contemptuously they have rejected all the external signs of religion, Christ has become nothing more than a superior human being.[37]

It is evident, that Dom Vonier cautions against the weakening of the Christological statements that would follow, if people failed to understand how symbols are employed to express authentic faith in the divinity of Jesus Christ. For, those who repudiate the use of symbols seem to lower their view of Christ by reducing divine Person to the human nature, because they find it impossible to conceive him as participating in the glory of the eternal Son. Likewise, once having rejected the divine signs of religion, Jesus Christ can easily become a virtuous human being like many others.

Dom Vonier assesses the earthly life of Jesus Christ from two different perspectives, and thereby he accentuates the signifying power of his human nature. Because of their profound sacramental sense, Christ's human words and acts, motivated by the Holy Spirit, have become the Church's infinite treasure of sanctity. As divinely accomplished, the salvific words and acts of Jesus Christ become "Christ-signs" to Christians and relate them to the "Christ-Person".[38] In other words, in and through the sacramental humanity of Jesus Christ, believers encounter the Son of God who redeemed the whole human race.

Moreover, by instituting the Eucharist by means of the finite rites and prayers of the Jewish Pasch, Jesus Christ gave himself to the Church as the redemption fulfilled. The Mass is thus the most apt means of keeping his *memoria* until he comes again in glory:

> The greatest act of religion, the Catholic Mass, what is it but an accumulation of symbols signifying the hidden mystery of the Redemption. We know, of course, that the Symbol of symbols, the Eucharistic Elements contain the divine Reality which is symbolized. But externally to the eye the Eucharistic Element is a symbol. To kiss a crucifix is a small act, yet the spiritual difference between two men, the one who kisses his crucifix and the other who refuses to do so, is truly abysmal. The symbol divides the world into the children of darkness and the children of light.[39]

Here, Dom Vonier states how external signs of the Mass justify the claim that the Eucharist re-presents the salvific deeds of Jesus Christ. Even though the consecrated bread and wine both symbolize and contain the Body and the Blood of Christ, their chemical or physical nature does not change, but only their essence so that they might remain effective symbols. However, in the context of the sacrifice of the Mass, these signs render present on the altar a true icon of Jesus Christ's unique physical immolation on the Cross. In other words, the salvific grace of the crucified and risen Christ is operative in the Church through its offering of the symbols bread and wine which have been consecrated. Further, the consuming of the consecrated elements provides the believers true entry into the unity and peace of Christ's glorious life.

In another passage, Dom Vonier remarks that the external symbols on the altar enable Christians to "treasure every one of his words and gestures, every act of his life, every detail of his death".[40] The spiritual effects of the power of signification aids the baptized to be better disposed to celebrate the Eucharist in a genuine way as the highest worship they can give to God. As a Benedictine, Dom Vonier insists on the necessity of comprehending the various Christ-signs employed in the Eucharistic liturgy. The salutation of the assembly with welcoming gestures, the readings from Scripture, the gift-offerings, the multiplied signs of the Cross over the elements, the words of consecration, the eating and the drinking of the sacrificial Bread and Wine, and the final benediction, unmistakably signify the presence on the altar of Jesus Christ who, through the power of the Holy Spirit, offered himself to the Father once-for-all on Calvary.[41]

Because of these considerations, Dom Vonier points out the moral and social significance of the Eucharist for the life of Christians. As this sacrament effects what it signifies, the union of all in the Body and Blood of Christ, the faithful become one at the rite of communion and are urged to extend this unity into society after the liturgy. Dom Vonier affirms that the union bestowed on the communicants through Eucharistic grace profoundly influences their character and behaviour to the point of transforming them into Eucharistic beings.[42]

This insight leads Dom Vonier to the conclusion that Christianity itself can be designated as Eucharistic way of being and acting: "The Christian has not only faith in the mystery of the Eucharist; he has a temperament, a character that makes him a member of that infinitely vast mystery, the sacramental state of the Son of God. How very different from the Christianity that we know would be a Christianity that was not Eucharistic".[43]

Thus, Abbot Vonier attributes the distinctive psychology of Christians to their reception of the Eucharistic bread and wine. They essentially live in or in virtue of the Son of God who offered himself for them on the Cross. Their incorporation into the Body and Blood of Christ fills their thought as they approach the altar, although the realities before their bodily eyes are natural elements of bread and wine. The sincerity with which Christians eat and drink the consecrated elements renders more credible their true incorporation in the mystical Body of Christ.

For Dom Vonier, union with Christ the Head and with the members of his mystical Body is the specific note of Eucharistic grace, as distinct from the supernatural graces bestowed on human beings through other means. Eucharistic grace raises Christians to such power and excellence that they are true companions of the Lord, having eaten and drunk with him.[44] In effect, they are as fully integrated into Christ's life as is possible before his second advent. Evidently, Dom Vonier attempts to imagine the fate of Christianity if it were not Eucharistic, that is, if it were not nourished and animated by the sacramental Body and Blood of Christ. In sharp contrast to authentically Eucharistic Christians, they would be like the infidels mentioned by St. Paul, who sacrifice to demons and partake of their table (1 Cor.10: 20-22). On the other hand, Christians who partake of the table of the Lord are his true companions and are united among themselves as a Eucharistic community bound by charity. Thus, they experience love and peace, and practice forgiveness and justice. Although the faithful may come from different social or cultural backgrounds, in virtue of Eucharistic grace, they are new creatures in Christ: "Such a perfect brotherhood, such a complete community of blood exists between Christians that racial differences, however, legitimate, are in no danger of becoming excessive".[45] In effect, the adherence to these human and Christian virtues, signify visibly the invisible inauguration of the Kingdom of God definitively established by Jesus Christ.

Dom Vonier reminds his readers that the first Christians, who gathered to keep the memory of the Lord, also shared their temporal goods with one another. This Christian generosity has been transmitted to generations of the followers of Jesus Christ, who eat the one Bread and share the same Cup. In this sense, the whole Eucharistic spirit is of great charity among the members of Christ. Furthermore, in explaining this truth in his article, "*Vinculum Charitatis*,"[46] Dom Vonier adds that charity is the behaviour of those believers who are admitted to the very table of God as His own children. Evidently, Dom Vonier accentuates the specific deeds of charity performed by the Eucharistic community of Christians, thereby distinguishing the social value of such corporate acts from that of individually undertaken ones. The charity which springs from the Eucharistic mystery is more universal in its scope and more credible regarding its public efficacy.

Dom Vonier adjoins the insight that the Eucharist is the origin of a whole new life for the Christian both subjectively and objectively. Evidently, the Abbot implies that a transformation takes place in the souls of Christians by the power of the Eucharist, because of which their outlook on the exterior world becomes more keen and mystical at the same time: "The '*Christianus Eucharisticus*' moves in a world of his own, has an atmosphere of his own, has a Presence of his own. As he goes about among his fellow men, as he mixes with the crowds, the taste of the mystery is in his mouth, the aroma of the Presence envelops him".[47] Such is the moral power of Eucharistic grace that it transforms Christians' entire attitude and behaviour, thereby making them share one mind and heart with Christ. In and through their activities, they give witness to the living presence of the Lord in this world and to his on-going mission on its behalf.

On the basis of the analysis of Dom Vonier's understanding of the Eucharist as essentially a divine gift to the Church for the spiritual and moral nourishment of its members, a justification has been proposed for his existential approach to the meaning of symbols. This has been shown by examining the Abbot's preference for a dynamic understanding of symbols which speak forcefully to human beings of divine things in a visible and tangible manner. Well acquainted with the thoughts of St. Paul and St Thomas Aquinas, Dom Vonier accentuates the truth that through sacred signs the faithful realize their distinctive existence as Eucharistic beings united to the crucified and glorified Jesus. Dom Vonier regards this transformation of Christians' souls as Eucharistic grace which influences their consciousness and their behaviour in relation to other human beings.

3. Towards a Chronological and Systematic Presentation of Dom Vonier's Eucharistic Theology

As a tribute to Dom Vonier's twenty-fifth anniversary as Abbot, the Jubilee edition of the *Buckfast Abbey Chronicle* (1931) classified his literary works according to how they corresponded to the intellectual capacity of readers to grasp certain fundamental truths of philosophy and theology. Thus, *The Human Soul* (1913), *The Personality of Christ* (1914), *The Christian Mind* (1920) and *A Key to the Doctrine of the Eucharist* (1925) were listed among the books which demand even by the expert philosopher and theologian solid preparation and hard concentration to grasp their basic truths.[48] Other works, such as *Death and Judgement* (1930), *The Angels* (1928), *The Life of the World to Come* (1926) and *The Art of Christ* (1926), were listed under an intermediary class because of their more direct literary style. Yet two other books, *The Divine Motherhood* (1921) and *The New and Eternal Covenant* (1930), were placed under either of the above mentioned categories.[49]

Aware of the inadequacy of such classifications, Bruno Fehrenbacher suggested a means to schematize fourteen of the Abbot's books so as to show the theological inter-connection among them.[50] The attempt here has been to include also other theological writings of Dom Vonier which, though published in various lesser known periodicals, are linked to his major works by their similar perspectives and purpose. Dom Vonier repeatedly argues that an innate spiritual power exists in every human person, which, transcending time and space, is able to border on infinity.

Thus, in his first book, *The Human Soul*, Dom Anscar Vonier enquires into the nature of this spiritual power which necessarily depends on the human body for its actualization. In explicitating the Christian doctrine on the human soul, he accentuates that its passive nature serves to highlight its relation to the body:

> The soul is neither conscious nor unconscious by itself; it is neither active nor inactive by itself; it is simply a principle of elevation to the bodily organism and to the activities of the bodily organism. It has no consciousness, peculiar to itself distinct from that of the whole human compound.[51]

Dom Vonier thus states that the soul, as the spiritual principle of human beings, elevates their existence to the point that they are open to God's self-revelation. The consequence of such openness is described in *The Personality of Christ*, which presents the God-Made-Man as a living sign of the salvation of humanity. By contemplating the earthly activities of Jesus, human beings can relate themselves spiritually to the Lord of their salvation, a theme also treated in *Christ the King of Glory*. Furthermore, to render the mystery of the Incarnation more comprehensible to contemporary persons, Dom Vonier traces the effects in Mary of the definitive presence of the Word of God in human history. Therefore, *The Divine Motherhood* was meant to illumine the sublimity between the experience of Mary and that of all believers in Church.

In *The Victory of Christ*, Dom Vonier exposed the manner in which the Son of God, by offering his Body to the Father, triumphed over human bondage to sin and death, and thereby redeemed the whole world from within. Thus, between God and humanity, there has been established a new and permanent relationship the characteristic features of which are depicted in *The New and Eternal Covenant*:

> There is a growing literature... concerning the respective importance in Christianity of the elements which are called "God-ward" and "Man-ward" ... This book is written to emphasize the "God-ward" side of Catholicism and as a consequence to enhance the institutional aspects of our holy faith.[52]

Evidently, the definitive victory of Christ initiated a new relationship, which is of divine institution between God and humanity. It follows that the same divine origin must be attributed to the external symbol by which Jesus Christ intended to signify the salvific and sanctifying dimension of his life and death. In turn, the Church participates in the redemptive person and mission of Jesus by enacting sacramental signs which by their very nature belong to the supernatural order.

Similarly, Dom Vonier's purpose in writing *A Key to the Doctrine of the Eucharist* is to locate the Eucharistic mystery in the sacramental character of the economy of salvation. In the Eucharistic sign of bread and wine, the definite redemptive act of Jesus Christ is sacramentally re-presented on the altar. The physical sacrifice of the Body and Blood of Christ on the Cross is, therefore, not repeated but rendered perpetually efficacious. Thus, the Eucharistic sacrifice for Dom Vonier is essentially a symbol-sacrifice, a visible manifestation commemorating through an ecclesial sign the definitive victory of Jesus Christ. By viewing the Eucharist as a sacramental celebration of the Paschal mystery, Dom Vonier was a forerunner of the late theologians who would render this aspect the core of their sacramental theology.

Moreover, in *The Spirit and the Bride*, Dom Vonier describes the manner in which the Spirit of the glorified Christ works both in individual believers as well as in their corporate existence as one people of God. In order to explain the profound significance of belonging to the Church, understood as the assembly of the elect, Dom Vonier wrote *The People of God* which emphasizes that the Christian Church is entirely permeated by the Spirit of the risen Christ. In other words, under the inspiration of the Holy Spirit the body of the Church learns to imbibe "the spirit of Christianity which is truly the art of Christ".[53] Thus, the manner according to which Christians should behave in their life is portrayed in *The Art of Christ*:

> This is truly the Christian art; to combine everything into one mighty beam of light; whether the things be material or spiritual, temporal or eternal, we gather up everything into the one great focus, and there comes forth a mighty light, worship, adoration. We prostrate ourselves before God in our bodily frame, and we give Him the homage of our minds.[54]

For Dom Vonier, this transformed mode of regarding the things of this world in the light of Jesus Christ is the central factor which distinguishes Christians from all other human persons.

In exposing this characteristic feature in *The Christian Mind*, Dom Vonier states that the Christian attitude "not only tends towards the great centre, God, but it is central... It occupies a central position from the very start. It is in Christ in a most excellent way, and from that great centre, Christ, it looks at all things".[55] Having Christ as the centre of all activities, Christians acquire a distinctive point of view and mode of behaviour. Dom Vonier developed this insight in the book, *Christianus*. Starting with *Christianus Discipulus* (I) and *Christianus Sanctificatus* (II), proceeding to *Christianus Sacrificance* (VI) and *Christianus Eucharisticus* (XI) and arriving at *Christianus Perpetuus* (XVII) and *Homo Naturaliter Christianus* (XVIII), Dom Vonier enumerated the characteristic feature of the followers of Jesus. Yet, he emphasizes that, while remaining individual, Christians should think and act in society as one people united by the same Holy Spirit.

Furthermore, Christians face the great crisis of human existence, that is, death, with equanimity and courage knowing that Jesus Christ has assumed and conquered it in his flesh; by faith and baptism they are already judged righteous in the Father's sight. Thus, in *Death and Judgement*, Dom Vonier offered "a most serene appraisement of the most dread realities",[56] while in *The Life of the World to Come*,[57] he emphasized the aspects of Catholic doctrine which strengthen the hope that Christians, as true sharers in the being of Jesus Christ, will at the end of time rise with him in glory. To depict this new state of life in a more comprehensible way, Dom Vonier treats in *The Angels*[58] the significance of being totally free to love and praise, glorify and enjoy God.

Although at first sight, Dom Vonier's writings might appear to consist of separate treatises written as occasion arose, they form a harmonious whole, because they have as a recurring theme the extension of the reign of Jesus Christ in the world and in the souls of believers. Essentially, Dom Vonier intended to encourage those people whose heritage is the faith and sacraments of the Catholic Church. In his writings, he unfolded this theme from different angles-historical, doctrinal, and mystical. By doing so, he sought to strengthen devotion by adapting to modern needs the classical exposition of the Fathers and Scholastics.[59] In a particular way, both the Abbot's intellectual vitality and fidelity to the heritage of Christianity are evident in *Sketches and Studies in Theology* (1940), a posthumous publication of articles and addresses selected and arranged by the author himself. The first article of this volume, "The Lesson of Ephesus," describes the manner in which the Council's dogmatic statement on the fullness of Christ's divinity, which was denied by the Nestorianism, was acclaimed by the faithful:

> It is stated by St. Cyril himself that when the Council of Ephesus rose at the end of its first Session, in which it had solemnly condemned Nestorius and his error, on June 22, 431, the Catholics of Ephesus heaped their marks of approval on the bishops as they came out of the Basilica of the Blessed Virgin, and accompanied them to their houses with torches and censers. The city itself was illumined in many places. After fifteen hundred years the grounds for rejoicing are still as real and the Catholic cities in the world would greatly honour themselves if they were illuminated to celebrate this fifteenth centenary.[60]

For Dom Vonier, the underlying issue at Ephesus was whether through Jesus Christ human persons now have access to participation in the Godhead itself: "So through Jesus' divinity our human race is exalted; through it, it is in the power of every man to become the son of God, not through oneness of personality, but through the resemblance of grace".[61] Thus, Dom Vonier concludes that the lesson of the Council of Ephesus is within human beings' power to be transformed through God's unconditional love for them in the Incarnation, passion, death and resurrection of Jesus Christ.

In various articles contained in *Sketches and Studies in Theology*, Dom Vonier explains what it means to state that Eucharist is the Church's commemoration of Christ's passion, death and resurrection. In this regard, he objects to the view of many Protestants by affirming that the anamnesis is not merely a mental recollection but a liturgical act which renders the sacrifice of Jesus Christ on the Cross sacramentally present on the altar:

> The Catholic "*commemoration*" of the Eucharist has had this faith in the presence of the objective reality; our commemoration, being a sacramental deed, has always held the thing commemorated... The words we say, the rites we perform, the bread and the wine, are all the sacramental "*commemoratio*," but they remain not unclothed but clothed upon by the divine reality, Christ's Flesh and Blood in the sacramental condition.[62]

Evidently, Dom Vonier asserts that the Eucharistic commemoration produces neither a helpful symbol, as some Protestants seem to believe, nor a physical change of the elements, as some Catholics seem to hold. Countering these two erroneous positions in an article entitled "Eucharistic Theology," Dom Vonier affirms that the Mass is neither a symbolic nor a physical sacrifice, but a sacrament-sacrifice. Thus, by forcefully accentuating sacramental character of the Eucharist, Dom Vonier prepares the ground for both Catholic and Protestant ecumenists, who would subsequently strive to arrive at a mutual understanding of the specific nature of the sacrifice of the Mass.

Convinced of the coherence of the themes in Dom Vonier's writings, Bruno Fehrenbacher attempted systematically to arrange ten of the more important among them in three volumes entitled *The Collected Works of Abbot Vonier*.[63] The value of these volumes is that they underline Dom Vonier's synthetic and spiritual approach to writing theology: this discipline exists to extend God's Kingdom on earth by rendering the mysteries of Christ and of the Spirit, by which human salvation was accomplished, meaningful to Christians. In and through the Church and its sacraments, they come to realize that their higher life in God is to be completely fulfilled on their entrance into eternal glory. Since the Eucharist is presented throughout Dom Vonier's corpus of writings, it has been decided to subdivide its analysis into three major periods in the subsequent, expository part of the work. The early period depicts Dom Vonier's understanding of the Eucharistic sacrifice from the perspective of the traditional teaching of the Church which viewed the immolation that takes place on the altar in sacramental terms. In order to substantiate this position, Dom Vonier grounded his theology of sacrament on St. Thomas' notion of an ecclesial sign which points to the cause, essence and goal of Christian sanctification, that is, the death and resurrection of Christ, thereby the bestowal of grace, and the access to future glory. Such reflection led Dom Vonier to arrive at the conclusion that all human persons, as constituted of body and soul, have the fundamental need to express their inner search for a divine reality through symbols:

> Very often man has worshipped false deities grossly and ignominiously, but one thing has never been absent from man, even in his most disastrous religious aberrations, he has tried to express his notion of God in a way that is invariably pathetic: his God has always been to him somehow his "best thing" or what he thought to be his best thing. His idolatry reveals his psychology as nothing else reveals it; his sentiment has arrived at this; how it arrived we cannot say, but he fears or admires or loves in that way, and his divinity, however grotesque, is truly the expression of his soul.[64]

Aware of the existing controversial debate between Catholics and Protestants with regard to the sacrificial nature of the Mass, because of the latter's insistence that such teaching denies the once-and-for-all sufficiency of the immolation of Jesus on Calvary, Dom Vonier re-examined the stance taken by the Council of Trent in *De Sanctissimo Missae Sacrificio*. The Abbot indicated the necessity of enhancing this teaching with insights drawn from scriptural, patristic and liturgical sources so as better to explicitate the soteriological import both of the physical offering of Jesus of the Cross and of its symbolic re-presentation in the Eucharist. Such an approach would stimulate Catholic and Protestant theologians to re-assess their polemical statements regarding the nature of the Lord's Supper, and to adopt a more ecumenical spirit. As one follows Dom Vonier's arguments closely, it becomes clear that he is a twentieth-century theologian who anticipated the subsequent ecumenical dialogue among the divided Christian Churches.

Furthermore, Dom Vonier grounded his Eucharistic theology in the person and the mission of Jesus Christ, in the nature of the Church and in its liturgical worship. Since the eternal Word of God assumed flesh in order to encounter and redeem alienated and sinful humanity in its concrete historical situation, Dom Vonier accentuates the historical prolongation of the redemption-in-person in the liturgical actions of the Church. To arrive at this conclusion, he argues that Jesus Christ achieved the redemption of humanity through his passion, death and resurrection, establishing the new and permanent covenant between God and humanity in his own Body and Blood. Thus, insofar as at the Eucharist the baptized re-enact in a sacramental manner the passion, death and resurrection of Jesus Christ, they efficaciously re-actualize the source of their salvation, and are conjoined to their Head and one another, thereby forming with him the *Totus Christus.*

By analysing the classical exposition regarding the signifying power of the sacrament of the Eucharist, Dom Vonier states that it symbolizes and effects the new and permanent relationship between God and His people. This is possible because the Eucharist communicates to the baptized who receive the salvific grace of the Cross, thereby enabling them to live in freedom and unity and to anticipate their future glory here and now. Thus, on the basis of this understanding of the Eucharist, Dom Vonier asserted that it forms the Church anew each time it is celebrated on the altar. This does not deny the equally valid truth that the Church confects the Eucharist, but does rediscover the dynamic force of this sacrament in the lives of believers; they gather to celebrate the Eucharist, but once they receive it, Christ gathers them to himself and renders them more perfectly his mystical Body.

Dom Vonier underlines the special role of the Holy Spirit at the Eucharist. Although the sublime sacrament was instituted by Jesus Christ so that he could be present to the faithful forever, it is through the power of the Holy Spirit that the bread and wine are transformed into his Body and Blood, and are thus the means by which the one Head in glory is conjoined to his many members in history. Dom Vonier argues that, since the Eucharist is made possible only by the power of the Holy Spirit, it exists in the economy of the supernatural order, and as such transcends time and space. Therefore, by re-enacting at the Eucharist in a symbolic manner the salvific and unifying acts of Jesus Christ, present-day Christians are united with deceased Christians who now enjoy uninterrupted unity with the risen Christ. Thus, on the basis of the Spirit's permanent presence and continuous activity in the Church so that the unique saving acts of Jesus Christ are communicated to the faithful through the Church's liturgical actions, Dom Vonier considers the Eucharist as both a Christological and a pneumatological event. This becomes clear in the way he relates the traditional teaching on the *anamnesis* to the patristic emphasis on the epiclesis of the Eucharistic liturgy.

Finally, Dom Vonier dwells on the relevance of this sacrament for the personal and public life of Christians. As regards to their spiritual benefit, the Eucharist nourishes their souls with the sacramental Body and Blood of Christ so that they are truly and yet only partially incorporated into his glorified life. Evidently, this elevated spiritual state constitutes the specific grace bestowed by the Eucharist, which enables Christians to identify themselves as those who while in history participate in the life and mission of their Lord in glory. It follows for Dom Vonier that Christians are to manifest in their public acts the virtues of charity, mercy and peace so that they become living signs of the Eucharistic Christ to whom they are conformed. Dom Vonier views the eschatological nature of the Eucharist as a stimulus to such self-giving behaviours on the part of Christians who receive this sacrament. Assured of their present and future union with Christ, Christians adopt an outlook on life and act in the world according to a law of love which are determined by their Eucharistic mission to direct all things to Christ who will come in glory.

Endnotes

[1] Wilfred Upson, "Abbot Anscar Vonier," *In Memoriam Abbot Vonier*, (Bristol: Buckfast Abbey Publications by the Burleigh Press, 1939), p. 4; the then Abbot of Prinknash remarks that Dom Vonier wanted to get back to the strong faith of the Middle Ages, when people knew the true implications of the dogmas of the Church, and spoke of the mysteries of their faith with ease and facility. For Dom Vonier this is "Classical Christianity" and he liked that his contemporaries relived it.

[2] Anscar Vonier, *The Human Soul: And its Relations with Other Spirits* (1913), 3rd ed. Revised (London: Burns, Oates & Washbourne, 1914).

[3] Bruno Fehrenbacher, "Foreword," *The Collected Works of Abbot Vonier*, I (London: Burns and Oates, 1952), pp. ix-x.

[4] Anscar Vonier, "The Worth of the Supernatural," "*Chimes*, VI (January-March 1926), pp. 259-69.

[5] *Ibid.*, p. 260.

[6] Anscar Vonier, "St. Martin of Tours," *BACh*, VIII (December 1938), p. 202.

[7] *Ibid.*, p. 203.

[8] *Ibid.*, p. 202.

[9] Anscar Vonier, "The Promise of the Spirit," *BACh*, IX (Winter, 1939), p. 190.

[10] Anscar Vonier, "The Worth of the Supernatural," *Chimes*, p. 260.

[11] "In Catholic theology the supernatural is the state into which the created and finite spiritual being is raised by a direct act of God, distinct from that act whereby He created the spirit, following upon that first act and making the Spirit inherently capable of seeing God face to face... The supernatural is a result of God's excessive liberality, making those that are happy, happier still, with a new happiness in comparison with which the first happiness seems unworthy of mention." *Coll. Works*, p. 134.

[12] Anscar Vonier, "The Worth of the Supernatural," *Chimes*, pp. 261-62.

[13] *Ibid.*, *Chimes*, p. 261.

[14] *Ibid.*, p. 262.

[15] *Ibid.*

[16] *Ibid.*, 264.

[17] Anscar Vonier, "St. Martin of Tours," *BACh*, VIII (December 1938), pp. 201-10.

[18] Anscar Vonier, *A Key*, p. 14; motivated by his principal objective to explain the Eucharist in symbolic terms, so as to place it against the spectrum of the economy of salvation, Dom Vonier had already perceived the idea of Christ as the primary sacrament of God. However, he did not offer his contemporaries the kind of developed theology of Christ as sacrament which Eduard Schillebeeckx presents in *De Sacramentele Heilseconomie* (Antwerp: H. Nelissen Bilthoven, 1952). He states that "because the saving acts of the man Jesus are performed by a divine person, they have a divine power to save, but because this divine power to save appears to us in visible form, the saving activity of Jesus is sacramental. For, a sacrament is a divine bestowal of salvation in an outwardly perceptible form which makes the bestowal manifest, a bestowal of salvation in historical visibility". *Christ the Sacrament*, trans., Paul Barret and N. D. Smith (London: Sheed and Ward, 1963), p. 15.

[19] Anscar Vonier, "The Blood of the Covenant," *The New and Eternal Covenant*, p. 98.

[20] *Ibid.*, "The Riches of the Covenant," p. 35.

[21] Anscar Vonier, "Sacramental Stability," *The New and Eternal Covenant*, pp. 122-23.

[22] Bruno Fehrenbacher, "Abbot Anscar Vonier," *In Memoriam Abbot Vonier*, p. 34.

[23] Anscar Vonier, "Sacramental Stability," *The New and Eternal Covenant*, p. 115.

[24] *Ibid.*, p. 252.

[25] *Ibid.*, p. 253.

[26] Anscar Vonier, "The Psychological Import of the Catholic Faith in the Eucharist," *The Catholic Medical Guardian*, t. 3 (1925), pp 112-14; *Sketches and Studies in Theology* (London: Burns, Oates and Washbourne, 1940), p. 90-100.

[27] Anscar Vonier, "The Worth of the Supernatural," *Chimes*, p. 259.

[28] *Ibid.*, p. 259.

[29] Anscar Vonier, "The Catholic Church and Progress," *Sketches and Studies in Theology*, p. 61.

[30] Anscar Vonier, "The Worth of the Supernatural," *Chimes*, p. 259.

[31] Anscar Vonier, "The Sacramental Role," *A Key*, p. 45.

[32] *Ibid.*, pp. 19-20.

[33] *Ibid.*, pp. 49, 56.

[34] *Ibid.*, p. 227.

[35] Anscar Vonier, "Symbolism in Religion," *BACh*, IV (December 1934), p. 210.

[36] *Ibid.*, p. 210.

[37] *Ibid.*, p. 211.

[38] Anscar Vonier, "Symbolism in Religion," *BACh*, p. 211.

[39] *Ibid.*

[40] Anscar Vonier, "Christianus Discipulus," *Coll. Works*, III, p. 191.

[41] In order to show the signifying power of the words of the unmistakable presence of the Lord, Dom Vonier notes the Church's use of the Latin demonstrative pronoun in the sacrificial utterances: "*Hanc immaculatam Hostiam; Hujus aquae et vini mysterium; Benedic hoc sacrificium; Haec dona, haec munera, haec sancta sacrificial illibata; Hanc igitur oblationem servitutis nostrae; Jue haec perferri; Ex hac altaris participatione*". Anscar Vonier, "Christianus Sacrificance," *Coll. Works*, III, pp. 218-19.

[42] Anscar Vonier, "Christianus Eucharisticus," *Christianus*, (London: Burns, Oates and Washbourne, 1933); *Coll. Works*, III pp, 248-54; "The Psychological Import of the Catholic Faith in the Eucharist," *The Catholic Medical Guardian*, t. 3 (1925), p. 112.

[43] Anscar Vonier, "Christianus Eucharisticus," *Coll. Works*, pp. 248-49.

[44] Anscar Vonier, *A Key*, p. 255. "Christianus Eucharisticus," *Coll. Works*, III, pp. 251-52.

[45] Anscar Vonier, "The New Creature in Christ," *Coll. Works*, p. 40.

[46] Anscar Vonier, "Vinculum Charitatis," *Chimes*, VI (October-December 1926), pp. 426-32.

[47] Anscar Vonier, "Christianus Eucharisticus," *Coll. Works*, III, p. 254.

[48] "The Abbot's Jubilee," *BACh*," I (Autumn, 1931), p. 156.

[49] *Ibid.*, pp. 156-57.

[50] Bruno Fehrenbacher, "The Works of Abbot Vonier: A Spiritual Edifice," *BACh*, VI (September 1936), pp. 157-63.

[51] Anscar Vonier, *The Human Soul, Coll. Works*, p. 23. In his lecture to the Catholic students of London University, Dom Vonier accentuates the co-existence and reciprocity of soul-body: "It is the soul's mission, not to have a life of its own, but to possess an isolated scope, not to work out a separate destiny, but to lift up, by its internal energizing as a spiritual power, man's organic nature to the highest possible plane of potentiality and activity. The soul is the *energia* of the body. The soul is a principle of energy to the body, a spiritual principle of external origin enabling organic

life to reach heights of perfection and delicacy which it never could reach out for the presence of such an energizing principle. The Creator wanted the living organism to arrive at conscious union with Himself, and in order to achieve this He breathed into it the living spiritual principle, the soul, made to His image and likeness". "The Spiritual Principle in Man," among the unpublished works of Abbot Vonier (not dated), pp. 2-3.

[52] Anscar Vonier, "Foreword," *The New and Eternal Covenant*, v-vi.

[53] Anscar Vonier, *The Art of Christ*, p. 2.

[54] *Ibid.*, p. 47.

[55] Anscar Vonier, "The Central Attitude of the Christian Mind," *The Christian Mind*, p. 96.

[56] Bruno Fehrenbacher, "Abbot Anscar Vonier," *In Memoriam*, p. 35.

[57] A reproduction of a series of essays contributed originally to *Chimes*, during the years 1921-1924.

[58] Anscar Vonier, *The Angels*, Vol. VIII of *The Treasury of the Faith Series*, ed. George D. Smith (London: Burns, Oates and Washbourne, 1928).

[59] Bruno Fehrenbacher, "Foreword," *Coll. Works*, p. xi.

[60] Anscar Vonier, "The Lesson of Ephesus," *Sketches and Studies in Theology*, p. 1.

[61] *Ibid.*, p. 11.

[62] *Ibid.*, p. 70.

[63] Bruno Fehrenbacher, "Foreword," *The Collected Works of Abbot Vonier*, Vol. I: *The Incarnation and Redemption*; Vol. II: *The Church and the Sacraments*; Vol. III: *The Soul and the Spiritual Life* (London: Burns and Oates, 1952), pp. x-xi.

[64] Anscar Vonier, "Symbolism in Religion," *BACh* IV (December 1934), pp. 205-7.

PART II

A Chronological Exposition of Dom Anscar Vonier's Eucharist Theology

The Early Period: The Traditional Teaching on Eucharistic Sacrifice in Sacramental Terms

Dom Vonier wrote and taught on matters pertaining to theology as occasion arose. His publications deal mostly with insights on the essential truths of Christian faith and on the nature of the sacraments, but they were never developed into a systematic body of doctrine.[1] One finds a particular theme treated in different places and under many apparently unrelated headings. This is certainly true of his presentation of the Eucharistic sacrifice in expressly sacramental terms. In fact, Dom Vonier never opted to compose his works in the formal method of theology. Rather, he adopted a free and open literary style which best suited his aim- an intense desire to instruct and inspire the intellectually trained men and women of his time. He sought to provide answers to their questions by combining the traditional teaching on faith and sacraments with the then emerging philosophical systems of thought which claimed competence in many areas of their life.[2] In other words, Dom Vonier's pastoral zeal on behalf of Christians both in England and on the Continent, urged him to write and preach in a manner quite different from that employed in the systematic treatises of the *ex professo* theologians. In contrast to such formal writings, he designated his own works simply as "theology".[3]

Based on his self-evaluation, to speak of a chronological exposition of Dom Vonier's Eucharistic theology may sound presumptuous. However, a close analysis of his works shows that Dom Vonier elucidated the traditional teaching of the Church on the sacrament of the Eucharist in three temporal stages. In the early period, he interpreted the Eucharistic teaching of St. Thomas Aquinas, the Council of Trent and the Post-Tridentine theologians for his modern Christians. Dom Vonier expresses his great appreciation for the way these theologians exposed the Eucharistic mystery which enabled him to adopt a missiological, ecumenical and soteriological approach to the understanding of the theology of the Eucharist. In fact, he laid the foundation for his sacramental theology on St. Thomas' insight that human persons have a psychological need for a sacramental system for they are led to things spiritual and intelligible through corporal and sensible realities.[4] Could it be possible that a philosophical principle and its implications might offer human persons sufficient reason to entertain the teaching of the Church concerning the mediation of divine salvation through sacramental realities? This query induced Dom Vonier to ground his theology of sacrament in the constitution of human persons as body and soul, matter and form.

Similarly, St. Thomas' definition of a Christian sacrament as an ecclesial sign signifying and effecting that faith through which believers in Jesus Christ are saved caused Dom Vonier to agree that all human persons express their inner search for a sacred reality through external sacred signs. Based on this principle, Dom Vonier proposed a concept of sacraments which could be applied to all human beings, irrespective of their particular religious tenets insofar as they seek to express their relationship to the sacred reality. Evidently, such a general concept of sacred sign indicates that Dom Vonier sought solidly to root his missiological concern of St. Thomas' theological assertion that the salvation attained by Jesus Christ is mediated through ecclesial signs.

Dom Vonier further underlined the common elements, found both in St. Thomas and the Council of Trent, with regard to the relationship between the sacrifice of the Mass and that of Calvary. In treating this subject, on the one hand, he accepts the validity of the Thomistic and Tridentine teaching, and appreciates what is original and dynamic in it; on the other hand, he reacts against the static notion of the Eucharistic sacrifice which later became dominant in the Post-Tridentine period. In order to lessen the controversy still existing between Protestants and Catholics concerning the sacrificial nature of the Mass, Dom Vonier lamented that the Council Fathers at Trent and their followers did not sufficiently expose the scriptural, patristic and liturgical sources in their presentation of the Eucharistic sacrifice. As one follows the arguments proposed by Dom Vonier in this regard, one recognizes in him a theologian who was open to the concerns of the then nascent ecumenical movement.

Furthermore, Dom Vonier makes an insightful observation of the Decree *De Sanctissimo Missae Sacrificio* of the Council of Trent, in which, while briefly mentioning the total self-offering of Jesus to the Father at the Last Supper, the Council Fathers give primary place to the sacrifice completed by him on the Cross, of which the Eucharist is the true representation. The unique death of the Son of God on Calvary is fully symbolized, commemorated and re-actualized by the offering of the consecrated bread and wine at the celebration of the Mass. Thus, Dom Vonier noted that the Council of Trent affirms the identity of the sacrifice of the Mass and the redemptive action of Jesus Christ on Calvary, while it distinguishes carefully that the sacrifice of the Cross is a natural one and the sacrifice of the altar a representational one. This affirmation of the Council of Trent, on the one hand, led Dom Vonier to urge Protestants to cease accusing Catholics of not believing in the all-sufficiency of the Cross, and on the other, to exhort Catholics to desist stressing the opinion that in the Eucharistic sacrifice Christ is both symbolically and physically immolated.

Dom Anscar Vonier reacts to the Post-Tridentine theologians' proposed speculative means by which to describe the special character of the immolation of Jesus Christ, which takes place on the Christian altar.[5] Against all such theories, Dom Vonier stated that while an explanation based on a merely symbolic understanding of immolation is insufficient, an excessively real concept of immolation is, in fact, impossible because of the glorified state of the Body and Blood of Christ in heaven. He concluded that the Eucharistic sacrifice is a sacrament-sacrifice. The sacramental sacrifice re-presents in a symbolic manner the duration of time in which Christ's

Body and Blood were once separated on the Cross. In glory, however, Jesus Christ enjoys impassibility and immutability so that the Eucharistic sacrifice does not imply that an actual separation of his Body from his Blood takes place in heaven. Thus, Dom Vonier, as an exponent of the Paschal mystery, perceives the permanent link between the passion and the resurrection of Jesus Christ both within history and in the liturgy of the Church.

1. The Influence of Thomism on Dom Anscar Vonier's Understanding of Sacred Signs as a Universal Phenomenon

Certain central themes in the sacramental theology of Dom Vonier are clearly indebted to his constant reflection of the teachings of St. Thomas Aquinas with whom he became acquainted during his training in sacred theology. For, until the second half of the twentieth century whoever studied for the priesthood was required to master the *Summa Theologiae* of St. Thomas. From this classical text, Dom Vonier learned not only the subtleties of Eucharistic theology but also the art of reasoning which subsequently determined his way of thinking and writing. In his life time, when there was much controversy regarding the nature of the Eucharistic mystery, the *Summa Theologiae* helped Dom Vonier to analyse the debated issues in a way which was truly his own.

St. Thomas offers three reasons to account for this need of human persons: first, by their nature they are drawn into things spiritual and intelligible through corporeal and sensible realities; second, by their choice of sin they subject themselves to material things; third, by their proclivity towards action they tend to be attracted to external things.[6] While Dom Vonier reiterates all three of these reasons by which St. Thomas grounded the sacraments of the Church, he preferred to reduce them to one: the psychology of the fallen human persons is structured in such a way that they simply cannot do without a system of symbols.[7] One can immediately observe that, while St. Thomas defends the specific sacramental practice of the Church, the system of symbols to which Dom Vonier refers is more general. St. Thomas centred on seven ecclesial signs by which the salvation won by Jesus Christ is applied to Christians throughout their lives. By placing this teaching against a broader religious horizon, Dom Vonier argues that all human persons, who are ontologically the same, have an inherent need to relate to the sacred through external signs. Therefore, Dom Vonier calls the latter sacred signs because they emerge from the inner, spiritual search of human persons for means by which to encounter the transcendent God.

Dom Vonier was quite aware of the traditional teaching of the Catholic Church regarding the immortality of the human soul. He also learned from Scholastic rational philosophy that human persons possess no direct consciousness of the existence and of the acts of the soul. Now, if the soul is truly a constituent dimension of the human personality, how do persons become aware of its existence and acts? Dom Vonier argues that such awareness is discovered only through a complex process:

> It is the verdict, not only of observation, but also of rational philosophy, and of Scholastic philosophy in particular, that there does not exist for man, here on earth, a direct consciousness of the acts and of the existence of the soul. The soul's acts are found out only through a careful process of mental sifting that reveals the

presence in man of activities which are higher than the highest sensitive activities.[8]

Here, one arrives at the heart of Dom Vonier's argument in defense of sacred signs as a universal phenomenon. Human intellect is a power of the soul, and is utterly dependent upon the body for any knowledge of itself. Thus, Dom Vonier firmly states that the functioning of the intellect is entirely determined by the objects provided for it by the bodily organs which, in their turn, are subservient to the intellect itself. However, one should note that Dom Vonier does not mean to imply that the intellect is a material reality: "the intellect possesses or requires a bodily organ for its operation; it is intellect for the very reason that it has no such bodily organ".[9] Dom Vonier emphasizes the fact that the intellect always works in co-operation with the senses; they alone provide the intellect with its proper object, so that human beings are led to intellectual growth through the channel of their senses. In other words, Dom Vonier affirms in a broader context the particular reasoning employed by St. Thomas so as to demonstrate that Christians are led to comprehend the spiritual and intelligible reality of salvation in Jesus Christ through exposure to the ecclesial signs, the seven sacraments. For St. Thomas, these sensible realities confront Christians with the inner, spiritual truth concerning the new and immortal existence of humanity which was attained by the passion and glorification of Jesus Christ. Desiring to communicate this insight to a greatly de-Christianized public, Dom Vonier found it indispensable to analyse the definition of the ecclesial signs offered by St. Thomas: "Sacraments are certain signs protesting that faith through which man is justified".[10]

Dom Vonier considered this an excellent definition, because it recognizes the efficacious role that ecclesial signs play in the spiritual process by which Christians constantly appreciate their definitive justification in Jesus Christ. Besides, this specific definition corroborates Dom Vonier's general notion of the world of signs and symbols which speak of God and of the things of God to every human person. Insofar as all sacred signs and symbols indirectly dispose human beings to accept the incarnational nature of Christian faith, they participate in various degrees in those supernatural realities on which Christianity rests. Thus, when Dom Vonier makes the following statement, he is conscious both of its quite specific and of its more general meaning: "A sacrament is always an external sign, that is, a most real witness of that more recondite quality of the soul, the faith that justifies man by bringing him into contact with Christ".[11]

On the one hand, Dom Vonier admits with St. Thomas that a Christian sacrament is an ecclesial sign of the internal reality, the faith in Christ which justifies and which is related to the patriarchal faith signified in the major rites of the Old Law.[12] On the other hand, Dom Vonier insists that, since each external sacred sign corresponds to an internal reality, it could legitimately be interpreted as a means willed by God so that human beings might be led to the sacred dimension of creation itself.

Thus, Dom Vonier's perception of sacraments is broader than that of St. Thomas, since it is concerned with the search of all human beings through symbols for the salvific nature of creation. In this sense, Dom Vonier was a nascent missiologist; he regarded all human beings as fabricators of symbols which speak to them of God and put them in contact with Him. In other words, Dom Vonier held the position that God enables all people to make use of external signs to discover in a partial way His salvific design for them. Of course, God could act in an entirely different way- for example, through direct illumination of people concerning salvation. But this decision would not be congruous with the symbol-setting inherent in human nature. Out of respect for human nature and its need to be creative, God uses external, visible realities as sacred signs which reveal the divine plan of salvation.

Viewed from this perspective, Dom Vonier proves to be a modern scholar open to fundamental sacramental questions such as whether salvation is possible outside the Church, in that God reveals Himself to all human beings in and through the symbolic quality of His creation. Through visible and tangible realities, God invites all people to a more profound realization of their inner, spiritual self which reflects the inestimable depth of the divine reality itself. God continually offers His salvific grace to all human beings in whatever situation they exist and enables their freedom to respond to grace or not. Yet, although Dom Vonier is convinced that God's sacramental activity is as ancient as the world itself, he employs chiefly examples from the Hebrew writings which serve as instances of God's sacramental way of using created things to lead people freely to come closer to Him.

Dom Vonier presents the salvific event of the Passover as "a great sign, a sign of God's omnipotence and loyalty into which all other signs were to be merged".[13] The Jewish Passover with all its rites - the slaying of the paschal lamb, the sprinkling of its blood on the door-posts, and the act of eating it in accordance with the command of the Lord - comprises an external sign of the profound faith of the people in their coming liberation by God from slavery (Ex.12: 2-14).

In the above example, Dom Vonier attributes a sacramental dignity to all the individual rites, because they respectively signify some dimension of the one event by which the people of Israel will be delivered from bondage and be brought to new freedom by the gracious power of God. Moreover, the paschal lamb itself, which the Israelites consumed, was a sacrifice in the real sense, since it perfectly symbolized the self-giving divine character of their delivery from injustice and oppression. Here, one observes that, in speaking of the external signs of the Hebrew Covenant, Dom Vonier employs the analogical dimension of the notion of a sacrament, by which St. Thomas refers to the rites of the Jewish Law as indicative of their fulfilment in Jesus Christ, God's definitive Passover.[14]

If Dom Vonier makes use of Hebrew sacramental concepts only by way of example, that is, so as to convey the truth that a sacrament is related to the interior faith of God's people, this procedure enables the Abbot more perfectly to understand the New Testament signs. In treating the infancy narrative of St. Luke, Dom Vonier perceives a sacramental significance in Elizabeth's divinely accomplished human motherhood for the parallel yet unique divine motherhood of Mary:

> Elizabeth's motherhood played a wonderful role in the mystery of the Incarnation; it was to Mary the one external proof of the possibility of a divine and virginal motherhood, and Mary's mind had the human satisfaction of possessing a visible evidence in favour of an incomprehensible spiritual fact. Elizabeth's motherhood was the Angel's argument to establish the veracity of his incredible message.[15]

Evidently, the role played by the external sign helps Mary to grasp the astounding spiritual truth of her new relation to God's Word. Elizabeth's inconceivable motherhood which surpassed all human laws lend to Mary's mind the *motivum credibilitatis* or the rational ground for her spiritual assent. The Angel's message of God's salvific presence in Mary's womb becomes more understandable to her because of an outward sign- Elizabeth's expected motherhood in her old age. This visible reality confirms the Angel's announcement of the hidden reality- the divine motherhood of Mary.

Dom Vonier further remarks in the course of reflecting on the Good News proclaimed to the shepherds at Bethlehem that the extraordinary event of the Angel's words enabled the shepherds to regard the humble child as a true sign containing a supernatural and thus invisible reality. By having believed in the Angel's words, the shepherds viewed the new-born babe as the tangible sign of the advent of the Saviour into the world (Lk.2: 8-20).

Dom Vonier points out several similar examples in the New Testament, and in doing so, he is also aware of a steady gradation or hierarchy of importance in the sign-value of the several sensible realities which are described. Nevertheless, the common element in all these external, sensible realities is their capacity to lend credibility to an invisible and provocative spiritual truth. However, Dom Vonier also perceived that if all the sacraments indicated in the Bible were merely to signify the mystery of genuine interior faith, there would be no difference between the Hebrew and the Christian covenants. Therefore, Dom Vonier relies on the teaching of St. Thomas concerning Christian sacraments as ecclesial signs. A Christian sacrament is not a mere sign, but effects within history the supernatural reality which it signifies. In other words, the sacraments of the new law besides pointing to grace, cause it:

> The sacraments of the new law are at the same time causes and signs; and on this account it is said commonly that they bring about what they figure. From this it appears also that they are sacraments in the most perfect sense of the word, because they are related to something sacred, not only under the aspect of sign, but also under the aspect of cause.[16]

Evidently, St. Thomas is explicating the Christian sacraments as essentially related to the Paschal mystery, in that they not only signify what has occurred once and for all in history but also cause the death and resurrection of Jesus to be existentially related to the lives of individual believers in Christ. This insight is important for Dom Vonier, because he perceives all visible signs of sacred reality not only to reveal some invisible truth, but to cause believers to participate in this truth. For, the great signs or sacraments of God not only remind us of the things of God, but they are powerful means to make things of God live again.[17]

Without denying the unique character of the Christian sacraments, Dom Vonier emphasizes that God's salvific grace is extended to the entire human race, which in various degrees is related to the specific signs of the Church. In this way, Dom Vonier reflects the concerns of a twentieth-century missiologist; interest in the salvation of all human beings makes him perceive the saving work of God the Father in every created thing. As a result of which, reality itself calls human beings to spiritual depth and to openness to God's offer of salvation: "The creative power of symbols, the productive efficacy of signs, the incredible resourcefulness of simple things in the hand of God to produce spiritual realities, nay, to reproduce them in their historic setting, this is the sacramental world, and it is profoundly unlike any other world".[18] Thus, Dom Vonier regards the signs and symbols of creation as having a general sacramental import. God the Creator renders them effective in producing faith in and relation to spiritual realities in various historic ritual settings. Here, Dom Vonier lends his approach to the concept of sacrament an interpersonal, even existential tone. The sacramental world of signs and symbols is an attractive reality, but until it is further illumined by divine revelation, one without "permanent and natural fixity of being".[19] The creation itself is endowed with a potential efficacy of signification in order to reveal to those who search for its ultimate meaning the manifold wisdom of God through Jesus Christ and the sacraments of his Church (Eph.3: 9).

To sum up briefly, Dom Vonier laid the foundation for his sacramental theology by broadening the philosophical insights of St. Thomas, namely, his assertion that all people have a psychological need to arrive at higher truths through sense experience; in the Christian dispensation specific ecclesial signs serve to point the baptized to the personal message of Christ by which they are saved. He concluded that all beings who sincerely express their search for God through external, visible realities are implicitly conjoined to the sacred signs of the Church:

> The wildest child of nature has ideals enough, shall I say has faith enough in some unknown greatness, to attract the attention of the Son of God, who is on the lookout for the feeblest signs of fire here on earth. He hears the prayers of the Bedouin; He listens

to the yearnings of the Hindu; He watches the conscience of the Buddhist; they are smoking flax, all of them, and none of them will He quench. It is not granted to us to see how many of them may be blazing forth into that true contrition which means supernatural justification. But one thing will ever be to me a consoling certainty: the God who cherishes the smoking flax has power to save every man in whom there is the least spark of goodwill.[20]

Dom Vonier interprets St. Thomas' philosophical assertion in terms of the data discovered through the modern study of other religions and adopts the stance of a missiologist whose concern is to relate the salvation won by Christ to the ritual practices of people throughout the whole world.

2. The Reiteration and Enhancement of the Tridentine Notion of the Sacrificial Character of the Eucharist

Dom Vonier, while exposing the Tridentine notion of sacrifice, places the Eucharistic mystery against the wide horizon of human symbolizing activity and thus arrives at the notion of the Eucharist as a sacrament-sacrifice. That the Lord's Supper is a true sacrifice identical in all but its external form with the physical sacrifice of Jesus on Calvary has perennially been the teaching of the Catholic Church. However, Dom Vonier knows not all theologians would account for the identity of the Eucharistic sacrifice and that of Calvary in the same way. He is equally appreciative of the spiritual force permeating the teaching of Protestants who would not accept the Mass as a true sacrifice because of their insistence on the once-and-for-all sufficiency of the immolation of the Body and Blood of Jesus on Calvary.[21]

In order to underline the Catholic teaching that the sacrifice of Calvary and the sacrifice of the altar are one and the same reality in different forms, Dom Vonier deemed it necessary that Catholics re-examine their appreciation of the celebration of the Mass so as better to grasp the relationship between the sacrifice made by Jesus on Golgotha and that made by them along with his at the Eucharist.[22] This process of re-examination was also to be done by Catholic theologians, who could suggest measures by which to correct many misconceptions of Protestants and thereby create an ecumenical spirit within the divided Churches.

In his attempt to contribute to such ecumenism, the Abbot of Buckfast concentrated his attention on the following words from the "Decree of the Sacrifice of the Mass" which was formulated at the twenty-second plenary session of the Council of Trent:

> At the Last Supper, in the night in which he was betrayed, Jesus offered to God the Father his Body and his Blood, under the appearances of bread and wine, so that he might leave to his beloved Bride, the Church, a visible sacrifice, proportionate to the nature of man, through which sacrifice the one which was about to be achieved once on the Cross might be represented, and its memory might remain to the end of the world, and its salutary power might be applied for the remission of those sins which are committed by us every day; thus declaring himself to be constituted a Priest for ever according to the order of Melchisedech.[23]

Dom Vonier observes that the principal feature is its unambiguous and intentional use of the verb *offerre* to indicate both the sacrifice made by Jesus at the Last Supper and that made by him on the Cross. Further, he remarks that the decree, though fully concerned with the Eucharistic mystery, gives primary place to the unique sacrifice of the Cross, which it obviously takes for the absolute act of Jesus which the Eucharistic sacrifice is not the repetition but the representation. In other words, the absolute sacrifice of the

Cross is continually made actual and efficacious throughout the time after the resurrection. The Abbot would insist then that through their faith in the sacrifice of the Mass, Catholics do not deny the all-sufficiency of the self-offering of Jesus Christ on the Cross. Rather, the Eucharistic sacrifice is properly viewed by them as the re-actualization of the sacrifice of Calvary by means of another form, that is, by the oblation of the bread and wine.

Dom Vonier notes that the promulgated decree marks an important shift from the previously much debated point concerning the relationship between the Last Supper and the sacrifice of the Cross to the relationship between the latter and the Eucharistic mystery. The Abbot observes that in the final decree there is no longer mention of the Last Supper being consummated on the Cross.[24] Regarding the nature of the debate on the relation between the Last Supper and the Cross, Dom Vonier assumes that the salient issue was whether a sacrifice was offered at the Last Supper, and if so, whether it was propitiatory, since it would be followed by the sacrifice of Calvary the day after. In explaining why the Council ignored the issue, the Abbot adheres to the comments made by Pallavicini,[25] that although the bishops at the Council of Trent could afford to leave aside the question of the connection between the Last Supper and the Cross, they felt constrained to declare that the sacrifice of the Mass is truly the re-actualization of the propitiatory sacrifice of Calvary:

> For the Lord being appeased by the oblation of the sacrifice and giving grace and the gift of penance, remits the most heinous crimes and sins; for it is one and same victim. The same Jesus is offering himself now through the ministry of the priests who then offered

> himself on the Cross, the differences being only in the way of offering.
> Of that offering, I mean the bloody offering, the fruits come to us
> most abundantly through the other offering (the unbloody one).[26]

While highlighting the propitiatory nature of the sacrifice of Mass, Dom Vonier insists on its sacramental character as opposed to the physical character of the sacrifice of the Cross. Aware that the sacrificial nature of the Mass remains a matter of controversy between Protestants and Catholics, Dom Vanier challenges all Christians properly to understand that the true meaning of the Eucharist is found in its power to signify, re-present, recall and apply one unique historic event. In the Eucharistic sacrifice, the same victim, Jesus Christ who once offered himself on the Cross, is sacramentally offered by the Church. Thus, the sacrifice of the Mass is neither a physical sacrifice, as some Catholics would seem to hold, nor a mere symbolic offering of gifts, as some Protestants would seem to believe. The Mass is rather a sacrament-sacrifice, one and the same sacrifice as that made on Calvary, but one different from it in the mode by which it is offered.[27] In other words, the Eucharist is a sacramental sacrifice, because the bloody self-gift of Jesus on the Cross is present and is offered in the Mass through the symbolic offering of bread and wine.

Further, Dom Vonier elaborates on this point by stating that the Body and Blood of Jesus made present in the Eucharistic sacrifice are actualizations of the event of Calvary when his Body was pierced and his Blood was poured out. In a similar way, the Abbot would affirm that the bread and wine employed by Jesus in the Cenacle were symbolically linked to the subsequent event of the Cross, and not to the physical state of Jesus during the Last Supper:

> The Body and Blood of the Eucharist are representations of the

> Christ in the state in which he was not whole and entire, but when he
> was broken up into parts on the Cross at his death. The Eucharistic
> Body and the Eucharistic Blood, therefore, at the Last Supper, were
> the representation, or to choose our word more accurately, the
> presentation, of the Christ who would be broken up the day after,
> not of the Christ who was there at the head of the table.[28]

Thus, Dom Vonier affirms that the sacramental representation of the Cross at the Mass is a real sacrifice. Sacramental representation is, therefore, not a mere image or an empty symbol. In this way, Dom Vonier intends to help Protestants understand that the symbolic commemoration of the passion of the Lord in the Eucharistic celebration is not a mental act, but a concrete reality. The Eucharist is the efficacious memory of the passion and death of the Lord, his Body and Blood separated from each other on the Cross.[29]

The Catholic Church has always believed and the Council of Trent re-affirmed that Jesus instituted the Eucharist at the Last Supper, so that under the appearance of bread and wine, his ensuing redemptive death would be effective in the Church by means of a visible sacramental sacrifice. After the words of consecration, the bread and wine on the Christian altar contain in a symbolic form the Body and Blood of Christ which were separated on the Cross. In assessing this teaching, Dom Vonier observes that it principally stresses the identity of the victim, that is, Jesus Christ, both on the Cross and at the Mass, and not the identity of the act of offering. While he accepts this emphasis, Dom Vonier points out that the act of offering is new every time the sacrifice is offered, even though the sacrifice itself is not new. For, by its very nature every sacrament represents a distinct aspect of salvation which is immutable. Therefore, Dom Vonier states that the newness in the act of offering the self-same sacrifice of the Cross is possible only in the sacramental sphere. The salvific act by which Jesus Christ instituted the Eucharist and offered himself on Calvary at the end of his public life must be distinguished from his reiterated self-offering in the sacrament of the Eucharist, which does not belong to his terrestrial but to his glorious existence. The newness of the act by which Jesus Christ offers himself at the Mass, therefore, can be attributed to the Church, the living sign of the glorious Christ, to which the Lord himself gave the command to act in his name.[30] By means of this analysis, Dom Vonier adopts a more decidedly ecclesiological and liturgical understanding of the sacrifice of the Mass. He intends to render it more meaningful for contemporary Christians, while at the same time adhering faithfully to the theological tradition. The result of his approach is that he fosters an appreciation of the dynamic and new way the Church unites itself to the act of Jesus' self-giving to the Father. Throughout his reflections on the doctrine of the Eucharist, Dom Vonier strives to accentuate the biblical, patristic and liturgical sources of the Catholic understanding of this sacrament.

The means Dom Vonier chooses to achieve this goal are to present objectively the common elements found both in the *Summa* of St. Thomas and in the decrees of the Council of Trent. These fundamental Catholic texts manifest a similar mode of conceiving and expressing the sacrificial and sacramental character of the Eucharist. Therefore, Dom Vonier does not hesitate to categorize the decrees of the Council as "an exact reproduction of the doctrine of St. Thomas".[31] The first article of the eighty-third question of the

Summa, regarding whether Christ is truly immolated in the Eucharist clearly forms the basis of the pronouncement of the Council. St. Thomas provides a twofold reason in favour of the immolation of Jesus Christ in the Eucharist, because of which this sacrament is also called a sacrifice. First, the Eucharistic species are the representative image of the passion of the Lord, which is his true sacrifice. Therefore, the sacrifice of the Eucharist can be properly designated as a sacramental immolation of Christ on account of the unmatchable efficacy of the sacrifice of the Cross which it re-presents. Second, through this sacrament, believers in Christ share in all the fruits of his salvific death for them. Thus, the sacrifice of the Mass is the symbolic form of the sacrifice of the Cross, and as such renders present anew, and in the life of each believer, the external merit of the sacrifice of Jesus Christ.

Furthermore, Dom Vonier affirms that these two temporally distinct yet essentially united modes of Christ's sacrifice should not be confused one with the other. The sacrifice of the Cross was indeed a complete act, and so is the Eucharistic sacrifice. The oneness of the two modes of Christ's sacrifice is, therefore, necessarily to be grounded in the belief that the Mass is the perfect sacramental representation, memory and application of the Cross. In the Tridentine pronouncements, there is no attempt whatsoever to regard the Eucharistic sacrifice as a substitute for or an enhancing part of the sacrifice of Calvary. Such an assertion should obviously have been a complete reversal of the traditional teaching of the Church on the nature of a sacrament. For, the latter is in no way viewed as a portion of the complete redemptive acts of Jesus Christ; it is essentially and solely a symbolic representation of the acts of salvation completed by Jesus during his life on earth. The sacrifice of the Cross is the complete re-presentation. In this sense, if the Eucharist were to add anything to the Cross, it would at once cease to be a sacrament, as it would no longer constitute a representation:

> Is not one of the basic principles of the Eucharistic sacrifice to be found in the very completeness and finality of the sacrifice of the cross? If Mass gave anything to the cross it would cease to be a sacrament, as it would cease to be a representation. Is not the very purpose of a monument to stand for the complete victory, the heroic deed, the final triumph? We do not erect monuments to failures or things half-achieved.[32]

Dom Vonier speaks here as a nascent twentieth-century ecumenist who challenges all Christians to dialogue on the nature of the Eucharist. By presenting the example of the relation between a monument and a victory, Dom Vonier urges Protestants and Catholics to understand both the connection and the difference between the sacramental sacrifice of the Eucharist and the physical sacrifice of the Cross. In effect, Dom Vonier is calling upon Protestants to cease criticizing Catholics for not believing in the definitive and unrepeatable event of the Cross. He is, likewise, challenging Catholics to cease giving the impression that the sacrifice of the Mass adds something new to the efficacy of Calvary.

In fact, even at the time of the Reformation, both Catholics and Protestants accepted the traditional teaching that the Eucharist is a sacrament, or symbolic salvific gesture, instituted by Christ himself. Therefore, the controversial point which divided them was not the sacramental nature of the Eucharist, but its sacrificial nature in the light of the proper yet unilateral emphasis of the Reformers of all-sufficiency of the sacrifice of the Cross. For Martin Luther, the Eucharist is primarily a sacrament and a testament of Christ's self-gift on Calvary but not sacrifice. The defenders of Catholic teaching mostly contented themselves with refuting the tenets of their opponents, rather than with comprehending the sound intention behind the accentuation on the Cross proposed by Luther and the other Reformers.[33] Nevertheless, when seen from the more positive point of view, the statement of the Council of Trent which, with the sacrifice of the Mass, can be said always to stress its sacramental nature. By means of Trent's emphasis on the notion of sacrament, it became easier for Catholics to speak of the anamnetical or sacramental sacrifice, a theme the eventual development of which could reconcile the theological stances of the divided Churches.

Another point which comes out forcefully in Dom Vonier's interpretation of the Council's position regarding the sacrificial nature of the Mass is that much attention was given to the innate need of human persons for a well-structured religious system. Therefore, in an attempt to attenuate the controversy between Protestants and Catholics, Dom Vonier would invite his interlocutors to reflect on the origin of sacrifice itself. The latter can be said to be rooted in natural law, and to have formed part of the rich heritage of the Hebrew Law. Evidently, the sacrificial death of Jesus on the Cross is the perfection of the Old Law; and the Eucharistic sacrifice is the perfect representation of the Cross. Moreover, this perfection is found in the symbolic, visible and institutional dimension of the Church's cult.[34] In this sense, then, relying on St. Thomas, the Council could assert that the symbolic application of redemption is exclusively a prerogative of the

Eucharist, the central sacrament of the New Law. Although the Council did insist that the offering of the Mass for the remission of the sins of the living and the dead was valid, it did not propose any particular theory of efficacy by which further to explain this traditional teaching.[35] Likewise, even though the Council emphasized the propitiatory value of the sacrifice of the Mass, it did not attempt to relate this theme to that of thanksgiving. It seems, then, that the application of the merits of the Cross for the remission of sin was the chief intention of the council's concern to highlight the propitiatory nature of the Eucharistic sacrifice.

In all these considerations, Dom Vonier observes that, while re-affirming the traditional stance of the Catholic Church, the Council of Trent attributed a more objective value to the Eucharistic sacrifice by regarding it as the sacramental commemoration of the unique sacrificial death of Jesus Christ on Calvary. While Catholic theologians strongly emphasize the commemorative dimension of the Eucharist, as do all Christians, they also give to the same commemoration inwardness and objectivity of reality so as to respond to the Protestant preference for interior conversion rather than for mere attendance at external rituals.[36] For Catholic theologians, however, the commemoration enacted at the Eucharist is not simply an act of reminiscence, but an actual rendering present in symbols of the past historic death of Jesus Christ. Dom Vonier is aware that the decree of the Council of Trent on the sacrifice of the Mass, although complete, was formulated in the theological terms prevailing at the time. This does not mean, however, that the Council fathers opted for one or the other school of theological opinion in their explanation of the Eucharistic sacrifice. Only in the centuries following the Council did Catholic theologians propose various theories of the type of immolation which takes place in the Mass.

3. The Restricted Eucharist of the Post-Tridentine Theology

After the Council of Trent, the theological efforts of the three subsequent centuries centred round the way in which the incomparable sacrifice of Jesus Christ on the Cross is made present on the Christian altar. For, the Post-Tridentine theologians were aware of the Reformers' argument that the mass could not be a sacrifice, much less a propitiatory one, because no real immolation takes place on the Christian altar. In answer to this objection, the Post-Tridentine theologians responded that the sacrifice of the Mass is in no way a derogation of the unrepeatable self-offering of Christ on the Cross, but that it does entail a true immolation of Christ. As a result, several immolationist theories by which to explain the sacrifice of the Mass were proposed. As a Benedictine, Dom Vonier instinctively reacted to all these theories as much too restrictive since the Eucharistic Sacrifice was not placed within the entire economy of the supernatural life. Thus, he evaluated the theories by employing sacramental notions which properly stress the supernatural and symbolic reality of the Eucharist.

According to Ulrich Zwingli, John Calvin and most of the English Reformers, the Catholic concept of the sacrifice of the Mass affirms that Jesus Christ has to be slain each time the sacred species are offered.[37] The Post-Tridentine theologians responded that the Mass is a memorial sacrifice in which the victim offered in Jesus Christ himself rendered sacramentally present on the altar. Therefore, the celebration of the Mass is not purely a spiritual commemoration of the Cross, but a truly objective memorial, in which through external signs the very event of Calvary becomes re-presented.[38] In other words, to counter the Reformers' objections, Catholic theologians set out to show that at the Eucharist the sacred species are actually offered up to God, a stance which would verify its definition as a sacrifice. Although Dom Vonier appreciated these efforts of Catholic theologians to dialogue with the Reformers, he resolutely held that the Eucharistic sacrifice involves neither a physical nor a virtual immolation of Jesus Christ, but a sacramental one. A more detailed account of these various theories of immolation, and of Dom Vonier's reaction to them, will demonstrate the consistent character of his position.

The first theory rested on the idea of a mystical slaying of Christ the victim. Gabriel Vasquez (d. 1604), in his commentary on the *Summa, III* of St. Thomas (Disputatio 220.3; 223.4: 37), argued that the Mass entails a mystical sacrifice because, by virtue of the double consecration of the bread and wine, not only Christ is made present in the sacred species but his death on the Cross is also re-presented in them. Like St. Thomas, Vasquez emphasized that at the Mass a commemorative rather than a physical sacrifice takes place.[39] This would mean that the Eucharist is a symbolic or a mystical offering of Jesus Christ as is indicated by the separation of the species of bread and wine. Dom Vonier basically adhered to this position but was concerned about modern persons who had lost an awareness of how the external, sensible elements of ritual, far from being empty signs, contain a profound spiritual reality. Thus, he regarded the mystical or symbolic understanding of the sacrifice of the Mass to be correct, but in need of further elucidation along more contemporary lines of thinking which would show the relation between external sign and invisible reality.

By relying on St. Thomas, Leonard Lessius (d. 1623) also argued that the double consecration of the bread and wine not only provides an apt image of the sacrifice of Christ, but by virtue of the power of the words of consecration, the Body and the Blood of Christ are actually separated from each other on the altar. This theory of immolation is based on the Thomistic notion of sacramental signification. Since the words through which bread and wine are changed into Christ's Body and Blood have a sacramental effect, they produce a real yet symbolic sacrifice which can be termed as a "virtual slaying" of Jesus Christ.[40]

With regard to this theory, Dom Vonier states that no change takes place in the Person of the glorified Christ, since he can no longer be sacrificed. Yet, in the sacramental Body and Blood of Christ a true sacrifice is re-presented through the external signification of the separated bread and wine which symbolize the historical event of the Cross. In the Eucharistic sacrifice, the offering of the Body and Blood of Jesus Christ to the Father is symbolized through the external forms of bread and wine. For Dom Vonier, then, the one sacrifice of Jesus Christ is rendered present and efficacious by means of a mystery or sacrament:

> To sacrifice in *mysterio*, in *sacramento*, is this: firstly, to do all the external acts of a natural, mortal sacrifice, as Melchisedech had done them, as the Levites in the Temple had done them; secondly, to have the external, natural things changed into an infinitely holier

reality, under the very hands of the priest, as it were, into the Body
and Blood of the beloved Son of God, so that the external rite is
merely the *signum*, the sign of a Thing infinitely greater.[41]

As a Benedictine liturgist, Dom Vonier fully recognizes the
import of the external signs employed in the Eucharistic
sacrifice; they help the faithful to understand their own
participation in the sacramental offering which Jesus Christ
makes to the Father. In this sense, Dom Vonier was concerned
that the rite of the Mass be solemnly carried out for the
sake not of external festivity, but of the faith of the gathered
assembly in the sacramental sacrifice of Christ present on the
altar in and through consecrated bread and wine.

The solemn words of consecration cause the bread and
wine to be transformed into the Body and Blood of Christ
sacramentally immolated so that Christians might receive
the full effect of the unique historical event of the Cross.
Thus, the Eucharistic symbols effect what they signify, the
re-presentation of the death of Jesus Christ on the Cross.[42]

Another theory proposed by the theologians to prove the
sacrificial character of the Mass was the *real slaying* of Christ
on the Christian altar. According to this theory, Christ is
really immolated at the Mass, as he is constricted by, and even
reduced to the Eucharistic species. In the Eucharist Christ
undergoes a kind of personal abasement which, although it
is contrary to his natural state of glory, he tolerates so as to
render his sacrifice on Calvary present to the Church. For these
theologians, therefore, this very state of personal humiliation
on the part of Christ constitutes the sacrifice of the Mass.[43]

Dom Vonier does not negate the general truth that a
state of abasement is one of sacrifice; but he does criticize the

application of such a truth to the sacrifice of the Mass. Such an explanation of the Eucharistic sacrifice does not properly correspond to the sacramental nature of the Mass. Humiliation and exaltation are indeed valid notions; however, they are aptly used not in sacramental theology but in quite another sphere of Christian thought. Such an analysis of the Eucharistic sacrifice comes not from the centre of the sacramental doctrine, but has been brought in from quite another realm of Christian thought and practice; it has been borrowed from the ethical world. In fact, humiliation or exaltation are not sacramental notions; they are ethical notions.[44]

Dom Vanier insists that theologians understand the precise meaning of the sacramental representation which is operative in the Eucharist. This sacrament renders present a concrete happening in the life of Jesus, and not merely an ethical experience he underwent. Dom Vonier is urging theologians not to attenuate the profound truth concerning the sacramental character of the sacrifice of the Mass in relation to Calvary for the sake of emphasizing an indisputable, yet not pertinent ethical experience of Jesus.

Still another theory concerning the Mass as a real sacrifice was based on St. Thomas' assertion that the breaking and eating of the consecrated host constitutes the validity of the Eucharistic immolation.[45] The ontological change brought about in the substance of the sacrificial gifts of bread and wine through the double consecration transforms them respectively into the Body and Blood of Christ. This fundamental change of the substances of bread and wine renders them the elements of sacramental sacrifice.[46] Dom Vonier agrees with this theory, but prefers to stress that through the words of consecration, Jesus Christ is contained in the bread and wine not in his own kind, that is, physically, but in the kind of the sacrament. Therefore, the Eucharist entails not the physical, but the sacramental sacrifice of Christ which is indeed as real as his immolation on Golgotha, because the external signs truly re-present this unique event. The Eucharistic bread and wine both signify and contain the Body and Blood of Christ so that the Mass is a real immolation brought about through sacramental sign. By insisting that Jesus Christ is sacramentally yet really immolated in the celebration of the Mass, Dom Vonier concludes that the Eucharistic mystery is properly understood as a sacrament-sacrifice.

All these various immolationist theories could be succinctly summarized by stating that they attempt in one way or other to unite the symbolic to the real nature of the sacrifice of the Mass. For Dom Vonier, a merely symbolic immolation is as insufficient as one based on a literal immolation is impossible. Since Jesus Christ now exists in a glorious state, and is, therefore, impassible, the literal immolationist theories are untenable. The Eucharistic sacrifice is always the joyful celebration of the Christ who passed from death to life. Therefore, the unique suffering and immolation of Christ on Calvary has been permeated by Easter victory; both the humiliation and the exaltation of Christ are thus re-presented in the celebration of Mass. By means of this analysis, one could rightly assess Dom Vonier as a forerunner of later theologians who accentuated the Paschal mystery as the central motif of the Eucharist.

Other theologians from the sixteenth century onward argued that the spiritual oblation of Christ was sufficient to render the Eucharist a sacrifice.[47] Later, this notion was developed by the so-called French school which did not deny the significance of the physical immolation of Christ, but emphasized his interior self-surrender to the Father, both throughout his earthly life and on the Cross. In glory, Christ continues this same act of self-giving; thus his immolation on Calvary was only an instance of this continuous and unchanging act of oblation. Since Christ exists in an everlasting state of oblation, his sacrifice is unceasing.[48] In the course of developing his own Eucharistic theology, Dom Vonier discusses at length this view of the French school.[49]

M. de la Taille argued that the unique sacrifice of Christ consisted in his oblation both at the Last Supper and on Calvary. Since after the resurrection Christ is forever in the glorified state, there is no possibility whatsoever that he can be made a Victim anew. The essential factor by which the Mass is a sacrifice is "the Church's renewed offering of this same Victim with the same act of oblation as at the Last Supper".[50]

Dom Vonier's assessment of such a view is that, in order to establish the reality of the sacrifice of the Mass in relation to that of the Cross, M. de la Taille, as well as M. Lepin, reacted consciously or unconsciously against the ultra-realists such as Juan de Lugo (d. 1660) and Franzlin (d. 1886). In their efforts and good faith to liberate the Eucharistic mystery from the incubus of this strange realism, they seem, unfortunately, to have become personalists.[51] Dom Vonier so evaluates them, because their theology of the sacrifice of the Mass first accentuates the ever present, glorious Person of Christ, and only thereafter the sacramental nature of his presence in the Eucharist. In other words, for the personalists the Eucharistic sacrifice is the ongoing actualization of the personal and unceasing oblation of the glorious Christ to the Father on behalf of humanity. According to the personalists then the present existence of Christ in heaven rather than his unique self-gift on Calvary, determines the Eucharist as a sacrifice.[52]

From these admittedly critical reactions of Dom Vonier to the personalists, it appears that he himself is drifting away from the traditional, Catholic presentation of the Eucharistic mystery in terms of the totality of Christ's Person. But the truth is quite the contrary. Without denying the fact that the totality of Christ's Person is the constitutive element of the Eucharist, the Abbot staunchly defends the manner in which the first millennium of Christianity understood the Eucharistic mystery; it was invariably explained in sacramental rather than personal terms. Dom Vonier, therefore, insists that in the Eucharist Christians do not have direct access to the person of Christ, but encounter him through a sacramental medium, that is, through the consecrated elements which, by virtue of the power and signification of the words of Christ himself, are changed into his Body and Blood. Thus, in the Eucharist, the reality of the person of Christ is present not in its natural form, but in and through efficacious signs.[53]

Dom Vonier emphasizes that the Eucharistic sacrifice, by means of sacramental signification, re-presents the Body and Blood of Christ on the Cross, that is, at the moment, when the perfect sacrifice of the now glorious One was achieved. The Eucharist is a perfect sacrifice because it renders the unique sacrifice of Christ present on the Christian altar. However, one should not say that during the celebration of the Mass Jesus Christ is physically immolated anew, for this would necessarily entail the unthinkable disintegration of his Body and Blood as they now exist in heaven. Instead, one should hold that Jesus Christ is sacramentally immolated in the Eucharistic sacrifice, because it re-presents for and applies to his followers the redemption he won for them on Calvary.[54]

Dom Vonier admits that these theological considerations attempt to make clear that the sacrament of the Eucharist contains only that which it signifies, the once-for-all self-offering of the Body and Blood of Christ on the Cross. Therefore, the sacrifice of the Mass consists in the re-presentation of that historic moment so that to speak of the sacrifice of the Eucharist as containing the personal oblation of the glorious Christ to the Father in heaven, as Lepin does, would be to do away with its essentially sacramental character: "The death of Christ on the Cross, if Lepin be logical, need not be Christ's sacrifice in an essentially higher way than, say, his fast of forty days, because the real inwardness of sacrifice is oblation, and that oblation, according to Lepin, was continuous, unceasing; is continuous and unceasing now in heaven".[55] What Dom Vonier observes is that although Lepin retains the word immolation to describe Christ's death on Calvary, he does not give it its full significance. For Lepin attributes to it a mere figurative meaning, while he designates the word oblation as "truly the one grandiose thing, everlasting, all-embracing".[56] The word oblation according to Lepin, therefore, aptly indicates Christ's on-going sacrifice.

In order to counter this position, Dom Vonier insists that throughout the centuries the Catholic Church has believed and taught that the three terms *Immolation*, *offerre* and *sacrificare* have the same meaning when employed in Eucharistic theology. In the Eucharist, therefore, Christ is immolated or offered or sacrificed in a mystery, in a sacrament, or in the elements of bread and wine. If the Eucharist is a sacramental immolation, this fact by no means excludes that it is a real oblation. If Lepin considered the concept mystical immolation to be figurative, it was because he failed to see any reality in the sacramental mysticism in the sacramental figure and sign.[57] Moreover, Lepin could not grasp the real meaning of the classical Eucharistic term, *repraesentare*. In fact, he always translated it into the modern French *répresente*, which expresses something merely imaged or symbolized. For Lepin then, the sacrifice of the Mass is essentially a figurative sacrifice, a stance, of course, which does not coincide with the traditional teaching of the Church that the Eucharistic sacrifice is the true sacramental re-presentation of the sacrifice of Christ on the Cross. It renders present again on the altar the Christ who offered himself once-for-all on the hill of Calvary.

As is evident from this analysis, Dom Vonier was convinced that the many more recent Eucharistic theories lack the simplicity of outlook which was characteristic of the thought of the first millennium. Although rich in themselves, the more recent theories are of a quite different theological strand.[58] In reiterating the mind of the Council of Trent regarding the Eucharist as the memorial of the sacrificial death of Christ on Calvary, Dom Vonier appreciates its faithfulness to the tradition of the Church, and especially to St. Thomas Aquinas.

At the same time, however, Dom Vonier perceives a certain lack of theological sensitivity on the part of the Council Fathers in their approach to the Protestant-Catholic division concerning the Eucharistic sacrifice. Both Protestants and Catholics based themselves on different authorities; while Protestants argued from the Scripture as the sole authority, Catholics relied for the most part on St. Thomas. Dom Vonier remarks that both Protestants and Catholics neglected Patristic and liturgical insights concerning the sacramental life of the Church as it was related to the faith of the people and to their salvation. Given the then extant controversial situation the Council of Trent could have certainly made a more effective attempt to preserve the unity of the Church, had it advocated the use of Patristic and liturgical understandings of the Eucharist. In this sense, one could rightly affirm that Dom Vonier, when viewed in retrospect, was a forerunner of ecumenism. By means of his analysis of the Eucharist as a sacrament-sacrifice, Dom Vonier attempts first of all to make both Protestants and Catholics understand the sacramental or symbolic character of the Eucharistic sacrifice; secondly, he urges Protestants to cease regarding Catholics as not believing in the all-sufficiency of the Cross, just as he urges Catholics to cease suggesting that the Eucharistic sacrifice adds anything essential to the sacrifice of Calvary. By stating that Christ is sacrificed in a symbolic manner, Dom Vonier anticipates the later emphasis to be placed on the notion of the Paschal mystery in sacramental theology. The Eucharistic sacrifice is viewed by him as the joyful celebration in which the death and resurrection of Christ is accessible throughout time by means of symbolic re-presentation.

Dom Vonier adds a final remark to what has been noted so far; he regards the Eucharistic sacrifice as essentially the Church's sacrifice. The Church in the sacramental dispensation of Christianity announces the sacrificial death of Christ through real symbols so to re-enact it on the altar for the spiritual well-being of its members. For, this is what Christ intended when he instituted the Eucharist and gave it to his Apostles at the Last Supper. Therefore, Dom Vonier is primarily concerned about the community of persons who take part in the celebration of the Eucharist according to the command of the Lord. In other words, Dom Vonier emphasizes the worldwide community of persons who gather around the Eucharistic table in order to become spiritually nourished. In such concerns, one perceives that Dom Vonier indeed intends to revitalize the traditional teaching of the Church. He appreciates what has always been regarded as the dynamic element in the Eucharist, and he rebels against the static theories which later somewhat distorted it. As a twentieth-century theologian, Dom Vonier grasped the connection between the Eucharist, the rediscovery of the Paschal mystery, the return to a liturgical spirituality and the engagement in ecumenical dialogue.

Endnotes

1 *The Collected Works of Abbot Vonier*, Vol. I (London: Burns and Oates, 1952), pp. ix-x.

2 Anscar Vonier, *A Key to the Doctrine of the Eucharist*, 1925 (Westminster, Maryland: The Newman Press, 1960), p. vi; Ernest Graf, "The Writer," *Abbot of Buckfast: A Study of Anscar Vonier* (London: Burns and Oates, 1957), p. 97.

3 Anscar Vonier, *The Personality of Christ* (London: Burns, Oates and Washbourne, 1934), p v; Ernest Graf, *A Study*, p. 97.

[4] Thomas Aquinas, *Summa Theologiae*, III, q. lxi, a. i.

[5] According to Gabriel Vasquez (d. 1604) and Leonard Lessius (d. 1623), a real yet mystical slaying of the risen Christ occurs in the sacrifice of the Mass. By virtue of the words of consecration, Christ is not only made present but his propitiatory death on the Cross is also re-presented. Francisco Suarez and Matthias Scheeben argued in favour of an actual destruction of, or at least a radical change in the gift-offering of the Church through the metaphysical transformation of the substance of the bread and wine into those of the Body and Blood of Christ.

[6] *Summa*, III, q. Lxi, a. i.

[7] Anscar Vonier, "Sacraments," *A Key*, p. 13.

[8] "The Mystery of the Soul's Unconsciousness," *Coll. Works*, Vol. III, *The Soul and the Spiritual Life*, pp. 20-21.

[9] *Ibid.*, p. 19.

[10] *Summa*, III, q. lxi, a. iv.

[11] Anscar Vonier, *A Key*, p. 10.

[12] *Summa*, III, q. lx, a. i; St. Thomas points out that sacrament belongs to the genus of sign; it could legitimately be used in an analogous manner.

[13] Anscar Vonier, an unpublished sermon preached at Buckfast on Easter Sunday, 1923. (Among the papers of Abbot Anscar Vonier, Buckfast Abbey, Devon, England).

[14] Anscar Vonier, *A Key*, pp. 14-15; "Divine Preparations," *The Clergy Review*, xiv (January 1938), 38-39; *Summa*, III, q. lx, a. ii.

[15] Anscar Vonier, *The Divine Motherhood* (London: B, Herder, 1921), p. 7; *Coll. Works* I, pp. 331-32.

[16] *Summa*, III, q. lxii, a. i; the quotation in its English translation occurs in Vonier, *A Key*, p. 28.

[17] Anscar Vonier, *A Key*, p. 28.

[18] *Ibid.*, pp. 35-36.

[19] *Ibid.*, p. 40.

[20] Anscar Vonier, "Homo Naturaliter Christianus," *Christianus* in *Coll. Works*, III, p. 297.

[21] Martin Luther accepted the Eucharist as a testament and a sacrament, but he denied its sacrificial character; for him Mass is only a testament and not a sacrifice; human persons can do nothing but accept the Eucharist as the last will of the Lord, and they do this through faith. Thus, Luther's

concept of the Eucharist is founded on his basic theory of justification by faith alone. The Eucharist, therefore, is a testament, a gift from God. Other reformers, like Huldrich Zwingli and John Calvin, while rejecting the Mass as a sacrifice, went further than Luther in also rejecting the Real Presence. Joseph A. Jungmann, *The Mass* (Collegeville, Minnesota: The Liturgical Press, 1979), pp. 82-84.

[22] Anscar Vonier, *A Key*, p. 145.

[23] Anscar Vonier, "The Final Act of the Council of Trent in the Matter of the Eucharistic Sacrifice," *The Tablet* (September 19, 1931), p. 363; *A Key*. P. 153-54; Josef Neuner and Jacques Dupuis, ed., *The Christian Faith* (London: Collins Liturgical Publications, 1983), p. 424.

[24] That the Last supper was consummated or completed on Calvary was the theory propounded by the Bishop of Hebron and his school of theologians. The relation between the Last Supper and Calvary indeed formed their central teaching on the Eucharist. And the relation they taught is that the Last Supper was not a distinct sacrifice, but only the ritual oblation of the one sacrifice of Calvary. Both the Last supper and the Mass are then related, but not additions to the sacrifice of Calvary. Anscar Vonier, *The Tablet* (September 19, 1931), pp. 363-64.

[25] Sforza Pallavicini (1607 – 1667) was the historian of the Council who, along with Massarelli and other diarists gave the account of the great debates of the Council Fathers.

[26] Anscar Vonier, *A Key*, p. 139; "The Final Act of the Council of Trent," *The Tablet* (September 19, 1931), p. 363.

[27] David N. Power, *The Sacrifice We Offer: The Tridentine Dogma and Its Reinterpretation* (Edinburgh: T. & T. Clark Limited), p. 119; Anscar Vonier, *A. Key*, pp. 154-55.

[28] Anscar Vonier, *A. Key*, p. 121.

[29] The notion of the separate consecration of the two species as the representation of the separation of Christ's Body and Blood on the hill of Calvary is stated by St. Thomas, *Summa*, III, q. lxxx, a. xii.

[30] Anscar Vonier, *A Key*, p. 136-37; *Summa*, III, q. lxxxiii, a. i.

[31] Anscar Vonier, *A Key*, p. 145.

[32] *Ibid.*, p. 139.

[33] Erwin Iserloh, *Der Kampf um die Messes in den ersten Jahren der Auseinandersetzung mit Luther* (Münster, 1952), p. 57.

[34] Anscar Vonier, *A Key*, p. 147-48.

[35] David N. Power, *The Sacrifice We Offer*, p. 131.

[36] Anscar Vonier, "The Concepts of Commemoration and of Immolation," *Sketches and Studies in Theology* (London: Burns, Oates and Washbourne Ltd., 1940), p. 63.

[37] Francis Clark, *Eucharistic Sacrifice and the Reformation* (Westminster: 1960), pp. 394-409.

[38] Josef A, Jungmann, *The Mass*, pp. 88, 104.

[39] St. Thomas asserted that the suffering of Christ was a true immolation, of which the Mass is merely a re-presentation. But since this sacrament is the re-presentation of the sacrifice of Christ, it has the nature of a sacrifice. He was the first to bring out the notion of the separate consecration of the two species which re-presented the separation of Christ's Body and Blood on the Cross. *Summa,* III, lxxix, xii; lxxxiii, i; the idea occurs in Jungmann, *The Mass*, p. 88.

[40] *Summa*, III, q. lxxviii, a. iv; Josef A. Jungmann, *The Mass*, p. 89.

[41] Anscar Vonier, "Christianus Sacrificance: The Christian at Sacrifice," *Chimes* I (New Series, January-March 1927), p. 11.

[42] Ernest Graf, *A Study*, p. 93.

[43] Anscar Vonier, *A Key*, pp. 56-57.

[44] *Ibid.*, p. 57.

[45] *Summa* III, q. lxxxiii, a. v; Vonier, *A. Key*, p. 94.

[46] Josef, A. Jungmann, *The Mass*, p. 89.

[47]*Ibid.*, p. 90.

[48] Anscar Vonier, "Eucharistic Theology," *The Tablet* (April 30, 1927), p. 576; Jungmann, *The Mass*, p. 90.

[49] M. de la Taille, *Mysterium Fidei* (1921); M. Lepin, *L'idée du Sacrifice de la Messe* (1926).

[50] Joseph A. Jungmann, *The Mass*, p. 90; Bernard Hall, "Our Sacrifice," *Bellarmine Commentary*, Vol. 1 (October 1956), p. 49.

[51] Juan de Lugo made the reality of the Eucharistic sacrifice consist in Christ himself. Through the words of consecration Christ is reduced to a lower state which is a *status deterior*, an abasement. And therefore the Mass is a sacrifice. Later, Franzlin expounded the same view by reducing Christ *ad punctum* and thereby completely abandoning the traditional sacramental aspect of the Eucharist. Anscar Vonier, *The Tablet* (May 7, 1927), p. 611.

[52] Anscar Vonier, *A key*, pp. 108-109; *The Tablet* (May 7, 1927), p. 611.

[53] *Ibid.*

⁵⁴ Anscar Vonier, *A Key*, pp. 125-26.

⁵⁵ Anscar Vonier, *The Tablet* (April 30, 1927), p. 576.

⁵⁶ *Ibid.*

⁵⁷ *Ibid.*

⁵⁸ *Ibid.*, p. 575.

The Middle Period: The Christological, Ecclesial and Liturgical Bases of Dom Anscar's Eucharistic Theology

Dom Vonier grounded his Eucharistic Theology in the person of Jesus Christ, in the nature of the Church and in that of its liturgical actions. In his Christological treatises, *The Personality of Christ, Christ the King of Glory: Tu Rex Gloriae Christe* and *The Victory of Christ*, Dom Vonier unites the person and the mission of Jesus Christ, God Incarnate by viewing him as being the redemption-in-person of humanity. Based on this soteriological understanding of Christology, Dom Vonier considers the mystery of the Church in such works as *The Christian Mind* and *The People of God*, the head of the mystical body. Thus, Dom Vonier argues that Jesus instituted the sacrament of the Eucharist so that this liturgical encounter might be the repeated event by which he effects the unity of the members of the Church. The efficacy of the Eucharist lies in its being the sacramental re-presentation of the final acts of the redemption-in-person, Jesus Christ, which constitute the cause, essence and goal of human sanctification.

Dom Vonier understands the Eucharist in relation to the passion, death and resurrection of Jesus Christ, so that this sublime sacrament of Christian faith is considered as the privileged encounter of the baptized with the person and mission of the Son of God and Redeemer of the whole human race. Christians who partake in this sacrament are enabled to read their life, their world, and their history in the light of Christ's redemptive person and mission. More precisely, Dom Vonier perceives how the desire of human beings for redemption by God finds in the Eucharist its definitive fulfilment.

Furthermore, Dom Vonier understands the Eucharist as effecting the unity of the mystical body in a triple way: first, the individual faithful are united to Christ insofar as they actively commemorate and participate in his passion, death and resurrection; second, the corporate body of the faithful is conjoined to Christ its head so that with him they form the *Totus Christus*; third, the members are united among themselves so that the Church herself is the one active personality in the Eucharistic celebration.[1] Thus, following the classical pattern, Dom Vonier treats the Eucharist as a commemorative sign of a definitive event in the past, that is, the Passover of the Lord Jesus Christ, which is the cause of human sanctification; then as a demonstrative sign of what is presently brought about in the Church, that is, the bestowal of grace which is the essence of human sanctification; and finally as a prognostic sign of the future glory to be enjoyed with Christ, that is, eternal life which is the goal of human sanctification. In these considerations, while Dom Vonier adopts Pauline and Thomistic approaches to understanding the mystery of the Eucharist, he reiterates the traditional teaching to advocate a Eucharistic way of life. For him, the Eucharist is indeed "the life of Christ, the death of Christ, the resurrection of Christ," presented in symbolic form in order to take concrete shape in the holy and dedicated lives of contemporary Christians. [2]

1.   The Living God Incarnate Encounters Humanity in the Eucharist

The doctrine of the Incarnation proclaims the fundamental truth that the Son of God, in assuming flesh, initiated the total transformation of humanity. Dom Vonier considers the sacrament of the Eucharist in relation to the concrete humanity of Jesus of Nazareth, which continually renders itself present and efficacious in the various historical situations in which human persons find themselves. Since the salvific events of Christ's life, passion, death and resurrection are contained in symbolic form in the Eucharist, Dom Vonier speaks of the living God Incarnate meeting humanity in this sacrament.

Dom Vonier distinguishes two fundamental aspects of the Incarnation: that the Son of God became flesh is the aspect which is *theoretical in nature*; that the Son of God assumed the concrete humanity of Jesus, in order to accomplish a definite mission, is the aspect which is *practical in nature*.[3] Both these aspects are essential, however, to the salvation of humanity, for the God Incarnate brings salvation to all the people of the world and to their history, and does this in his unique person and mission. In effect, this redemption-in-person, both as sacred event and as saving grace, is aptly symbolized and re-actualized in the liturgical actions of the Church:

> In celebrating the Christian festivities we not only remember a past event on the world, but we enter into the very grace it has left behind, which remains forever and which can never be driven away from this world by men's iniquities because the sacred incident has changed forever the conditions of heaven and earth.[4]

Dom Vonier affirms the permanence of grace, the newness of life of the redeemed humanity, effected by the redemptive death of Christ so that the sacraments are not mere remembrance of the past historical event, but permanent saving realities. In the celebration of the sacraments, the definite words and gestures signify and re-actualize particular aspects of Jesus Christ's redemption in its absolute meaning and efficacy. In other words, the sacraments render present in Christians the salvific acts and graces which Jesus Christ, the Incarnate Word of God accomplished both in his divinity as well as in his humanity:

> The aim and goal of the whole drama of the Incarnation, from the conception through the Holy Ghost in the Virgin's womb to the glories of the risen Jesus on Easter morning is this, that the God-Man, Christ Jesus, Son of God and Son of Mary, true God and true Man, should be, both through his human as well as through his divine element, man's eternal life; and all the parts of that divine drama, with such a wonderful chief Actor in the centre of it, are indispensable to that crowning achievement, that he, Jesus of Nazareth, is man's life substantively, and not only life-giver to man.[5]

With this understanding of the Incarnation of the Son of God, Dom Vonier emphasizes that human beings find in Jesus Christ the substance, or the metaphysical basis of their lives. Both through his divine and human elements the Word

Incarnate was a concrete sign or symbol of the salvation of humanity. Thus, Dom Vonier argues that Jesus Christ brought not only salvation but also life to the world. If it were only the matter of human beings' salvation, the Word of God would not have needed to become flesh, for only an act of God's eternal omnipotence would have sufficed. Then, Dom Vonier states: "but to be life to man necessitated a Christ, who is the Son of God born of a Virgin, who suffered under Pontius Pilate, who died, was buried and rose again from the dead".[6] In each of the sacraments, an essential aspect of the life brought to humanity by Jesus Christ is symbolized and communicated.

In the Eucharist, the summit of the Church's sacraments, the living God Incarnate gives to human beings his Body and Blood, symbols of his life-giving immolation on Calvary:

> The two elements are indispensable to the integrity and full meaning of the Eucharistic mystery. Without the Body, the Blood would lack that profound signification of being poured forth from a living Body; without the Blood the Body would miss the signification of being offered up or immolated, as its offering and immolation was essentially the pouring forth of its life Blood.[7]

One clearly observes here that the organic relation between the living Body and the poured forth Blood of Jesus Christ gives the Eucharistic mystery its proper saving significance. From the perspective of sacramental efficacy, the integral union of the Body and the Blood is indispensable in the Eucharist. For, from the living Body of Christ his sacrificial Blood is poured out, and the new Covenant between the Father and humanity is thus established once-and-for-all. For this reason, Dom Vonier states that the measure of human beings' redemption was full when Jesus Christ had shed the last drop of his Blood on Calvary.[8]

When Dom Vonier states that the Eucharist is "the endless repetition of Christ's sacrifice on the altars of the Church from sunrise to sunset, until the end of the world", he notes that this sacrament is possible primarily because of the mortal life of Jesus, and not because of his divine nature:

> It may seem a paradox, yet the truest way to state the matter is to say that the Eucharistic renewing of Christ's death is a result of that infinite fullness of redemption that is in his mortal life. Because Christ merited infinitely, and atoned with a generosity superabundant, we have the real Presence, we have the daily sacrifice of the Christian altar.[9]

Jesus Christ achieved fullness of redemption for humanity in and through his weak mortal flesh. The Eucharist is a sacramental renewing of the ignominious death of Jesus Christ on the Cross. Dom Vonier intends to emphasize the role of the human nature assumed by the Word of God in his becoming the redemption-in-person of humanity through his sacrificial immolation on Calvary. As the risen Lord, Jesus Christ continues to be the redemption and the life of humanity in the Eucharist, since by its very nature it re-presents the unique event on the altar of the Cross. In other words, the sacrament of the Eucharist inherently contains "an active power, bringing about in the Church and in souls the full effects of the New Testament".[10] In the Eucharist, the faithful receive the Body and Blood of Christ, and are bound more perfectly to his person and mission so as to be able to commit themselves to his kenotic way of life, dying to self, in order to rise with him in eternal glory.

In order to synthesize these soteriological reflections on the Eucharist, Dom Vonier asserts that Christ's humanity is as indispensable to his role as the life of the world as is his divinity.[11] Thus, the universality and permanency of the higher life made possible in the world by Christ's unrepeatable death can be fully understood only through further reflection on the meaning of his humanity for that of human beings:

> The Incarnation is adequately appreciated by those only to whom Christ's humanity is the marvel of marvels, a superb creation, in which they have their being, in which they live, work, die, and in which they hope to rise again, in which they find the fullness of the Godhead, as Moses found the fire in the bush. The astonishing frailty of human nature being made to blaze forth the glory of eternal godhead, and yet remain unconsumed and keeping its native greenness, is the ever amazing paradox of Christ's humanity.[12]

By affirming that the humanity of Christ is a superb creation in which human beings find their authentic existence, Dom Vonier highlights the fundamental truth that the Son of God manifests his divinity to human beings not apart from but through his humanity. It is evident that, since the Eucharistic mystery contains both the divinity and humanity of Christ, both these elements create a life-giving encounter between him and his people. Yet, lest the divinity of Christ be affirmed to the point that his humanity seems secondary in the Eucharist, Dom Vonier makes an analogy between the humanity of Christ and the bush witnessed by Moses (Ex.3: 1-6); in both cases, the blazing glory of God breaks forth through the apparent frailty of a plant or of a mortal being.

Furthermore, Dom Vonier, as a Benedictine monk, insists that the Eucharistic celebration does not emphasize the Paschal mystery so much as an historical event but as an omnipotent reality:

> To celebrate the mystery of Christ's redemptive act merely as an historical event is certainly no full explanation of the Church's attitude. Even the desire and the effort to have a share in the fruits of the Church's temper; there is more, there is a celebration of redemption in its absolute meaning, as an ever-present, omnipresent reality which creates a mentality in the Church which is truly consummate religious genius.[13]

Evidently, the mentality to which Dom Vonier refers here is explained by him in another passage as "that spiritual estate, that world of light and liberty which was created by the fact of Christ's Death and Resurrection".[14] In other words, the ongoing and everlasting Covenant, which was first established by God in the Body and Blood of Jesus Christ, is the absolute meaning of the Eucharist. Thus, Dom Vonier states that the Eucharistic celebration should create in the baptized a sense of possession, a feeling of certainty and a note of triumph and victory, since they are already within history the redeemed people of the Kingdom, eating and drinking at the table of their heavenly Father. The Eucharist, as the ever-present reality of divine redemption, is "the feast of love, the sacrament of union and the banquet which Christ with a great desire wished to eat with his disciples".[15] Thus, by perceiving the Eucharist, as the continuation of the definitive victory of Jesus Christ on behalf of humanity, Dom Vonier is clearly one of the theologians who anticipated the eschatological themes of more recent Catholic sacramental theology.

Dom Vonier goes on to argue that, although the act by which the second Person of the Trinity became flesh might appear weak, and the renewal of humanity through his death on the Cross folly, "one thing is beyond doubt, that through the accidents of his mortal life he carried out his work of the redemption with supreme perfection....Moreover the things he suffered were so appointed that through them he entered into his glory".[16] The contrast between the words *mortal life* and *supreme perfection* in this text captures the similar paradox which an unpublished sermon of Dom Vonier employs as its central theme; the implications for the Eucharist and for the life of those who receive it are quite striking:

> Nothing has so deeply modified Christian sentiment as has this determination of God to work out the salvation of man in the infirmity of the flesh. It is the peculiar spirit of Christianity, the blending of majesty and infirmity, of power and weakness... It is the Christian, and the Christian only, who adores power in weakness, and wisdom in the folly of the Cross.[17]

By making use of paradoxical phrases, power in weakness, majesty and infirmity, wisdom in the folly of the Cross, Dom Vonier intends to underline that in his humanity Jesus entered into the sinful world of human beings, and took upon himself on the Cross all the burdens, and chief among them is the burden of death. In this humanity is re-born as new people of God while the Word of God dies by being engulfed in its weakness.

Dom Vonier, therefore, states that the human blood of Christ shed on the Cross in utter humiliation is rendered symbolically present in the Eucharist so as to become the sign of humanity's victorious inheritance:

> The Eucharistic drinking is a showing forth of the death of Christ and therefore the divine Will becomes operative, we enter into our inheritance. Testament, Blood, Death – or better still, Death through the effusion of Blood – and inheritance, these are the pivotal ideas, not only of the Pauline theology but also of that of the whole New Testament.[18]

Dom Vonier emphasizes the drinking of the Eucharistic wine which, in sacramental significance and meaning, indicates that Christians are inheritors of God's eternal Covenant with humanity. On the basis of this consideration, Dom Vonier states that Jesus' experience of shedding Blood on the Cross in perfect love and obedience to the Father for the redemption of humanity attracts the attention of his followers in a more intense way than does any other act of his life. In other words, Christians recognize the unconditional love of the Son of God for them in his sacrificial pouring out of life on the Cross. For, as Dom Vonier poignantly affirms, "a Christ who did not share human conditions to the full or who in his life and death had experiences which were not human at all would not be the Christ of Catholic theology".[19] The Son of God poured out his Blood on the Cross in order to guarantee the sanctification of the human race and its privileged inheritance of divine life.

Although Dom Vonier does not fail to show how each of the sacraments of the Church draws its efficacy from the grace of Christ attained on the Cross, he accentuates the special feature of the Eucharist, namely, that in it the personality of Christ is the means of the conferral of his grace:

> The Eucharist is the grandest and truest result of his holiness, as it is the grandest and truest union with the Person of Christ. All the sacraments derive their spiritual power from Christ's death. That one of them, instead of merely containing Christ's grace, contains Christ himself shows the wonderful efficacy of his death. In the Eucharist, the Personality, which is the pivot of Christianity, has become not only a centre and source of grace, but a means of grace.[20]

This statement of Dom Vonier can best be illumined by referring to another in which he affirms that the seven sacraments of the Church "besides signifying the grace which is the inheritance of faith, also contain that grace and cause it".[21] However, in accentuating the unique character of the Eucharist, Dom Vonier states that it contains Christ himself, the source of life and grace. And all those faithful who participate in the celebration of the Eucharist "enter into direct and physical communion with Christ's life and death".[22] The use of the word "physical" might lead the reader to deem here Dom Vonier an ultra-realist. But far from being the case, he simply advocates the importance of the encounter of Christians with the human life of Jesus for their meaningful participation in the Eucharist. For, the continual tendency of believers to view Jesus Christ only from the perspective of his divinity mystifies his death without stressing its practical relevance for their daily existence. In contrast, Dom Vonier maintains that the Eucharist reveals Christ as truly living in the baptized, once he was raised to glory by the power of the Holy Spirit. The continual access to Christ's humanity in the Eucharist enhances the truth that grace is a dynamic self-communication of both Christ and his Spirit.

Next, Dom Vonier explains more fully the manner in which the living God Incarnate encounters humanity while in majesty he enjoys the glory of heaven: "Christ's Resurrection means more than the vivifying of a dead body; it means above all things that mode of existence which is called the life of glory... It is a newness of life that transforms the whole history of mankind".[23] Dom Vonier undoubtedly considers Christ's resurrection as his unique mode of existence which, in turn, transforms the very meaning of human history. Elsewhere Dom Vonier states that Christ's resurrection is more than "a glorious event that crowned his earthly career; it is part of the dispensation of grace and salvation, and not only unimpeachable evidence of Christ's divinity".[24] In each of these texts, and in many others like them, the main theme is that the Incarnate Word of God, by entering into newness of life, opens up an unexpected possibility of humanity: its transformation from a self-made dispensation of sin and nothingness to a God-given one of grace and salvation. With this insight, Dom Vonier goes beyond the narrow Post-Tridentine concern with the passion and death of Jesus, and the salvific import of the glorification of the Crucified One. In stating that the resurrection is far more than the vivifying of Jesus' dead Body or the undeniable verification of his divinity, Dom Vonier means that the assumption of glory on the part of the Incarnate Word is as important for humanity as is that of having assumed flesh, suffering and death. In brief, Dom Vonier advocated the relevance for human salvation of both the humiliation and the glorification of the Body and Blood of Jesus in the Paschal mystery.

This insight, far from remaining an abstract principle, decidedly influenced Dom Vonier's understanding of the Eucharist as the memorial of Jesus Christ's victorious death; the Christ who is present in the Eucharist comes to the Church not from the realm of death, but from that of eternal life:

> Coming now to the great memorial of the Lord, the divine Eucharist, it is as much the sacrament of Christ's Resurrection as of his death, because it is the monument of that Death like unto which there is no other death. It is a commemoration of that victorious passage into the Father, that new and supreme Passover, of which the first Passover was but a faint figure. "Therefore as often as we eat that Bread and drink of that Cup we show forth the death of the Lord

until he come"; a Death that is in every respect a triumph, because the advent here alluded to is not a coming from the realm of the dead, but from the kingdom of eternal life.[25]

Dom Vonier affirms the Eucharist as the sacrament which re-actualizes the death Jesus understood as a victorious passage to the Father. Thus, the salvific grace operative in the Eucharist effects the newness of life or the total transformation of humanity conjoined to the glorified Christ. Unlike then contemporary theologians who seemed to devaluate the Resurrection as an agent of redemption, Dom Vonier adhered to the classical soteriology of St. Paul and the Fathers of the Church. He considers Christ's resurrection as an indispensable motif of Eucharistic theology, insofar as this sacrament is a memorial of the saving power of his life-giving death.

Furthermore, because of the soteriological efficacy of all the sacraments, Christ's resurrection remains a present reality within history, a continuous act by which human beings are renewed:

> Through Christ's resurrection something has taken place in the world of spirits, in the world of souls, nay, even in the world of bodies, which is ever active and which never can be checked any more: the resurrection is with us, so to speak... We have in the resurrection a permanent upraising; we glory in it as in our supreme inheritance; through it our whole life receives a loftiness which would not be believable if we had not God's word for it.[26]

By reflecting on the unique event of Christ's resurrection, Dom Vonier accentuates its permanent ability to uplift the spiritual life of the baptized, because they share in the glorification of their Lord. Dom Vonier argues that, although Jesus Christ personally enjoys the glory of the Godhead, he extends this privilege to the world through the sacramental gestures of the Church. For, the Word made flesh has assumed the intended glory of Humanity and became human redemption-in-person forever. The difference, however, between Christ's glorification and the resurrection with us lies in the temporal mode of his presence. Throughout history, the glorified Christ is more significant in the Eucharist as this sacrament is in a more direct manner the monument of Christ's victory.[27] In another passage, Dom Vonier reiterates the insight that the Eucharist in particular renders the triumph of Christ accessible to humanity with a directness which surpasses that of the other sacraments:

> From the right hand of God, through the sacraments, Jesus enters into the very flesh and bone of the human race as an assimilating power binding man to himself. But there is one sacrament which may truly be called the sacrament of Christ's victory, because through its very constitution it is a monument of the great achievement of the Son of God, our liberation from all evils through his blood. This sacrament is the Blessed Eucharist. In it we celebrate Christ's triumph with a directness that leaves nothing to be desired as to the true significance of that venerable sacrament.[28]

While stating that all the sacraments of the Church are the monument of Christ's victory, Dom Vonier emphasizes the traditional Catholic belief that the glorified and living Word Incarnate encounters humanity in the Eucharist in a special manner; it is the liturgical re-enacting of his Passover which contains what it signifies. Although sacraments of the Christian dispensation manifest the continued presence of the risen Jesus in history, the Eucharist excels because it renders his Body and Blood more directly available to the members of his Church so as to guarantee the permanence of their spiritual renewal in and through him.

Now, when Christians partake of the Eucharistic bread and wine, they are in perfect union with their risen head "not indeed in his own kind, but in the kind of the sacrament".[29] Thus, Dom Vonier concludes that, although the presence of the glorified Christ in the Eucharist is real, it always remains a sacramental one. The glorified Christ encounters humanity in the Eucharist through symbols which indicate that the union between his death and resurrection which has but one purpose- the perfect redemption of human beings from shame and death unto glory and majesty. Although this gracious divine plan has been accomplished once-and-for-all in the person and mission of Jesus Christ, it continues to be prolonged in the world through the Church's liturgical words and gestures.

2. The Eucharistic Event as Effecting the Unity of the Mystical Body

In his Christological treatise, *Christ the King of Glory*, Dom Vonier states that "Christ in his humanity has power to communicate to the souls of the redeemed the kind of supernatural life that is in himself, to communicate it in its very essence, homogeneously, identically".[30] By employing what might appear to be static philosophical concepts such as essence, homogeneity, identity, Dom Vonier emphasizes the dynamic relation between Christ's life and that of redeemed humanity universally though not explicitly affected by his redemptive grace. It is in the Church that Christ, with all his grace and power forms an acknowledged organic whole with redeemed humanity, the Church. In these considerations, Dom Vonier adopts both the Pauline and the Thomistic approaches to the mystery of the Church so as to show the intrinsic relationship of Christ the head with the members of his mystical body.

Furthermore, Dom Vonier does this by having recourse to sacramental notions, for he argues that the communication of life and grace between Christ and Christians takes place in the Church through sacraments. This process reaches its culmination in the Eucharist; this sublime sacrament not only symbolizes but also contains Christ himself, the source of salvific grace. Moreover, as the Eucharist is the objective memorial of Christ's unique Passover, it repeatedly becomes the decisive redemptive-event effecting, on the one hand, the union between the Redeemer and the redeemed humanity into an organic whole, and on the other, that of the individual members among themselves into one body under one head. Because of its sacramental nature, the Eucharist renders present on the Christian altar the self-same event of Calvary at which Christ's Body was pierced and his Blood poured out. Significantly, Dom Vonier states that the Church maintains its identity by consuming the sacramental bread and wine on the altar which re-present Christ's sacrificial Body and Blood.

Accentuating the necessity of being conjoined to Christ, Dom Vonier insists that the primary response to the Eucharist is eating and drinking of it: "We must always remember this pivotal fact in Eucharistic theology, that at all times and everywhere the Body of Christ and the Blood of Christ in the Eucharist must be eaten and must be drunk sooner or later by a Christian; there is no other known way of consummating the sacrament".[31] Thus, Dom Vonier indirectly refutes those who would adore rather than eat and drink of the Eucharistic elements; chiefly in this way do Christians express their inner need to participate in the passion and resurrection of Christ. The verbs, "must be eaten and must be drunk", reveal the Abbot's conviction that receiving the Eucharist is the *sine qua non* of taking part in the death and resurrection of the Lord, until he come (1 Cor.11: 26). Dom Vonier, then, argues that, although the sacrificial death and glorious exaltation of the Lord is rendered actual on the Christian altar through the consecration of the elements, its full efficaciousness is attained in the act of consuming the sacrament. Through this symbolic action, Christians know that they are incorporated in the New Covenant which has been established in the Blood which flowed from Christ's Body.

In other words, well before partaking in the chalice, on the part of the laity, was permitted, Dom Vonier viewed such full participation in the Eucharist as the privilege of the people of God:

> In the Eucharistic mystery the Cup, the Blood of the Lord, is not only an indispensable part, but is the most characteristic part, because through it, in sacramental significance and meaning, that thing is rendered present whose presence is for us of supreme importance, namely, the Death of the Lord in a mystery. Through that death on the Cross... we become the heirs of the Covenant in that general and absolute way which is proper to the redemptive work of the Cross. On the Christian altar, through that same Blood we enter individually into our inheritance, into the Covenant, because sacramentally and mystically there is the Death of the Lord as his Blood is poured out.[32]

While Dom Vonier admits that "those events in Christ's career which are called his life's consummation, the passion, the death and the resurrection" are re-actualized through the consecrated bread and wine on the altar, he is primarily concerned that the Eucharist be understood as enabling

Christians personally to inherit all the graces of the New Covenant. In other terms, for all his emphasis on the ontological presence of Christ's saving Blood on the altar, Dom Vonier does not lose sight of the inherent existential and eschatological sense of the Eucharist.

In a graphic passage, Dom Vonier explains the existential power of the Eucharist by which the Christian soul is nourished and given its true heredity. "The Blood of Our Lord is drunk by our soul in the mystery of the Holy Eucharist, is drunk by that highest and innermost part of ourselves, where spiritual temperament, or conscience is to be found; and it gives to that part of our being, by a new kind of heredity, its own nobility; it makes us have God in our blood."[33] Dom Vonier forcefully highlights the supernatural efficacy of the act of drinking the sacramental Blood of Christ. It transforms the entire life of Christians by enabling the salvific act of Christ on the Cross to penetrate their souls. Yet lest he be misunderstood as holding that the Blood of Jesus Christ simply nourishes individual souls, Dom Vonier mentions "our blood" so as to stress that the whole reality of human persons, their physical and spiritual dimensions, enters into a dynamic salvific relationship with the Son of God. For this reason, he speaks of the effect of the Blood of Christ "on the innermost part of ourselves"; but he goes on to state that the whole human person acquires a new kind of heredity, that is a nobility which comes from being holistically united to the salvific outpouring of Christ's Blood.

This insight is deepened in another passage in which Dom Vonier conjoins partaking in the Blood of Christ to having access through him to the Father. For, just as the innocent blood of Abel prefigured that to be shed by Christ, the value of the first sacrifice in God's eyes cannot be compared to that offered by His Son:

> The Blood of Christ as shed on Calvary, as shed on the Christian altar, is an absolute spiritual quantity; through it we have access to Christ first, and through him to the Father and to everything that is holy in heaven and on earth; we have been admitted to "Jesus the mediator of the new testament, and to the sprinkling of blood which speaketh better than that of Abel" (Heb.12: 24).[34]

In these considerations, Dom Vonier concentrates on the efficacy of the Blood of Christ for the salvation of human beings. In effect, Dom Vonier argues that the Blood of Christ as the divine instrument of human salvation is a theme dominant in the Scriptures (Eph. 1: 7; 2: 13; Heb.9: 14; 1 Pt.1: 18-19; 1 Jn.1: 7; Apoc.1: 5; 12: 11).[35] Christ's Body or Flesh is mentioned in some of these texts, but not with the same force which is attached to his Blood. However, this fact does not mean that the Body of Christ is to be regarded as less important for the mystery of human salvation. For, Christ's Body is the abode of the gratuitous event of the redemption, since from it there issued forth Blood by which the divine liberation of humanity was consummated.

In all these considerations, Dom Vonier adopts both Pauline and Thomistic views in describing the organic relationship between Christ the Redeemer and the redeemed humanity. He views the special relationship between Christ and the Church, as head to body, as both sacramental and functional. From the sacramental point of view, the Church as the assembly of redeemed people is a sign to the world of the perduring value of Christ's passion, death and resurrection. The Church is "a continuation of the Christ's Person and his salvific mission in the world".[36] From the functional point of view, this continuity is made visible whenever believers live in such a way in society that they extend the efficacy of the Eucharist to all people. "Only in this way can Christ's world redeeming action attain its goal. It is here that mankind is integrated in Christ's death as well as in his resurrection."[37]

As the commemoration, participation and ratification of the New Covenant on the part of the Church, the Eucharist can be the offering and the gift made to God along with Christ and in the name of all humanity which is included in it in an implicit way: "We cannot give the Eucharistic sacrifice a scope wider than the Church, because it is the Church only that offers it, and it offers it as its own gift. The sacrifice of the Cross belongs to the whole world, but the Eucharistic sacrifice belongs to the Church only".[38] Although Dom Vonier considers the Eucharistic sacrifice as essentially the liturgical act of the Church, in the last analysis he professes the universal applicability of the saving event of Calvary. Thus, the efficacy and grace of the sacrament of the Eucharist reach all human beings through the action of the Church: "If the Eucharistic sacrifice is a power in this world that affects even those who are not in the body of the Church, it is still through the body of the Church that the power is exerted. The Eucharistic sacrifice reaches the infidel, not directly, but through the Church".[39]

Thus, while admitting the universal applicability of the grace of the Eucharistic sacrifice, Dom Vonier insists that this truth is grounded in the reality of the social body of the Church as it is united to Christ, its head. Evidently, as the mystical body of the Lord, the visible Church proclaims and represents in and through its sacramental actions, the salvific deeds of the Lord on behalf of all humanity. From that analysis, Dom Vonier arrives at a heightened appreciation of the sacramental words and rituals of the ecclesial body:

> It is in this that the Church has shown to the fullest extent her talent of expressing the divine things. The history of her Lord's life has been couched by the Evangelists in language truly inimitable; she has only to remember the phrases in which the greatest of all careers has been described by those who were either the eyewitnesses or their disciples. But to show forth in words, in rites, the sense she has within herself of the divine victory of the Redemption – that is the Church's own art.[40]

While admitting that the Church has been graciously endowed with knowledge concerning supernatural realities, Dom Vonier ponders the creative manner in which it expresses them in each age so as to render the divine victory of the redemption more comprehensible and relevant for the world. Evidently, the Church manifests the divine salvific events of Christ by acting them out in definite words and rites, that is, in its liturgical proclamation of the Word and celebration of the sacraments. Thus, in the case of the Eucharist the Church's efforts to make this sacrament meaningful and relevant in the life of each of its members through their active participation leads Dom Vonier to conclude that the Church makes the Eucharist.

Next, Dom Vonier considers the Eucharist as effecting the unity of the mystical Body of Christ from the perspective of its ability to signify the communion of Christians with Christ and with one another. Dom Vonier states that this communion is brought about as the baptized gather around the altar and share the one cup:

> In the celebration of the blessed Eucharist we have the Covenant brought home to us in the very element that, so to speak, is the mother of that Covenant, the Blood of Christ... to hold the Cup of that Blood as we do in the sacrifice of the Catholic altar is the most solemn, most drastic, most realistic assertion of the superb fact that we are redeemed in Christ and that we believe in our redemption. The Christian chalice is the most perfect symbol of the greatest of all victories... To drink of it abundantly, freely, as sons and daughters drink of the wine that is on the table of their father on a festive day, is the natural way for us to enter into participation of all the riches of the covenant.[41]

In a manner then uncharacteristic of Catholic theology, Dom Vonier describes how the new and eternal Covenant established by the Blood of Jesus Christ on the Cross is rendered present on the altar in the real symbol which is the consecrated wine. Dom Vonier states that, insofar as the Eucharist is an objective gift of Christ to the Church, it also has the existential purpose of helping Christians to realize that they are indeed the people of the New Covenant, the assembly of the elect of God, a great new society, whose head is the Lord; and "he is head because the life that is in him is communicated in its identity to the Church". In another text, Dom Vonier likens the Eucharistic elements in the altar to "a divine fire[42] which burns in virtue of its own inner force and all that man can do is to come within the radius of the heat of that fire".[43]

By employing such phrases, Dom Vonier accentuates the divine power operative in the sacrament of the altar, and affirms that sacramental grace is derived from it. Christians who receive the Eucharist attain to a most personal and communitarian experience of redemption. On the basis of these considerations, Dom Vonier states that the sacrament of the Eucharist effects the sanctification and the unity of Christians as true members of the one Body of Christ.[44] In other words, the sacramental grace conferred by the Eucharist makes recipients of the sacrament members with Christ and the whole community of believers.

Dom Vonier proceeds to consider this state of unity as the specific characteristic of Eucharistic grace:

> We become all members of one Body, eating one Bread: this is the classical, traditional concept of the Eucharistic assemblies of Christians. The society of the elect here on earth are gathered in love and brotherhood, performing such mysterious rites as will open the portal of heaven itself, and make Angels and men come together.[45]

Here and in similar texts, Dom Vonier presents the Eucharist as furthering the great cause of Christ's mystical Body, the society of the elect. And, if this sanctified society is, through charity and brotherhood, to extend the redemptive mystery of Christ to many others, their membership in the mystical Body of Christ is also a foretaste of their eternal happiness in the Kingdom of Christ and of God the Father. For this reason, Dom Vonier logically argues, in the paragraph under investigation, from eating and drinking the Eucharistic species, to becoming all members of one ecclesial Body, to practicing love and brotherhood as visible signs of being the society of the elect, to regarding such a way of life as an eschatological reality.

Dom Vonier's statement concerning the Eucharist as an eschatological sign is, of course, true of all the sacraments of the Church:

> The sacramental graces taken in their most specific aspect, has this characteristic of being a pledge of the eternal splendours of the life

> to come... Not only do we receive graces through the sacraments
> which give us strength to fight the battle of our soul and to conquer
> eternal life, but in them we are marked and sealed for eternal life.[46]

Dom Vonier asserts that all seven sacraments of the Church in their respective modes are prognostic signs of eternal glory. However, the Eucharist excels in this regard, because it is the symbolic re-actualization of the glorification of the crucified Christ so that his new life is communicated to his followers in a real, true and substantial manner. Therefore, Dom Vonier emphatically declares "that of the Eucharist on earth cannot be different in the smallest matter from the Christ who is in the glory of the Father, except in the sacramental appearance".[47]

On the basis of all these considerations, Dom Vonier would affirm that the Eucharist makes the Church, insofar as it effects the unity of its members, just as the Church makes the Eucharist, insofar as it is the active subject in carrying out the Lord's command to do what he did in the Cenacle. This understanding of mutual relationship between the mystery of the Eucharist and that of the Church demonstrates once again the truth of the assertion that Dom Vonier was a forerunner of later developments in Catholic Eucharistic theology. While affirming the truth of the metaphysical change of the elements, he added to it the further truth that this change was for the Church, that is, for the existential conviction on the part of Christians that they are united to their head and to one another in a society of the elect. Furthermore, such unity is a foreshadowing of the total oneness to be enjoyed in the Kingdom at Christ's victorious banquet table.

3. Temporal Aspects of Redemption as Symbolized in the Eucharist

That the redemptive act of Christ, the Paschal mystery continues to be efficacious in the life of human persons through the sacraments of the Church is a basic teaching of Christianity. Relying on this assumption, Dom Vonier considers the sacraments of the Church from the perspective of "a much higher degree of signification that has effectiveness associated with it".[48] Dom Vonier states that sacraments, besides signifying Christ's grace through which all human beings are sanctified, actually render it operative in the lives of believers. Following the classical thought pattern of St. Thomas Aquinas, Dom Vonier presents the power of sacramental symbolization from three perspectives:

> The sacrament, properly so called, is the thing ordained to the purpose of signifying our sanctification; in this three phases may be taken into consideration, namely – the *cause* of our sanctification, which is the passion of Christ; the *essence* of our sanctification, which consists in grace and virtue; and then the ultimate *goal* of our sanctification, which is eternal life. Now these three things are signified by the sacraments; therefore a sacrament is a commemorative sign of what has gone before, I mean the passion of Christ, and demonstrative sign of what is being brought about in us through the passion of Christ, that is grace, and prognostic, that is a prophetic sign, of the future glory. [49]

Evidently, Dom Vonier understands the effectiveness of sacramental signification in terms of the cause, the essence and the goal of human sanctification. Although Dom Vonier bases his sacramental theology on metaphysical principles, his primary concern is the integral salvation of all human persons. Yet, human beings would not know fully their salvation, which is an invisible reality, if it were not proclaimed to them through words and signs which are audible and visible. Thus, Dom Vonier affirms that the Christian concept of sacred sign essentially rests on the ability of such signs to announce graphically a hidden truth: "If the sacrament did no longer proclaim as a sign something which is not seen, it would not be a sacrament".[50]

With these reflections, Dom Vonier plumbs the very nature of the sacrament as signs. Because of their power of signification, they render present a past historic reality, the death of Christ, which is the sole source of the sanctification of human being, and they anticipate the goal of human sanctification in the glory of God. Having enunciated this general principle, Dom Vonier dwells on its relevance for the Eucharistic symbol: "The Eucharist would not be a sacrament if it were not causative, a bringing about again of the mystery of the death of Christ; nor would it be a sacrament if that mystery of the death of Christ thus brought about in the Eucharist were not done under signs and symbols".[51] No doubt, then, that Dom Vonier treats the sacrament of the Eucharist as the commemoration of the death of Christ from the perspective of the two inseparable concepts of signification and causation. At the Church's celebration of the Eucharist, both words and actions signify Christ's Body and Blood, and produce them on the altar under the signs of bread and wine. Following the Scriptural narrative of the Lord's Supper, Dom Vonier argues that the liturgical words and rites of the Eucharist re-present the event of the Cenacle, where Jesus Christ, in the context of a Jewish meal, employed bread and wine as symbols of his own Body and Blood, blessed and gave them to his disciples to eat and drink with an explicit command to do so in his memory.

On the basis of this historical event, Dom Vonier then states that Jesus Christ gave to the assembly of his disciples, a definite rite, made up of actions and words, symbols and expressions by which to commemorate his Passover:

> God's omnipotence does not place directly, immediately, through an imperative *fiat*, the Body and Blood of Christ on the altar; but God – i.e., the Son of God – at the Last Supper first, and through the priestly minister after, says things and performs rites which signify the sacrifice of his Body and of his Blood; and we conclude that there is in that sacramental act of signification the sacrifice of the Body and Blood of Christ, otherwise the divine signification would be a falsehood.[52]

Dom Vonier makes a distinction between God's absolute act of omnipotence and His bestowal of sacramental power on the Church. In the Eucharist, God works through mediation by making the external signs to have full and complete internal truth.[53] Therefore, this sacrament is performed, not through the divine imperative, but through the divine communication of the power to symbolize. More precisely, the unique sacrifice of Jesus Christ on the Cross is rendered present on the altar through the words and gestures of the ordained minister who acts *in persona Christi capitis ecclesiae*.

Viewed from this perspective, the Eucharist is explained as the liturgical commemoration of the passion, death and resurrection of Christ; the ecclesial remembrance of these saving events is clothed in the sacramental presence of Christ who accomplished them in his Body and Blood: "The words we say, the rites we perform, the bread and the wine, are all the sacramental *commemoratio*, but they remain not unclothed but clothed upon by the divine reality, Christ's Flesh and Blood in the sacramental condition".[54] By evidently employing a metaphor, Dom Vonier designates the sacrament of the Eucharist as a *vestita commemoratio* which would be a mere mental act or sign without containing the reality. In the Eucharistic celebration, Christ's Flesh and Blood are made actual in the Church through the sacramental signs of bread and wine. However, Dom Vonier cautions that the Church celebrates the Eucharist in such a manner that it does not perform simply a dramatic representation of what the Lord Jesus said and did at the Last supper; on a more profound level, the entire celebration of the Church becomes a commemorative sign of the Paschal mystery, the passion, death and resurrection of Christ. As one follows Dom Vonier's exposition of the classical notion of the Eucharistic mystery, one finds in him a theologian undauntedly faithful to the tradition. On the other hand, insofar as he frequently accentuates the desire that the re-enactment of the Paschal mystery in a symbolic manner should adopt a "suitable structure, to the extent that Jesus himself has made provision for such development and adaptation",[55] Dom Vonier appears to be a pioneer exponent of the later liturgical movements.

Dom Vonier then describes the manner in which the essence of human sanctification, the salvific grace accomplished by Jesus Christ on Calvary is symbolized and rendered present in history through the Eucharist. In this sacrament, Jesus Christ the redemption-in-person, shows forth his sacrificial death under symbols, and thus provides his followers a demonstrative sign of their sanctification. This specific sacramental grace was caused precisely by his self-surrender in love to the Father. This unique event is re-presented and offered to God in the Eucharistic celebration under the appearance of bread and wine, unlike that of Christ's physical offering to the Father on Calvary.[56] Dom Vonier emphasizes that the unrepeatable sacrifice of Jesus Christ on the Cross is effectively re-actualized on the altar through the external signification of the separation of the Body from the Blood, in order to remind his readers of the "existence, the presence of a spiritual order of forces which come from Christ's life and which are always with us.[57]

When Dom Vonier turns to the prognostic dimension of the Eucharist, he begins with reflections on the manner in which Christianity celebrates with symbols and ceremonies the heavenly feast of the glorified Christ:

> The Christian Church not only believes but symbolizes her belief, makes of it a Feast, has found many wonderful symbols and ceremonies to express almost adequately the hidden glories of Christ. The constancy of that celebration is, of course, its most overwhelming aspect. In all its essentials the Church celebrates today the mysteries of Christ and the hidden things of God as she has done for ages without number.[58]

Thus, Dom Vonier affirms that at the Eucharistic celebration, as at all the sacraments, the Church makes the invisible glory of Jesus Christ visible for the faithful through the re-enactment, in a symbolic manner, of what he said and did while on earth. Dom Vonier states that, through the symbolic actions of the Church, the salvific events accomplished by Jesus in the past become not only a present reality but also a prognostic sign of the final union of his followers with him. Thus, along with all the sacraments, the Eucharist is the sure pledge of the feast of eternal life in the presence of the glorified Lord Jesus. By stating that the future life of glory is symbolized in the Eucharist, Dom Vonier anticipated the importance which eschatology would later enjoy in Catholic sacramental theology.

In another text, Dom Vonier designates the liturgical celebrations of the Church as directing the faithful in their pilgrimage towards the final destiny of the Church, which is essentially life in Christ. This pilgrimage is one led by Christ himself who through grace allows his followers to find the fulfilment of the past in the future:

> Catholic Liturgy has its feelings as well as its definitions, and there is in the Christian people an abiding sense that in the celebration of each step in the forward march of the One who goes forth like a giant, we are actually moving along with him through glorious spheres of grace, that we are not simply looking back to the regions whence he started.[59]

In the Eucharistic celebration, therefore, the Church acts out through words and gestures all the hidden mysteries of Jesus Christ, thereby, moves ahead with Christ towards the final consummation of every temporal feast in the messianic banquet.

The sacraments are, therefore, viewed by Dom Vonier as being confined to history where Christians are united to Christ through effective signs which prepare them for their entrance into eternal glory:

> They are the tools of God to bring about definite results, and when those are completely achieved the tool will be laid aside by the divine Artificer. Sacraments are part of the work which Christ does here on earth; they are not permanent glories of the everlasting triumph, when God shall be all in all. They belong to that definite opus which Christ achieved here below, a task very clearly set him by the Father, to be done in its own hour.[60]

By assigning an instrumental role to the sacraments, Dom Vonier highlights the purpose for which they were instituted, that is, in time and history, re-actualize in a symbolic manner the redemptive mysteries of Jesus Christ. Thus, insofar as God the Father makes use of the sacraments so as to communicate to humanity his salvific plan as it was revealed in the Word Incarnate, crucified and Risen, they are prognostic signs of human beings' permanent union with Christ in the glory of the Father.

On the basis of this analysis, Dom Vonier challenged then contemporary theological views which presented the sacrament of the altar as "a heavenly prolongation, not in the sense of all things reaching consummation through the power of the Eucharist, but in the sense of a real continuation of the Eucharistic immolation in its proper kind".[61] Convinced of the sacramental nature of the Eucharistic sacrifice, Dom Vonier emphatically declared that:

> Sacrifice belongs to the period of faith and hope, where things are seen in a dark manner. To introduce sacrificial elements into the clarity of divine vision is to give to the notion of sacrifice an arbitrary extension. In heaven sacrifices are ratified, are received, are remembered, but they are not celebrated; heaven sings the glory of the sacrifice as the triumph of the past, as one remembers the day of battle of long ago on which a nation was born to liberty.[62]

By placing the sacrifice of the Christian altar within the economy of the history of salvation, Dom Vonier defended its truly sacramental nature, so that the Eucharist is a commemorative sign of the death of Jesus Christ, a demonstrative sign of the accomplished grace operative in the present, and a prognostic sign of the future glorious life which is something greater than the Eucharistic mystery itself.[63]

In conclusion, it can be affirmed that Dom Vonier based his comprehension of the Eucharist as a mystery on the person of Jesus Christ, the Church and its liturgy. In order that his identity as the redemption-in-person be extended to his faithful followers, Jesus Christ instituted the Eucharist, whereby he continually gives his Body and Blood to them as food and drink under the signs of bread and wine. By partaking of one Bread and one Cup, Christians profess their union with Christ, both as individual believers and as one sanctified body. In this sense, it has been noted that the Church makes the Eucharist, and the Eucharist makes the Church. From the perspective of the power of signification, the Eucharist has been considered as a commemorative sign of the cause of human sanctification, that is, the death and glorification of Christ in a definite moment of history. The Eucharist as a sacrament necessarily signifies the past salvific events and re-actualizes them under symbolic forms. Moreover, since the Eucharist contains Christ himself, the redemptive grace attained by him becomes a present reality in the Church. In this sense, the Eucharist has been considered as a demonstrative sign of human beings' sanctification. Finally, in the Church's Eucharistic celebration, the words and gestures symbolize the participants' forward movement with Christ towards their future glory in heaven. On the basis of these considerations, a justification has been made of Dom Vonier's thesis that the Eucharist is a transient reality which leads all created things to their final consummation.

Endnotes

[1] Anscar Vonier, "The Concepts of Commemoration and of Immolation," *Sketches and Studies in Theology* (London: Burns, Oates and Washbourne Ltd., 1940), pp. 64, 72.

[2] *The Collected Works of Abbot Vonier*, Vol. I (London: Burns and Oates, 1952), p. 91.

[3] *Ibid.*, pp. 4-5.

[4] Anscar Vonier, *The New and Eternal Covenant*, p. 84.

[5] Anscar Vonier, *The New and Eternal Covenant*, p. 84.

[6] *Ibid.*, p. 9.

[7] *Ibid.*, p. 103.

[8] Anscar Vonier, *The Personality of Christ, Coll. Works*, I, p. 222.

[9] Anscar Vonier, *The Personality of Christ, Coll. works*, I, p. 223.

[10] Anscar Vonier, *The New and Eternal Covenant*, p. 101.

[11] Anscar Vonier, *The Christian Mind, Coll. Works*, I, p. 11.

[12] *Ibid.*, p. 12.

[13] Anscar Vonier, *The New and Eternal Covenant*, p. 87.

[14] *Ibid.*, p. 86.

[15] Anscar Vonier, *A Key*, p. 249.

[16] Anscar Vonier, "The Certainties of Christ," *The New and Eternal Covenant* (London: Burns, Oates and Washbourne Ltd., 1930), pp. 154-55.

[17] Anscar Vonier, "The Passion of Our Lord," an unpublished sermon preached in January 1923. (Among the papers of Dom Anscar Vonier, Buckfast Abbey, Devon, England).

[18] Anscar Vonier, *The New and Eternal Covenant*, p. 98.

[19] Anscar Vonier, "The Congruity of the Incarnation," *Christ the King of Glory: Tu Rex Gloriae Christe* (London: Burns, Oates and Washbourne Ltd., 1932), pp. 10-11. Dom Vonier's use of the terms, *Christian* and *Catholic* could be somewhat misleading. But one should keep in mind that Vonier is unanimously using them with qualifications, such as *Christian mind* and *Catholic theology*. On the one hand, therefore, it has nothing to do with the universality of the God Incarnate over the whole of human race. And yet, on the other hand, it is a reality that Christians and Catholics are all human beings. However, in this particular case, Dom Vonier is treating the acts and facts of the Incarnation from a Christian perspective.

[20] Anscar Vonier, *The Personality of Christ, Coll. Works*, I, p. 223.

[21] Anscar Vonier., "Sacraments," *A Key to the Doctrine of the Eucharist*, 1925 (Westminster, Maryland: The Newman Press, 1960), p. 15; *Summa, III*, q. 1xi, a. iv.

[22] Anscar Vonier, *The Personality of Christ, Coll. Works*, I, p. 223.

[23] Anscar Vonier, *Christ the King of Glory*, p. 137.

[24] Anscar Vonier, *Christ the King of Glory*, p. 141; *The New and Eternal Covenant*, pp. 41-42.

[25] Anscar Vonier, *The Victory of Christ, Coll. Works*, p. 309.

[26] Anscar Vonier, *The New and Eternal Covenant*, pp. 42-43.

[27] Anscar Vonier, *The Victory of Christ, Coll. Works*, I, p. 306.

[28] *Ibid.*, p. 307.

[29] Anscar Vonier, *A Key*, p. 92.

[30] Anscar Vonier, *Christ the King of Glory*, pp. 58-59.

[31] Anscar Vonier, *The New and Eternal Covenant*, pp. 269-70.

[32] *Ibid.*, pp. 99-100.

[33] Anscar Vonier, *The Personality of Christ, Coll. Works*, I, p. 228.

[34] Anscar Vonier, *The New and Eternal Covenant*, pp. 102-3.

[35] *Ibid.*, pp. 94-96.

[36] Anscar Vonier, *The Personality of Christ* (London: Burns, Oates and Washbourne, 1914), p. 235.

[37] Josef A. Jungmann, *The Mass*, p. 115.

[38] Anscar Vonier, *A Key*, p. 228.

[39] *Ibid.*

[40] Anscar Vonier, "Liturgy," *The New and Eternal Covenant*, p. 89.

[41] *Ibid.*, p. 101.

[42] Anscar Vonier, *The People of God*, p. 166.

[43] Anscar Vonier, *The People of God* (London: Burns, Oates and Washbourne Ltd., 1937), p. xii; *Christ the King of Glory*, p. 58.

[44] Anscar Vonier, *A Key*, p. 255.

[45] Anscar Vonier, *A Key*, p. 255.

[46] By the specific Eucharistic grace Dom Vonier means Christians' membership with Christ and the entire mystical Body of Christ, as distinguished from other graces of Christian dispensation. Anscar Vonier, *A Key*, p. 258.

[47] Anscar Vonier, "Christianus Gaudens," *Christianus, Coll. Works*, p. 228.

[48] Anscar Vonier, *A Key*, p. 15.

[49] *Summa*, III, q. 1x, a. iii; the quotation appears in Vonier, *A Key*, pp. 19-20.

[50] Anscar Vonier, *A Key*, p. 20.

[51] Anscar Vonier, "The Doctrinal Power of the Liturgy of the Catholic Church," *Sketches and Studies*, p. 31.

[52] Anscar Vonier, *A Key*, p. 101.

[53] *Ibid.*, p. 99.

[54] Anscar Vonier, *Sketches and Studies in Theology*, p. 70.

[55] Josef A. Jungmann, *The Mass*, p. 115.

[56] Anscar Vonier, *The People of God*, pp. 162-163.

[57] Dom Vonier, *The New and Eternal Covenant*, p. 84.

[58] Anscar Vonier, *Sketches and Studies*, pp. 148-49.

[59] Anscar Vonier, *The New and Eternal Covenant*, p. 85.

[60] *Ibid.*, p. 259.

[61] *Ibid.*, p. 261.

[62] Anscar Vonier, *A Key*, p. 261-62.

[63] *Ibid.*, p. 259.

CHAPTER - 4

The Late Period: Eucharist as Oriented by the Spirit to Rendering the Life of the Glorified Christ Accessible to Christians

Dom Vonier viewed the special role and mission of the Holy Spirit in the Eucharist, as it enables the life of the risen Christ continually to be extended to Christians through this sacrament which symbolizes and actualizes the unifying power of the Paschal mystery. Although *The Collected Works* of the Abbot attests that he never wrote a separate treatise on the mission of the Holy Spirit, yet he invariably treated this theme in relation to the person of the Incarnate Son of God, the Church and the Eucharist. In *the Victory of Christ*, he emphasized the role of the Spirit as the herald of Christ's victory. The Incarnate Son of God, as already noted earlier, became the redemptive-act-in-person through his passion, death and resurrection, but on this earth he never assumed the glories of that triumph. It is the work of the Pentecostal

Spirit to glorify Christ (Jn.16: 14), that is, to externally to manifest all the hidden achievements of the risen Lord.[1]

Through his death and resurrection, the God Incarnate obtained from the Father the Holy Spirit as the abiding divine gift to human beings, so that they could witness the efficacy of the Paschal mystery throughout subsequent history. The Spirit is to vivify the individual souls of the faithful and to gather them collectively as the Church which rallies around the Eucharistic altar to be nourished for its mission of witness. Dom Vonier has depicted the manifold activity of the Holy Spirit in the Church in *The Spirit and the Bride*, and in *The New and Eternal Covenant*. The Holy Spirit is described as universally protracting the bond of life and union between God and the elect which has been established in the Blood of Jesus Christ, the saving presence of which the faithful encounter at the Eucharist.

Here, it would be presumptuous to attempt to bring out all of the Abbot's comprehension of the link between pneumatology and eschatology. This section exposes only those aspects of his understanding of the person and mission of the Spirit, insofar as he is active in effecting the Eucharist through which the glorified Christ continues to live in Christians and to grant them a true anticipation of their future glory.

The Abbot forcefully underscores the continuing presence of the one Divine Spirit in the Jesus of history and in the Christ of glory. Unlike some modern theologians who speak of the Holy Spirit as if he succeeds the person and mission of Jesus of Nazareth by completely replacing him, Dom Vonier advocates the absolute identity of the Spirit given to the Church at Pentecost with the Spirit who filled the Jesus of history and raised him to glory. The Spirit who acted in Jesus is the one whom the Father and the glorified Son send as the Paraclete to continue, by means of extension to many, what Jesus Christ did and said during his earthly life. The Pentecostal Spirit does not mark the end of Christ's victory, but the prolongation of the future of the Paschal mystery in the lives of many human beings.

The principal mission of the Pentecostal Spirit is then to manifest the hidden glory of the Lord Jesus visibly and tangibly through the sacramental actions of the Church, and most specifically through the Eucharist which contains in symbolic forms the Body and the Blood of the exalted Christ. What Jesus established in the Cenacle and on Calvary is now re-actualized by the Spirit in the Eucharist of the Church, and therefore, the presence of the glorified Christ is experienced most intensively by Christians in this sacrament. Dom Vonier's attempt to base his Eucharistic theology both on Christology and on pneumatology will be appreciated as a pioneering work in the field of modern sacramental theology.

Next, Dom Vonier understands the Eucharist as the real symbol conjoining the one glorified Christ to the many Christians in history. He explains the relation of the two parallel mysteries of Incarnation and Pentecost on which the originality of Christianity is based. From the perspective of divine revelation, these mysteries are fundamentally united; they differ, however, in their external manifestations. The Son of God assumes human flesh; the Spirit of God is clothed in ecclesial charisms and signs that originate in the Spirit's descent in the Apostles at Pentecost and culminate whenever the Church assembles to celebrate the memory of the Paschal mystery of the Lord at the Eucharist.

Further, Dom Vonier perceives the Eucharist as the locus where Christians are incorporated into oneness of life with Christ and with one another. By partaking of the Eucharistic Body and Blood, the faithful profess that their unique redemption by Christ on Calvary is renewed by him in the sacramental re-presentation of his death. Moreover, Christians are incorporated into the resurrected life of Christ as members of one body united to their victorious head.

On the basis of the affirmation that through the Eucharist the Spirit enables the glorified Christ to live in individual Christians in entire aspects of their life, that is, psychological, social and economic dimensions. Dom Vonier admits that the Eucharistic elements are effective in and by themselves, independently of Christian faith; the belief of Christians in the sacramental presence of Christ gives them a definite identity and mission, thereby distinguishing them from adherents to people of other faiths.

Again, Dom Vonier asserts the specific virtues which Christians acquire through their partaking of the Body and the Blood of Christ. Christians themselves are to become Christ-like, in that they inherit an entirely new mode of behaviour which is marked by charity and mercy, peace and rest of soul. In society where the neediest, affected human beings are often marginalized, the Eucharist urges Christians to practice charity and mercy to bring about concrete signs of the equality of the children of God. Amid the strain and suffering of modern life, the Eucharist allows Christians to find peace in them, hope of attaining eternal life in heaven.

In fact, at the Eucharist, Christians already anticipate their future life here and now because of their union with Christ who will come again in glory. This insight into the relevance of the Eucharist for the personal and social life of Christians who are led by the Spirit of Christ makes Dom Vonier a forerunner of modern Eucharistic theology which accentuates the connection between pneumatological and eschatological explanations of this sacrament.

1.   The Spirit of the Glorified Christ Realizes the Eucharist

In *The Victory of Christ*, Dom Vonier states that "the external form of Christ's resurrection is the last evidence of the resolve of the Son of God that here on earth at his first coming he would not show forth the majesty of the divinity that was in him".[2] Evidently, by means of this statement Dom Vonier emphasizes both the continuity and the difference between the Incarnate Son of God in his mortal state and the Risen Christ in his glorified state. At the resurrection, the glory of the Word of God broke out, whereas during his earthly life it was hidden and could be grasped only by faith. His present glory reveals his former humility. He first comes as a member of the human race, but he now exists as its universal Lord. For, the God Incarnate is not merely an historical personality; he is ever present in all parts of the world until the end of time.

Dom Vonier alludes to the united yet distinct states in the life of Jesus Christ by explaining that the Holy Spirit, who was all along in and with Jesus during his earthly life, is now still united to him and reveals his hidden glory as the Christ through the visible symbolic actions of the Church, of which the sacrament of the Eucharist is the most complete and expressive:

> It is the Holy Ghost who saves the life of Christ from being merely
> an historical event. Through the Spirit all things that Christ did
> and said are permanently with us. Through the Spirit we have the
> Eucharist... in the sense in which he is at the root of the Incarnation
> itself, for it is through the power of the Spirit that bread is changed
> into Christ's Body and wine his changed into Christ's Blood.[3]

Obviously, the primary truth affirmed here is the permanent presence of the life of the glorified Christ in the world through the activity of the Holy Spirit. This truth is, then, exemplified and made more concrete by pointing to the epicletic role of the Holy Spirit in the Eucharist. The self-gift of Jesus Christ in the Cenacle and on Calvary is still available to the world through the power of the Spirit at work in the liturgy of the Church. Viewed from this perspective, the Eucharist understood as the permanent *memoria* of Jesus' divine redemption-in-person, is to be attributed to the act of the Spirit. Therefore, the Eucharist is the objective memorial and not simply the result of a mental or spiritual phenomenon.[4] In other terms, the personal Spirit of God, who brought about the Incarnation, transforms the bread and wine offered by the Church into the sacramental Body and Blood of Christ.

Well before these insights had been regained in the larger theological community, Dom Vonier affirmed that the Spirit of the glorified Christ realizes the Eucharist through the epiclesis pronounced by the ordained priest over the gifts of the people. Yet, Dom Vonier articulates this theological stance while he attempts to rectify some then contemporary theories which viewed the Holy Spirit, "not [as] another Paraclete who receives from Christ and announces to us, but [as] a new power, succeeding the personal Christ and completely replacing him".[5] Dom Vonier asserts that such a view is not consonant with the pneumatology developed throughout Christian tradition. The descent of the Spirit is neither a superseding of Christ nor a succession of one power following upon another:

> The Spirit who came down at Pentecost is essentially the Spirit of Jesus... The Spirit who was in Christ all along, now rules the Church, and rules it with an energy and efficiency that make him into something that is again almost palpable and outward, for if there is a characteristic of that Epiphany of the Spirit which began at Pentecost it is this, that he acts and speaks manifestly and that his works are visible.[6]

Thus, Dom Vonier states that the Spirit of Pentecost can be properly conceived as none other than the Spirit of Jesus. The Spirit now gives testimony to the Lord by revealing his own presence in the Church by means of external and palpable acts, such as that by which Peter could declare that his preaching to the crowd was a tangible manifestation of the Holy Spirit (Acts 2: 33). Evidently, Dom Vonier intended this fundamental reflection as a means of assuring his readers that between the action of the Spirit of Pentecost and that of the Christ there is not discontinuity, but there "inwardness taking the place of outwardness".[7] In another text, Dom Vonier succinctly expressed the unity of the divine person revealed to the world through Christianity, a teaching which clearly distinguishes it from other religions: "The one and the same dispensation can be expressed in terms of flesh and blood and in terms of the Spirit; the work of Christ is the work of the Holy Ghost in all things that are the Church's sanctification".[8]

The achievement of the redemption-in-person, Jesus Christ the Son of God in flesh and blood, is now carried out by the Holy Spirit for the sanctification of human beings.

After Pentecost the Spirit of Christ, who had always been with him throughout his ministry, is inwardly active in his followers. To underline this truth, Dom Vonier clearly conjoined the outward and the inner dimensions of the Christian dispensation: "flesh and blood", and "Spirit"; "the work of Christ is the work of the Holy Spirit". In keeping with Christian tradition, Dom Vonier admitted both the distinction and the identity between the two major theological tracts of Pneumatology and Christology.

In order to understand the relevance of this viewpoint for Eucharistic theology, a further observation should be made concerning Dom Vonier's process of thinking about Christology and Pneumatology. Since Jesus Christ, the redemption-in-person, was accomplished by the Spirit in offering himself on Calvary, Dom Vonier emphatically declares in *Christianus*: "We do not say indeed, that the Holy Ghost redeemed the world, but we say very truly with St. Paul that "Christ by the Holy Ghost offered himself unspotted to God as the victim of our redemption".[9]

In his analysis of Heb.9: 14, Dom Vonier distinguishes between the specific role of the Word and that of the Spirit in attaining the redemption of humanity. The redemption of the world is primarily the work of the Word of God who assumed humanity. Yet, this mission was brought to its finality, that is, to the self-offering of Jesus to the Father as the victim of our redemption only in and through the power of the Holy Spirit. Thus, in the process by which the redemption of humanity was procured once-and-for all, the Holy Spirit is assigned the role of fully sanctifying the flesh and blood assumed by the

Word at the Incarnation, and of directing the Word to the final act of offering and to his new state of glory.

Here, it might also be observed that Dom Vonier relies on the theology of the Greek Fathers insofar as the Incarnation and the transformation of the Eucharistic elements are the work of the Holy Spirit.[10] Dom Vonier states that at the Eucharist the Holy Spirit can be said to have a determining role in the consecration of the elements: "In the Eucharistic mystery the Spirit, by appropriation at least, is invoked as the power that will bring about the great presence of Christ... The Sanctificator is, of course, the Spirit, the Holy Ghost".[11] The words "by appropriation at least" draw one's attention immediately. What evidently means is that, in the economy of salvation, the creation, redemption and sanctification of humanity represent one divine operation. Strictly speaking, therefore, salvific activities are not proper to one Person but are common to the three Persons of the divine Trinity. According to the defined teaching of the Church, however, it is by appropriation that the sanctification of humanity is attributed to the Holy Spirit.[12] Thus, insofar as the Eucharistic mystery entails the work of sanctification, the Holy Spirit is invoked by appropriation to sanctify the gift-offerings and transform them into the sacramental Body and Blood of Christ. By means of this analysis, it becomes clear that Dom Vonier insists on the continued presence of the glorified Christ in the faithful through the Eucharist, which is realized by the power of the Holy Spirit, the divine Sanctificator. After being informed of Dom Vonier's teaching on the central role of the epiclesis in the Eucharist, one must look to his theology of Pentecost for further insights into the foundation of this teaching. In fact, Dom Vonier offers a penetrating understanding of the role of the Holy Spirit in effecting the Church and the sacraments, realities which are intrinsically related to the person of Christ.

The connection between the Spirit and the Church, on the one hand, and Jesus Christ and the Church, on the other, is best expressed by Dom Vonier in *The People of God* and *The Personality of Christ.* Concerning the reality of the Church, Dom Vonier states that it stands "as an unsurpassable power of sanctification, as a pillar and column of truth, as a continuation of Christ's Person, as an organism vivified by the Paraclete".[13] Evidently, Dom Vonier is highlighting the Church's intrinsic relationship both with Christ and with his Spirit. Dom Vonier would thus consider two of the phrases mentioned above as key to the present discussion: The Church is "a continuation of Christ's Person" and is "an organism vivified by the Paraclete".

By asserting that Christ's person is the real inwardness of the Church, Dom Vonier means that one cannot speak of the essential nature of the Church without relating it to the glorified Christ. Yet, he acknowledges that the inner life of the Church is also a gift of the Holy Spirit, who enables Christians in history to be united to the Son of God in glory. Dom Vonier, then, goes on to state that the Holy Spirit renders the glorified Christ present to the Church until the eschaton. The Spirit serves as the glorification of Christ within time:

> It is very necessary for us to remember this aspect of the descent of the Holy Ghost; from the moment of his coming to the end of times, nay, for all eternity, he will be to the Church the Spirit of Jesus. It is his work and his mission to manifest the Jesus who has been taken away, who has hidden his glory and who himself refrained from

> declaring to the world the greatness that was in him; the Spirit has
> to do it all until the Lord come in the full splendour of his glory.
> In one word, the glorification of Jesus has not been seen by the
> world; it is the Spirit that glorifies Christ or more accurately still,
> he is the glorification.[14]

Dom Vonier reflects on the activity of the Spirit in the Church since Pentecost in terms of the mission to manifest the hidden glory of the Lord Jesus. In other words, the Spirit glorifies Christ by making him known to the entire world. Understood in this way, the Holy Spirit is the Glorifier of Christ. In another passage, Dom Vonier concludes that "the Spirit is essentially and unalterably the radiation in this world of Christ's glorification".[15] In yet another passage, Dom Vonier states that the Spirit brings Jesus Christ so near to us.

All these considerations lead Dom Vonier to stress the relationship between the Holy Spirit and the *Resurrection Church*.[16] This synthetic term indicates that the newness of the life enjoyed by the risen Christ is accessible to and operative in the Church by the power of the Holy Spirit. In other words, the Spirit enables the Church to exist as the continuation of Christ's glory in the world. Dom Vonier describes the specific initiative role of the Spirit of the risen Christ as that of "creating the Church, of making the sons of God to be gathered into one".[17] Although Dom Vonier admits that the hidden grace and manifest gifts of the Spirit have been bestowed on the world all through the ages since creation, he maintains that the Church alone is the definitive gathering together of all people into one assembly of the elect. In this sense, Dom Vonier attributes the birth of the one Church to the work of the Holy Spirit who at Pentecost extended the merit of the resurrection of Christ to many: "The newness and the originality of the work of the Holy Ghost at Pentecost is expressed in the idea of birth. It is said by the Fathers and Doctors that the Church was born on that day. The Bride dates her age from the fiftieth day after Christ's resurrection".[18] Thus, Dom Vonier characterizes Pentecost as the definitive event at which the Church was animated by the life of the glorified Christ through the Holy Spirit. He stresses the fact that the activity of the Spirit of Pentecost is indispensable in effecting the permanent access of the Church to the life of the risen Christ.

Perceived from this point of view, the day of Pentecost marks the beginning of the entirely new life of the Church which is characterized by holiness:

> When we say that the Church was born on the day of Pentecost, we mean of course that the beginning of a life which is a total life, which is the whole new sanctity of Christianity, was started then; not only were external signs given of the presence of the Spirit, but an internal holiness, the holiness of the Church, began its mighty career on that day; it is the birth of Pentecostal holiness, a sanctity which has all the elements of the ancient godliness and much more... the essence of the new holiness is this: the oneness of charity of all those who invoke the name of Christ and constitute the Church.[19]

Evidently, Dom Vonier emphasizes that the essence of the holiness of the Church consists in the unity of all those who profess Christ. Dom Vonier is concerned not only with the internal sanctity of the Church but also with its external expression as the human society united in charity by the Holy Spirit.

Insofar as the Church owes both its internal holiness and external charity to the Spirit given to it at Pentecost, it can rightly be called sacrament of the Spirit. Furthermore, through the sacraments, and through the Eucharist, the Spirit constitutes the Church again and again as a dynamic gathering of people. On the basis of this truth, Dom Vonier affirms that through the sacrament of the Eucharist the Spirit renders effective in the Church "what Jesus did meritoriously through the power of his blood".[20] Evidently, Dom Vonier thus posits that the work of the redemption-in-person, Jesus Christ is continually brought to its fulfilment through the Spirit of Pentecost at work in the sacraments of the Church, in particular that of the Eucharist:

> The Holy Ghost is everywhere in the working of the sacraments; and though at first sight there might seem to be an opposition of character between the Spirit and the material thing, in reality the material sign is the means preferred by the Holy Ghost for his operations as well as for his manifestations. As he showed himself at Pentecost under external signs, so likewise He operates in the Church under the visible elements of the sacramental order.[21]

Although Dom Vonier admits the seeming contradiction between the Spirit and the material world, he nevertheless states that the Spirit conjoins his sanctifying activity to the external signs, first chosen by Jesus and then later furthered by the Church. With regard to the Eucharist, Dom Vonier would affirm that the ensuing internal and external union of the faithful is certainly the manifestation of the effective operation of the Spirit. The words and symbols of the Eucharistic celebration do indeed bring about the real presence of the glorified Christ in the transformed bread and wine. Yet, all this is possible since the Holy Spirit, invoked at the epiclesis, enables the material realities of bread and wine to become visible manifestations of the Body and Blood of the glorified Christ.

Furthermore, by receiving the Eucharistic species at communion, the believers participate in the life of the risen Jesus. This invisible participation shows itself in the collective union of the faithful as the visible assembly of the members of Christ's Body. This bond of union with Christ and with each other is the result of the creative working of the Spirit, who from the day of Pentecost conjoins the head to his members in the world. On the basis of Dom Vonier's analysis of the role of the Spirit in realizing the Church at the Eucharist, the Abbot's attempt to describe the unifying power of the grace of the Holy Spirit in this sacrament can be comprehended.

2.   The Eucharist as Conjoining the One Glorified Christ to the Many Christians in History

One of the chief aims of Dom Vonier's theology of the Eucharist is to show how the Spirit operates through this sacrament, so as to communicate the saving grace in the form of the union between Christ and human beings after the resurrection. In order to demonstrate how effective this uniting mission of the Spirit is in the world through the Church, Dom Vonier draws a parallel between the mystery of the Incarnation and that of the Pentecost:

> The Incarnation is an entirely new way for God to be with man; the abiding of the Paraclete in the New Testament belongs to the same plane of reality; it is as new, as original, as the birth of the Word in time. It would not be allowable to call it the Incarnation of the third Person of the Trinity, because the Spirit did not take flesh as the Word took flesh. What I say is this, that the advent of the Paraclete is of the same kind as the coming of the Son of God; in both instances there is a true *descensus de coelo*, a true coming down from heaven, as had not been before. In what way this new advent differs so profoundly from the whisperings of the Spirit in the ancient world before Christ, theologians have tried to

understand and explain; but they are faced with as great a mystery as the mystery of the Incarnation. As it is God's secret how the Son of God dwells in man, but in both of these instances it is literally true that a divine person and no one else has been seen and has conversed with man here on earth.[22]

In this striking passage, Dom Vonier places the Spirit's presence in the Church since Pentecost on a par with that of Son of God in the flesh since the Incarnation. In both instances God personally communicates himself to human beings: in the Person of the Word and in the Person of the Spirit. The way the Spirit of God dwells in human beings is a mystery equally as great as the manner in which the Word of God assumed human nature. However, the fundamental truth is that a distinct divine person has respectively revealed himself to human persons through the Incarnation and through Pentecost. The Abbot's conception of the parallel between two mysteries calls for further analysis.

At the outset of the passage just cited, it appears that Dom Vonier is tempted to speak of the descent of the Holy Spirit in terms of an Incarnation of the Third Person of the Trinity in human beings. But he realizes that at Pentecost the Spirit did not assume humanity in the same way as the Word took flesh. What fascinates Dom Vonier is that the parallel with the Incarnation enables one pointedly to speak of the self-communication of the Spirit in visible, tangible forms.[23] In another powerful text, Dom Vonier speaks of the presence of the Spirit in symbolic terms:

> The Spirit was incarnated in the Church, as the Second Person of the Trinity was *incarnated* in an individual human nature. The only exception we take to such a phrase is the use of the word *incarnate* with regard to the Spirit... the Spirit's coming is as literal

as the coming of the Word; but instead of his taking flesh, he clothed himself in signs. If those signs be permanent, the Spirit is permanently with men.[24]

Dom Vonier considers the act by which Spirit of God clothed himself in signs as real as that by which the Son of God assumed unto himself human flesh. On the one hand, Dom Vonier deliberately avoids referring to an incarnation of the Spirit, but on the other, he insists on the permanent presence of the Spirit in the signs of the Church. The Abbot perceives no difference in the completeness and realism of the advents of the Word and of the Spirit, because in both cases a divine Person united himself definitively with external forms.

Dom Vonier being consistent in his approach to both Christology and Pneumatology has no qualms about asserting the fundamental parallel between the thought patterns which characterize them. In fact, Dom Vonier's theology of the Spirit pivots on the words of the Apostles at Pentecost as palpable indications of his presence in them: "The Holy Ghost himself came on that day under all those signs which are enumerated by St. Luke, the wind, the parted tongues of fire, the power of speech, the ecstasy of the mind, which made the Apostles pour forth words over the marvels of God. Those signs were the immediate indication of the presence of the Spirit".[25] Through these signs the mission of the Spirit to vivify and to unify the members of Christ's Body is revealed. Thus, whenever the Gospel is preached and the sacraments celebrated, the Spirit himself brings about the life and unity of the Church through such external signs. The gathering of the Christian community at the celebration of the Eucharist is the experiential indication of the life-giving self-communication and the unifying presence of the Spirit.

Yet, Dom Vonier objectively remarks that even at Pentecost these signs were not recognized and accepted by all. For, not all the people were given the grace to know the Spirit of truth (Jn.14: 17) in the same measure:

> It is, of course, possible for men to fail to see the kingdom of the Spirit in spite of its notes and signs. Not all men in Jerusalem at Pentecost gave a right explanation of what was before their eyes. This blindness of man in no ways diminishes the evidence of the Spirit's presence. It is the world's peculiar curse to be ignorant of this obvious fact just as it is the grace of the children of God to know "the Spirit of truth, whom the world cannot receive because it seeth him not, nor knoweth him. But you shall know him; because he shall abide with you and shall be in you".[26]

Dom Vonier affirms that the descent of the Spirit, which is independent of human being's faith, can nevertheless be recognized only through the gift of faith. This same interconnection between the objective presence of the Spirit in signs and the personal reality of faith is applicable to the operation of the Spirit at the Eucharist. The Spirit renders Christ present in the signs of transformed bread and wine, but the faithful can recognize the unifying activity of the Spirit in the Body and the Blood of Christ only through faith.

Furthermore, Dom Vonier considers the entire social body of Christians as the principal sign of the real advent and permanent presence of the Holy Spirit: "The Church of the New Testament, and it alone, is so constituted that whoever looks at her must say truly that the Spirit, the Lord, the Vivifier, is upon this earth. The Bride is a sign".[27] Evidently, Dom Vonier refers to the fundamental relationship between the visible reality of Church and the efficacious self-communication of the Spirit. Since the Church has its origin in the mystery of Pentecost, it is a sign of the Spirit insofar as its life and activity proclaims the glory of the risen Christ and gives witness to the unity of all humanity in him.

The Spirit who was poured out at Pentecost is understood by Dom Vonier as the unifying factor between all Christians in history and the one glorified Christ:

> The Spirit of God, a divine Person, is to the scattered Christian souls of all times and all climes a bond of life and union that is not thinkable elsewhere. The presence of that Spirit amongst the faithful... is more than the separate sanctification of many thousands, nay, many millions, of individual souls. There is the mystery of the one life; nature has nothing analogous.[28]

Dom Vonier affirms that a Divine Person of the Spirit is operative in Christians both as individuals and as a collective group. On one hand, Dom Vonier admits that individual Christians of every age receive the Spirit, while on the other hand, he insists that they are incorporated into one Spirit-filled Body of Christ, so that "there is the mystery of the one life".[29] In other texts which have already been examined, Dom Vonier perceives the concrete realization of the mystery of the one life in the assembly of Christians who are unified through their participation in the celebration of the Eucharist.

Dom Vonier proceeds to deepen his explanation of how the incorporation of Christians into the one life of Christ is affected by the Spirit. Assuming that all Christians are redeemed once-and-for all by the death and resurrection of Jesus Christ, Dom Vonier underlines that they also continually die and rise with him. This on-going incorporation of Christians into the salvific life of Jesus Christ is realized by the Holy Spirit who sanctifies the members of the Church through sacramental grace:

> Our sanctification is this: that we participate more and more in his life, that we are more and more his… All the graces of the sacraments are ours which bring about that incorporation and carry it to perfection. The Holy Ghost proceeds from Christ, and gives us the very nature of Christ and draws us all into Christ. Christ is twofold, in his own personal nature and in his mystical nature; the true Body of Christ and his mystical Body.[30]

The sanctification of Christians consists in their ever greater union with the life of Christ, a union which is brought to perfection by the Holy Spirit through sacramental grace. The same Spirit who had united the flesh of Jesus to the Word throughout his earthly life is given to Christians after his death and resurrection. The glorified Christ now sends his own Spirit to Christians in order to draw them ever more effectively to himself, and thus grant them a fuller share in his divine glory.

Dom Vonier further specifies that Christians participate in the personal nature of Christ through incorporation into his mystical nature. Dom Vonier, obviously, has in mind the truth that the whole assembly of the Church, "being rooted and established in the resurrection from the dead of the Son of God, through the Spirit of glory", undergoes an invisible yet real transformation through the reception of all the sacraments, and especially by being nourished with the Body and Blood of Christ in the Eucharist. Here, Dom Vonier decidedly adopts the Pauline and Augustinian notion of the corporate manner whereby Christians are made one with Christ by the Spirit. Thus, distancing himself from excessive forms of Scholasticism, which would prefer to think more in terms of individual union with Christ, Dom Vonier emphasizes the corporate dimension of such union. Through the sacraments, all Christians throughout history are joined into the one life of the glorified Christ.

Yet, Dom Vonier is not aware of the diversity existing among those vivified by the same Spirit of the Lord:

> Shall we say then that it is the Spirit who makes Christ live in the hearts of chosen men and women according to their capacity, and that moreover the Spirit impresses the sentiment and the effective powers of Christians differently and at different times; that he truly creates in them a Christ entirely in conformity with that truth which is his very essence, yet with wonderful variety?[31]

Dom Vonier treats the reality that the Holy Spirit unites Christ to individual Christians in the proportion to their capacity to reflect his one essence through various charisms. Thus, their own personalities mirror the glorious fullness of the Person of Christ. Through the creative workings of the Spirit, the living Christ is united to all generations of Christians so that, while not losing their individuality, they are members of the one body. Despite subjective differences, Christians of all times share in the one essence of Christ, die and rise with him, and are assured of entrance into his glory. This mystery of the union of Christians to their head is clearly attributed by Dom Vonier to the universal activity of the Holy Spirit.

Turning to the specific effects of the action of the Spirit of Christ in Christians, Dom Vonier concentrates on the sacraments of the Church as vivifying realities:

> Through the presence of the Spirit each sacrament is linked up, through all space and all times, with the cause of all sacramental grace – the death of Christ on the Cross. Sacraments are also sources of special graces which are certainly a portion of the Pentecostal dispensation, graces not known before Pentecost. From these graces is born the social order of the New Testament, the union of all

Christians in one Body, Christ. Now it is the Spirit who has, so to speak the special mission of vivifying the Body of Christ.[32]

Dom Vonier associates the efficacy of the sacraments throughout the centuries with the efficacious presence of the Spirit in the Church. Since Christ obtained the gift of the Holy Spirit through his redemption-in person, the Spirit conjoins all the sacraments with the death of the Redeemer, which, in fact, is the sole cause of sacramental grace. Moreover, the graces bestowed by the sacraments are gifts of the Spirit, which as such were not granted to humanity before Pentecost. Through sacramental grace, the Spirit vivifies the social or mystical Body of Christ, and thereby conjoins its members to the one life of their head. Dom Vonier thus perceives the continuing celebration of the sacraments as oriented by the Spirit to ever greater union between Christians and the glorified Christ.

Dom Vonier, then, applies these truths to the presence of the Lord in the Eucharist. The Spirit renders this sacrament much more than a mere commemoration of a salvific event in the past. Thus, Dom Vonier insists that there is "a profound distinction between the commemoration of the historic fact and the celebration of an actuality".[33] In the Eucharist, the faithful experience Christ's death as actual for them in and through the sacramental presence of his Body and his Blood given for them on Calvary. Therefore, the self-gift of Christ is as actual at the Eucharist as it was on Good Friday when his Body was broken, and Blood was poured out on Golgotha. In order to render this mystery of one life between Christ and the faithful more comprehensible, Dom Vonier emphasizes the Eucharist as the sacramental eating of Christ's Flesh and sacramental drinking of his Blood:

> In the death we all were born and it is still with us. We are so closely incorporated with him, we are so much part of his life, his history, that whatever he did must be given to us in reality, that we have actually the mystery of his death on our altars each morning, and we enter into that death, that sacrifice. We sit at the table of the Lord, and we eat his Flesh and drink his Blood, because if we did not eat the Flesh and drink that Blood our incorporation would be less complete.[34]

Evidently, this text treats Dom Vonier's understanding of Christians' ever more complete incorporation in the death of Christ by which he redeemed human beings and made them one with himself. This incorporation is possible because the Holy Spirit transforms the bread and the wine offered by Christians into the sacramental Flesh and Blood of Christ their head. This sacramental communion with Christ guarantees their ever-full participation in his glorious life. As a twentieth century liturgist, Dom Vonier emphasized the Eucharist as the continual re-enactment of a unique event of history so that even the least liturgically-minded Christian might be helped to distinguish sharply between the Eucharist understood as a mere mental recollection of the past fact and as an efficacious celebration of its permanent actuality.[35] He concludes, then, that each time the faithful participate in the Eucharistic celebration they deepen their oneness with the life of Christ; the Paschal mystery of their head becomes their own identity as they die with him and rise with him.

This insight into the living bond between the Christ in glory and the Christians in history is rooted by Dom Vonier in the continuous presence of the Spirit of Christ to the faithful since the day of Pentecost:

The Spirit is always with us, he has not gone away, his coming is as actual today as it was when Peter rose and spoke to the multitude. So we have liturgy there in the very act of dealing with a present reality: The Church celebrates the Spirit that is hers as one entertains a guest who has come and who stays… It is not to the Spirit that the bride says, "Come": He is always with her; the invitation is to Christ, to return to the earth which he has left.[36]

Obviously, Dom Vonier affirms that the Church possesses the Spirit as its own privileged guest who, in turn, keeps the whole body of the Church united. Therefore, in its liturgical celebrations, the Church does not invite the Spirit but Christ to come into its midst. This truth concerning the permanent presence of the Spirit of Christ in the Church is ritually expressed in the epiclesis of the liturgical celebration. The Spirit is invoked to transform the bread and the wine which symbolizes the Church into the Body and the Blood of Christ. Indeed, through the epiclesis and the *anamnesis*, Christ is sacramentally present to the faithful in a manner like his being physically with them on earth. The sacramental bread and wine thus signify and contain Christ's redemptive presence in his Body and Blood. Eating and drinking of Christ's Body and Blood is then the act by which Christians are made "one with Christ, flesh of his Flesh and bone of his Bone". [37]

Dom Vonier concludes that, although the liturgical form of the Eucharistic celebration may have varied since its institution in keeping with different times and situations, it has always remained the supreme means by which the Spirit enables Christians to be united to the one glorified Christ. By reflecting on this observation, one can conclude that Dom Vonier, the theologian is primarily concerned about the transcendent destiny of all Christians both within and beyond history, that is, their ever more complete union with God. He views the full achievement of this union in the future as being realized in history through the ecclesial mission of the Spirit who at the Eucharist conjoins the one glorifies Christ to his many mystical members. To further develop this theme, Dom Vonier elucidates some of the positive effects of this union on the ecclesial and social life of Christians.

3.   The Relevance of the Eucharist for the Personal and Public Life of Christians

Relying on insights culled from the Scripture, Dom Vonier presents the life of the glorified Christ as being continually extended by the Holy Spirit to Christians through the sacraments. Furthermore, Dom Vonier enquires into the nature of this extended life of Christ by considering the relevance of the Eucharist for the personal self-awareness and public behaviour of Christians. Therefore, he emphasizes Eucharistic grace as the union of Christians with Christ, with each other and with the entire human race. Since all people seek peace, love and justice, the Holy spirit orients Christians who have received the Eucharist to a way of life, which announces that Jesus Christ embodies these desired realities. In a further related reflection Dom Vonier states that living according to Eucharistic grace is an anticipation of the share in the glorious life of Christ hoped for by all Christians. Dom Vonier's understanding of the present and the future implications of Eucharistic grace as being grounded in the action of the Holy Spirit makes him a forerunner of contemporary theologians who stress the relation between the epiclesis over the bread and wine and that over the community which is to live according to the personal and social dimensions of Eucharistic grace.

Dom Vonier first assesses the existential relevance of the Eucharist from the perspective of its sacramental power. First, he demonstrates the inseparable link between human psychology and sacramental grace:

> The Christian sacrament is essentially a power that transforms a man's soul, giving it supernatural qualities of the highest order and enriching it with divine vitalities which have far-reaching results in man's conscious life. All sacraments are therefore intimately connected with human psychology, as they bring about a radical change and transformation of man's powers through divine grace.[38]

Applying this truth to the sacrament of the Eucharist, Dom Vonier states that it produces supernatural grace in the internal being of Christians which, in turn, influences their character and behaviour. Since the Eucharist is an instrument of divine grace and is meant to cause perceptible changes in the lives of Christians, Dom Vonier finds it imperative to view Eucharistic grace in connection with human psychology.[39] At this juncture, Dom Vonier neither fully explains what he means by a sacramental power, nor does he analyse how it operates. However, one can infer from the context that he intends to underline the traditional teaching that the grace conferred by each sacrament signifies the respective manner in which Christians are saved and sanctified through its reception.[40] Dom Vonier purposely avoids any fuller explanation, because here he is not dealing directly with the supernatural grace; rather his concern is to view faith itself as containing a psychological freedom which enables Christians to grasp the Eucharistic realities objectively.

Dom Vonier then asserts that the belief of the faithful in the supernatural power of the sacraments is in itself based on the objective order and is, therefore, not a product of their psychological search for value:

> Whatever our intensity of faith, we know that there is something outside ourselves that corresponds with all our spiritual desires and anticipations. We do not read spiritual worth into the sacraments – we know them to possess innate power. We do not give the sacraments their value by believing them to be of value – they are of value in their own right, and our faith is nothing else than the acceptance of that great fact.[41]

Evidently, in this consideration, Dom Vonier insists on the objective spiritual worth of the sacraments, independent of the faith which Christians have in them. The sacraments are valuable *per se* because of the power of signification which Jesus Christ bestowed on them. Each of the sacraments he instituted can create the effect which they signify. Thus, the sacrament of the Eucharist is capable of nourishing Christians with Christ himself, as it objectively contains the reality it signifies, that is, his Body and Blood given for the life of the world. Therefore, Eucharistic faith consists in the personal acceptance of this revealed truth. The faith of Christians in the presence of the redemption-in-person in the Eucharist is grounded on the divine initiative to grant them sanctification and eternal life through its reception. Based on this truth, Dom Vonier notes that the Eucharist is for Christian life a *sine qua non*.

Once again, it can be pointed out that Dom Vonier bases the effect of the Eucharist on its sacramental character, that is, on its commemoration of a divine reality through a material sign:

> The thing that is bread one moment is truly the Body of Christ
> the moment after, in virtue of the consecration; the thing that is
> wine is truly the Blood of Christ in virtue of the consecration. The
> Eucharist is not Christ brought down from heaven; the Eucharist is a
> sacrament, a thing of material elements which are changed through
> transubstantiation into an infinitely high thing, the very elements
> which make Christ in heaven what he is. We have therefore in the
> Eucharist this marvel, that one kind of being, bread and wine, is
> changed, is transubstantiated, into another kind of being, the living
> Body and the living Blood of Christ.[42]

Bread and wine consist of natural elements refined by the labour of human beings so as to become their food and drink. At the Eucharist, in virtue of the words of the consecration, they are changed into the higher realities of the living Body and the living Blood of Jesus Christ who exists in the glory of heaven. Yet, the Eucharist is meant, through the very words of its institution, to be a commemoration of something that is past - the death of Christ on Calvary. In other words, as Christians partake in the Body and Blood of the glorified Christ, they are redeemed and sanctified by him who died so that they could have life. Thus, when viewed from the psychological perspective, the Eucharist is for Catholics the supreme means by which the Holy Spirit correlates the life of the crucified and risen Lord with the entire life of Christians.[43] Dom Vonier employs psychology insofar as it helps him to explain how the sacramental objectivity of the Eucharist exerts an influence on the whole of Christian life. When Dom Vonier treats the relevance of the Eucharist for the practical Christian life, he relies on the New Testament's description of the basic Christian virtue, namely, social love or charity:

> The essence of the new holiness is this: the oneness of charity
> of all those that invoke the name of Christ and constitute the

> Church. This is what St. Paul calls "drinking the same Spirit," it is a profoundly social godliness, it is the "new commandment," the precept of mutual love which the Spirit with flaming power forces the disciples to obey: "A new commandment I give you, that you love each other as I have loved you." It is the one heart and the one soul of the Christian community.[44]

In this text, Dom Vonier relates the oneness of Christian charity to its special function as the characteristic mark of the people who constitute the Church. The divine source of the oneness and the sociability of charity is the Spirit of the glorified Christ. Furthermore, instead of merely explicitating the precepts of mutual love, Dom Vonier emphasizes their theological source, significance and goal. The oneness of Christian charity is rooted in the communication of the Holy Spirit who raised Jesus from the dead; its existential significance is that the Spirit unites all the faithful to each other in a social godliness which reaches its highest expression in and through the sacrament of the Eucharist; the goal of this oneness of charity is to extend the benefits of the resurrection to all humanity through the witness of Christians themselves.

Dom Vonier remarks that the union of Christians in Christ is an entirely new life which springs from worship and sharing:

> As we watch the apostles in their mode of life in the days that followed the pouring down of the Holy Ghost, we observe a double current of religion; they still keep the rites of the faith in which they had been brought up; they go up to the temple to pray as they had always done; they partake of the sacrifices as they had been accustomed from their childhood. But there is also the entirely new life, the new prayer, the new doctrine, the new rite of the "breaking of the bread," the new love, that makes the disciples give up their possessions; in fact, their religion is a new religion... it is the *via*

nova, the new way, in which Christians alone walk, it is the way of the Lord.[45]

Dom Vonier explains how at Pentecost the Holy spirit definitively prepared the apostles to adopt an exclusively Christian way of life. The unity of all the baptized in the one Body of Christ is the typically Christian element. Therefore, the social or external symbolism of the Christian life has its internal significance in the oneness created by the Spirit of the Glorified Christ. This internal reality of the Church is manifested visibly in its celebration of the Eucharist. First, the congregation itself, gathered in the name of the Lord, is the external sign of the internal reality of the Church: union of mind and heart brought about by the Spirit. Second, the prayers, readings, epiclesis and anamnesis which comprise the Eucharist are the external signs of the faith of the people in the presence of the risen Christ whose unique self-offering on Calvary is re-presented in the consecrated bread and the wine. Finally, the consumption of the elements effects the ever more prefect incorporation of Christians into the life of Christ.

However, for Dom Vonier the Eucharist is not a static reality; it grants Christian life a nobility which enables the baptized to worship God in and through their very existence in the world:

> There is nothing in your daily life which cannot be made the worship of God in spirit and in truth. You know God in your mind, and your external actions are transformed into the service of God. You have your external worship but an external worship which has an internal reality in the Holy Ghost. You know the Holy Spirit is with us, so that whatever we do in external symbolism has its internal significance. When we assist at Holy Mass with its various rites and ceremonies of external worship, we know that behind all and

> in it all is an infinitely spiritual thing- the Body and Blood of our
> Lord offered up in sacrifice. And so your whole life has the nobility
> which belongs to the children of God.[46]

Dom Vonier underlines the power of the Holy Spirit to sanctify everything in the life of Christians so that it becomes service to God. The Spirit unites the spiritual and the material, the internal and the external dimensions of existence so that Christians might adore God in spirit and in truth.[47] The Eternal actions of the baptized become symbols of their internal union in the Holy Spirit. In the Eucharist Dom Vonier finds the supreme example of this truth, for the external gestures of eating and drinking the sacramental body and blood indicate the participation of Christians in the redemptive death and glorious life of Christ. Moreover, Dom Vonier states that, since "the Eucharistic sacrifice is profoundly a corporate act," eating and drinking of the sacramental body and blood, which follows the sacrament-sacrifice as a communitarian meal.[48] Evidently, then, besides its characteristic note of being spiritual nourishment, the Eucharistic banquet has a decidedly social significance. It unites the whole Christian community so that it might extend to the world the brotherhood of Christ.

Thus, Dom Vonier relates the Eucharist to the needy and the poor since the transcendental value of the love of Christ stimulates Christians to promote greater equality in society. It is generally true that to sit at table is an experience of human inter-subjectivity by which the participants come to understand the disharmony within their inner selves as well as in their external behaviour. At the Eucharistic table, Christians likewise discover the disharmony within themselves, with their co-participants in the ritual, and with

Christ. Therefore, the sharing of the *sacrament-food* becomes a medium of reconciliation with self, with others and with God. Furthermore, already here on earth the Eucharist provides a foretaste of the heavenly banquet where all human beings will be children of God and exist in prefect equality. By means of this consideration, Dom Vonier appears to anticipate later developments of the practico-social and eschatological dimensions of the Eucharist.

One can consistently note that in this sacramental theology Dom Vonier attributes equal importance to external signs and to internal realities. For, at worship "everything is sanctified in the Spirit of God and in the truth of the Gospel".[49] Since the Eucharist is the sacrament of the Body and the Blood of the Lord, it is the most powerful means of sanctifying Christians and of infusing in them the virtues of Christ whom they receive:

> Because we have that mighty spiritual possession, our incorporation in Christ, our union in Christ, we can afford to bear things patiently, to deal gently with everyone, to have those thoughts of mercy, long suffering and tolerance, and to wait with the utmost confidence for the hour of God, knowing with absolute certainty that he cannot fail.[50]

Thus, Dom Vonier clearly grounds the virtuous life of Christians in their sacramental incorporation into Christ. Patience, gentleness, mercy, tolerance in suffering, and hope in the coming of the Lord are not ultimately based, as many would hold, on a sense of human misery and suffering. Christian kindness, while it is moved by human misery, is founded on the possession of spiritual wealth. Since Christians know that all people have been made children of God by being united to his Son made man, they realize that at the Eucharist they draw courage and strength to exercise virtue in daily life. Here, Dom Vonier appears to be a pioneer of the contemporary emphasis on the link between Eucharistic orthodoxy and orthopraxy, since he affirms that the sacramental union of Christians with Christ through the Eucharist reaches its fulfilment in the moral readiness to place others before themselves.

In another passage, Dom Vonier deepens his reflections on this insight:

> We are kind to each other through the fullness of our riches in Christ, we give of the abundance of our possessions. God is kind through the abundance of His essential love, He pours out His mercies upon all His creatures because He is infinitely rich in Himself. His children are given that Spirit also; they are kind and merciful, forbearing and forgiving, simply because they have been united to that wonderful power – the Son of God made Man; and in that power they find strength and courage to bear all things.[51]

Obviously, Dom Vonier refers to Eucharistic orthopraxy, in that he seeks to encourage Christians to labour for the solutions to human problems by relying on the spiritual power which they receive in the Eucharistic mystery. On the basis of his insistence on the spiritual, social and eschatological relevance of the Eucharist for the life of Christians, Dom Vonier concludes that "the world's salvation is in the Eucharist".[52] Since God redeemed the world through the passion, death and resurrection of His Son and since this redemptive mystery continues in the Eucharist through the action of the Holy Spirit, it follows that, if the Eucharistic mystery becomes "the constant occupation of human society, its daily deed, its chief concern, its highest aspiration, then society is saved".[53]

As a conclusion, it can be affirmed that its three interrelated sections of this chapter highlight Dom Vonier's approach to the Eucharist as oriented by the Holy Spirit to rendering the life of the glorified Christ, whose effective presence was manifested to the Christians of the Apostolic age, still inspires the faithful to break bread together at worship and to continue this through social charity. Since the Eucharist is associated with the Pentecostal as well as with the Paschal dispensation, the Holy Spirit acts at the liturgy to unite all Christians in the one Body of Christ, the Church. For this reason, Dom Vonier affirms that at the Eucharist the Spirit conjoins the life of the one glorified Christ to the many Christians in history. The constant and devout partaking of the Body and the Blood of Christ moulds the life of the faithful and gives them a specific Christian identity which is characterized by love, forbearance and forgiveness. This new life hoped for by all human beings at the end of the world is anticipated here and now by Christians in and through the Eucharist.

Endnotes

[1] *Coll. Works*, I, p. 288; Dom Vonier considers the Pentecostal Spirit as a permanent revelation of the triumph of Christ thereby distinguishing him from all other advents of the Spirit in the earthly life of Christ. In fact, twice during his mortal life the Spirit appeared over Jesus, and on both occasions he manifested himself as the glorifier of the Incarnate Son of God (Mt.3: 16-17; 17: 5). However, of this Jesus would not allow his disciples to speak before the resurrection (Mt.17: 9). The permanent revelation of his glory came on the day of Pentecost and took possession of the Church and the entire world. In this sense the glory of the Lord here on earth is more than just the memory of what he did and was: "His glory is a divine person; the Paraclete came to do this very thing which Christ had always shunned, to appear glorious" (*Coll. Works*, I, p. 289).

[2] *Coll. Works*, I, p. 286.

[3] *Coll. Works*, III, pp. 206-207; see also Vonier, *The New and Eternal Covenant*, p. 74.

[4] This is the Catholic notion of the Eucharist. For the Protestant, the mystery of the Last Supper in the Cenacle is exclusively a spiritual or mental matter. *Coll. Works*, III, p. 207.

[5] Anscar Vonier, *The New and Eternal Covenant*, pp. 74-75.

[6] *Coll. Works*, III, p. 206.

[7] *Ibid.*, p. 206.

[8] Anscar Vonier, *The New and Eternal Covenant*, p. 74.

[9] *Coll. Works*, III, p. 206.

[10] Edward J. Kilmartin, *Christian Liturgy*, p. 166.

[11] Anscar Vonier, *The Spirit and the Bride*, pp. 220-21.

[12] According to Edward J. Kilmartin, M. J. Scheeben's attempt to renew Pneumatology in theology does not transcend the traditional Catholic view concerning the mission of the Spirit in the work of sanctification only by appropriation. However, Scheeben argues that "the Spirit is personally present in the just by an indwelling that is proper to him, and not appropriation". Further, Kilmartin remarks that this aspect is commonly accepted by theologians today. "But the possible implications for a theology of the personal mission of the Spirit, still remains unfinished business". Kilmartin, *Christian Liturgy*, pp. 218-19.

[13] Anscar Vonier, *The People of God*, p. xvi.

[14] Anscar Vonier, *The Spirit and the Bride*, pp. 60-61; *Coll. Works*, III, p. 207.

[15] *Ibid.*, p. 62.

[16] *Coll. Works*, p. 60.

[17] *Ibid.*, p. 80.

[18] *Coll. Works*, III, p. 80.

[19] Anscar Vonier, *The Spirit and the Bride*, p. 82.

[20] *Ibid.*, p. 80.

[21] Anscar Vonier, *The Spirit and the Bride*, p. 80.

[22] *Coll. Works*, III, "Christianus Spiritualis," *Christianus*, pp. 203-4.

[23] Charles Froehle, "The Signs of the Activity of the Holy Spirit," *The Idea of Sacred Sign*, p. 132.

[24] Anscar Vonier, *The Spirit and the Bride*," p. 28.

[25] *Ibid.*, p. 21.

[26] *Ibid.*, p. 24.

[27] *Ibid.*, p. 31.

[28] Anscar Vonier, *The Spirit and the Bride*, p. viii.

[29] Anscar Vonier, *The Art of Christ*, p. 101.

[30] *Ibid.*, p. 101.

[31] Anscar Vonier, *The Art of Christ*, p. 55.

[32] *Ibid.*, p. 220.

[33] Anscar Vonier, *The New and Eternal Covenant*, p. 87.

[34] Anscar Vonier, *The Art of Christ*, p. 106.

[35] Anscar Vonier, *The New and Eternal Covenant*, p. 87.

[36] *Ibid.*, pp. 87-88.

[37] Anscar Vonier, *The Art of Christ*, p. 105.

[38] Anscar Vonier, *Sketches and Studies in Theology*, p. 90.

[39] *Ibid.*

[40] Anscar Vonier, *A Key*, p. 18; *Summa*, III, q. 1x, a. v.

[41] Anscar Vonier, *Sketches and Studies in Theology*, p. 93.

[42] *Ibid.*, p. 96.

[43] The use of the two terms, *Catholic* and *Christian* is to show the difference of opinions between the Catholic teaching of the Eucharist and that of the traditional Protestants. "It is, of course, a sad fact that among Protestants there are innumerable individuals to whom the Catholic doctrine of the Eucharist has become unacceptable simply because it demands faith in the supernatural, in the divine power. They reject the Eucharist primarily on the grounds on which it was first rejected by the Jews when they strove among themselves, saying 'How can this man give his flesh to eat'". Anscar Vonier, *Sketches and Studies*, p. 91.

[44] Anscar Vonier, *The Spirit and the Bride*, p. 82.

[45] Anscar Vonier, *The Spirit and the Bride*, p. 83.

[46] Anscar Vonier, *The Art of Christ*, pp. 47-48.

[47] Dom Vonier takes pain to explain the meaning of the worship of God in spirit and in truth. "To adore in spirit does not mean the elimination of all external worship. To adore in spirit means to have as our final purpose in all things a spiritual insight, to see the things of the spirit, to believe in the world of the spirit, to have absolute faith that, besides the material world, there is a spiritual world, infinitely greater; that the material world, whatever its bulk, is made subservient to the spiritual world. This is to adore in spirit, to make the spirit the supreme thing, to know that there is a world of spirits, and that God, who is spirit, is the King of that mighty

world; that the material things are merely helps and props to spiritual things". Anscar Vonier, *The Art of Christ*, p. 46.

[48] Anscar Vonier, *A Key*, p, 256.

[49] Anscar Vonier, *The Art of Christ*, p. 48.

[50] *Ibid.*, p. 10.

[51] *Ibid.*, p. 12.

[52] Anscar Vonier, *A Key*, p 257.

[53] *Ibid.*, p. 257.

PART III

Evaluative and Prognostic Synthesis of Dom Vonier's Eucharistic Theology

The Notable Advantages and Inherent Limits of Dom Anscar Vonier's Approach to the Eucharist

If one were to attempt an evaluation of the principal achievements of Dom Vonier in the field of Eucharistic theology, one would have to begin by affirming that the traits of all his writings are reflected in those which specifically treat this sacrament. Appreciating Dom Vonier's intellectual and spiritual approach to theology, Aelred Graham remarked, "there is evident the characteristic generosity and breadth of vision, the depth of faith and zeal for the Church's honour... the same power of casting light on the theology of Christ's Person, the same insistence on the intrinsic holiness of the Church, the same insight into the meaning and implications of the Eucharist".[1] Dom Vonier's ability to present fundamental theological insights in a concise and forceful manner adapted to the situations of then contemporary Christians constitutes the chief characteristic of his genius. Although grounded in the scriptural, liturgical and dogmatic heritage of the Church, his approach to the Eucharist represents a fresh elucidation of this sacrament and prophetic indication of its future development.

Dom Vonier's Eucharistic theology is founded on the Pauline, Benedictine and Thomistic intuitions and approaches. His familiarity with the Pauline corpus enabled him to perceive the connection between Christology, Pneumatology and Ecclesiology.[2] St. Paul states that Christians gather around the Eucharistic altar to share the one bread and the one cup so as to be joined to the Body and Blood of Jesus Christ, their head. So nourished, the faithful are conjoined also to their brethren with whom they build one body.[3] These Pauline insights, which depend on the interconnection of the mysteries of Christ, the Spirit and the Church, greatly aided Dom Vonier in comprehending the dynamic nature of the Eucharist. Furthermore, they enabled him to rediscover for his time the inextricable link between sacramental grace and moral action. Sanctified by the Spirit of the risen Christ through participation in his Body and Blood, Christians are challenged to express their spiritual transformation by adopting an ethical and prophetic style of life.[4]

Next, it will be depicted how Benedictine spirituality enabled Dom Vonier to appreciate the importance of sacramental symbols as means of relating Christians to the mysteries of Christ. Dom Vonier perceived the entire Christian life as constituting a living sacrifice to God, because the baptized participate in the once-and-for-all physical offering of Jesus through its re-presentation in the Eucharist. As a sacramental sacrifice, the Eucharist is the symbolic re-enactment of the death and resurrection of Jesus Christ so as perpetually to extend the fruits of the Paschal mystery to

Christians until their Lord comes in glory.[5] In order that these truths might be better known, Dom Vonier insisted on the need to teach Christians that the Eucharistic liturgy reveals the mystery of their incorporation into Christ. Furthermore, the liturgical celebration of the Eucharist affords them the greatest means by which they might praise God for the redemption won by his Son and for the sanctification being achieved by his Spirit.[6]

Then, it will be highlighted how following the Thomistic teaching - the Eucharist contains the reality which it signifies – Dom Vonier arrived at a new awareness of the Eucharist as a real symbol.[7] By pointing out the unity-in-distinctness between the unique sacrifice of Jesus on Calvary and the repeatable means of re-presenting it on the altar, Dom Vonier defended the Eucharist as a true sacrifice, and yet differentiated the physical presence of Christ from his sacramental presence. Thus, he countered the excessive teachings of those theologians who advocated that a physical immolation of Jesus takes place in the sacrifice of the Mass. By rediscovering the true meaning of a real symbol, that is, an entity into which another being exists and dwells reveals itself and acts, Dom Vonier directed Catholic theology towards an authentic appreciation of the Eucharist as a sacrament-sacrifice.[8]

Furthermore, Dom Vonier's understanding of the role of the Holy Spirit in the Eucharist is underlined. By stressing the significance of the epiclesis, Dom Vonier correlated Christological and Pneumatological dimensions of the Eucharist. The Holy Spirit is invoked to transform the gift-offerings into the Body and the Blood of Christ as well as to sanctify and unite those who are to receive the consecrated elements. In this sacrament, according to Dom Vonier's views, the Holy Spirit acts as mediator between Christ and his followers through the epiclesis, an agent of unity by allowing Jesus Christ sacramentally present in the sacred species, to be joined to Christians, and as harbinger of prophetic action in society by urging Christians to be Eucharistic in their moral lives. Thus, Dom Vonier accentuates how in the Eucharist the specific mission of the Holy Spirit is fulfilled; he enables Christ who exists *extra nos*, that is, in the glory of heaven to be *in nobis*, that is in the recipients of sacramental communion with him.[9]

After pointing out some of the inherent limits of Dom Vonier's Eucharistic Theology, a few complementary viewpoints are suggested, which could well have been adopted by the author himself. Although Dom Vonier's writings are full of dispersed dogmatic insights into the Eucharist, these are not sufficiently organized into a systematic framework. No doubt, the teaching of Dom Vonier which mostly relies on St. Paul and St. Thomas Aquinas, could have been considerably enriched, had he incorporated the Eucharistic themes dominant in the Synoptic, John and Augustine. By analysing the Synoptic Gospels and that of John, he could have treated Jesus' eating with sinners, the multiplication of the loaves and fishes, the Last Supper and the washing of the disciples' feet. From Augustine, he could have been exposed to the much neglected teaching concerning the real sacramental presence of Christ as well as of the entire Church in the Eucharistic elements. As a concluding remark, Dom Vonier's insufficient emphasis on the Second Coming of Jesus and the immortal life of Christians could have been avoided had he been more cognizant of these viewpoints as they are stressed by St. Paul and St. Irenaeus.

1. Pauline, Benedictine and Thomistic Insights Dominant in Dom Vonier's Eucharistic Theology

The long period of formation in Benedictine spirituality, in Scripture studies and in the thought pattern of St. Thomas Aquinas inevitably determined the main lines of Dom Vonier's Eucharistic writings.[10] In general, it can be said that "he was influenced principally by St. Paul and St. Thomas Aquinas… He had no time for writers who waffled, or who tried to bring forward their own ideas rather than founding their writings on Scripture… It must be understood that Abbot Anscar always based his thoughts on those of St. Paul".[11] Following the Pauline understanding that Jesus Christ is present and active through the Holy Spirit's activity in the Church, Dom Vonier perceived the essential link between Christology, Pneumatology and Ecclesiology. In particular, he appreciated the way St. Paul presented the person and mission of the Spirit as the divine power who raised Jesus Christ from the dead. Just as the Spirit saved the life of Jesus from remaining an isolated historical event by raising him from lowest humiliation to highest glory, so the Holy Spirit continually extends the fruits of the passion and the resurrection to all human beings who come to faith and to baptism.[12]

From St. Paul, Dom Vonier also grasped the dynamic or ecclesial dimension of the Eucharist. Brought about by calling on the Holy Spirit, the Eucharist is the locus of the specialized or sacramental encounter between the living Christ in glory and his many members in history. The Holy Spirit assures that the faithful assemble around the Eucharistic table so that nourished by the sacramental Body and Blood of Christ they become one not only with each other but also with their glorified head. Thus, just as through his universal mission the Holy Spirit prolongs the bond of union between Christ and Christians, so at the Eucharist the Spirit renders the life of the glorified Christ accessible to Christians struggling within history. By being incorporated at the Eucharist into the Paschal mystery, Christians are to become efficacious signs to the world of the victory of Jesus of Nazareth over sin and death. The Pauline link between Christology and Pneumatology enabled Dom Vonier to perceive the dynamic nature of the Church which is attained at the Eucharist.[13]

The dynamic relationship between this sacrament and the Church led Dom Vonier to appreciate other Pauline insights which are closely connected to it. The encounter with the glorified Body of Christ through the Lord's Supper is a unitative experience which enables the baptized to live the Christian life fully, that is, to give witness to the Paschal mystery by making known to the broader society its saving power. Thus, Dom Vonier perceived the necessary link in Pauline thought between recognizing Christ's Body on the altar and assuming moral responsibility for Christ's social body around the altar. The Eucharistic presence of Christ should induce Christians to transform their relationships with one another as well as with adherents of other religious tenets. The sacramental union with him should completely outweigh the force of unjust social customs and especially the inequality between classes.[14]

Having grasped this Pauline insight, Dom Vonier appropriately applies it to the social existence of his contemporaries. In the Eucharistic presence the Christ who though rich became poor for the sake of granting humanity divine grace; the sacrament reveals that those who have less are not unequal to those who possess much. The Christian charity which springs from the Eucharist can bridge the gulf between the wealthy and the poor, if true fraternity becomes the practical norm of the lives of those who are nourished by the sacramental Body and Blood. Thus, Christians should prolong the self-sacrificing charity of Christ to the most needy in the society as the concrete sign of the in-breaking of the Kingdom of God initiated in the death and resurrection of Jesus Christ. For this reason, Dom Vonier forcefully underscores that the Eucharistic celebration necessarily involves the sharing of material and spiritual goods by Christians as a means of giving witness to their participation in the eschatological glory of the risen Christ. As one follows Dom Vonier's arguments, one recognizes that he accentuates what is presently called the *realized eschatology* of Paul, for the Abbot advocates the present reality of the kingdom within history because of the Paschal mystery. No doubt, Dom Vonier reflects the theological preference of early twentieth-century Catholicism for the notion of *realized eschatology*.

As a Benedictine, Dom Vonier understood the efficacy of the sacramental symbols employed in the Eucharist, that is, their power of signifying and containing the unique historical sacrifice of Jesus Christ. Since Dom Vonier emphasized that the human person is composed of soul and body, he perceived the absolute necessity of external signs both as expressions of their inner selves and as means to relate to the supreme reality. Thus, Dom Vonier attributed to the entire cosmos the character of a sacred sign. Because of his Benedictine training, Dom Vonier had no difficulty in describing the Eucharist as a symbolic reality. In this sacrament, the words and gestures of the Church serve to enable the elements of bread and wine to signify and contain the Body and the Blood of Jesus Christ. Therefore, the *epicletic* and the *anamnetic* words and gestures pronounced and enacted during the Canon of the Mass by the ordained priest cause the natural elements of bread and wine to become the efficacious symbols of the Body and Blood of Christ. Moreover, the eating and the drinking of the Eucharistic species by the faithful constitute the concrete sign of their incorporation into the once-and-for-all sacrificial death of Jesus on Calvary and into the victory of his resurrection.[15] Thus, in re-affirming the essential nature of the Eucharist as the sacramental sacrifice of Christ, Dom Vonier emphasizes that its liturgical enactment prolongs the salvific effects of the death and resurrection of Jesus Christ and grants Christians a sure pledge of entering into eternal glory with him.

Since Dom Vonier's spirituality was strictly Benedictine, that is, centred on the relationship of Christ to the Church, he viewed the liturgy as the primary means by which the Church participates in the mysteries of the Incarnation, the death and the resurrection of the divine Son, and thus renders the highest praise to the Father.[16] At a time when the liturgical movement was in its nascent stage, Dom Vonier rediscovered the existential significance of scriptural and sacramental symbols, and thus contributed to its growth. Dom Vonier considered Worship as the supreme means of professing the economy of supernatural order and of acknowledging the creative redemptive and sanctifying power of the divine

Trinity. Worship is, thus, an admission of what the triune God is in Himself, of what He is to human beings, and of what they are to Him. Such truths of the supernatural order are expressed by the Church in adoration and thanksgiving, in praise and admiration, and indeed, in every possible choice of moral behaviour in society.[17]

Having thus explicitated the meaning of worship in terms of acknowledging and accepting divine realities, Dom Vonier concentrated on the manner in which the Eucharist enables the Church both to give supreme honour to God and to render the entire life of its members a constant sacrifice. He underlined the Eucharist as the prolongation of the New Covenant which, God established in the Blood which was poured out of the Body of His Son. Since the Eucharist symbolizes and contains the sacramental Body and the Blood of Jesus Christ, its liturgical celebration permits the eternal Covenant to be effective in the lives of Christians. For, in this sacrament, not only do the baptized profess the reality of the Paschal mystery, but they take part in its salvific effect and are incorporated into its divine Subject, Jesus Christ. In the symbolic acts which comprise the Eucharist, Christians attain an intimate union with Christ, offer themselves with him to the Father, and extend the salvific mysteries of Jesus Christ to those with whom they share their lives in society.

On the basis of these considerations, Dom Vonier stated that the primary object of the liturgical movement is the renovation of the manner of celebrating the Eucharist, which is meant to render the mysteries of Christ meaningful in themselves and relevant to all the dimensions of human life. The liturgy fosters the proper exposition of the sign-character of the Scriptures and of the sacraments. Dom Vonier being a convinced Benedictine made the liturgy "the springboard for many of his thoughts; he loved great liturgical services; the grander they were the more they gave honour and praise to God".[18] Here, it can be remarked that the constellation of Pauline and Benedictine intuitions into the Eucharist enabled Dom Vonier to assert that this sacrament causes Christians to exist in and for Jesus Christ, and that it renders such a state of co-existence apostolically effective in the world. The external grandeur of the liturgy was viewed by Dom Vonier as the most appropriate means of appealing to the interiority of Christians. Seeing the mysteries of Christ enacted symbolically enables Christians to enter into them spiritually, to undergo interior conversion, and to manifest the latter through moral commitment in public life.[19]

The originality of Dom Vonier's writings on the Eucharist also lies in their point of departure. Based on St. Thomas' definition of a Christian sacrament as a sacred sign witnessing to that faith through which the baptized attain salvation, the Abbot broadened his understanding of the fundamental concept of symbol and of its applicability to many dimensions of human life. Constituted as soul and body, as spirit and matter, human beings necessarily strive towards the cooperation of these components, one physical and the other metaphysical, in order to express themselves adequately. Dom Vonier views the body as an external reality on which the soul acts. In other words, the body is the visible sign of the existence of the spiritual element in human persons. On the basis of this Thomistic insight, Dom Vonier asserted that all human persons have the fundamental need to express their inner desire for the Divine. Furthermore, insofar as the created realities of the world potentially relate human beings with Him, they can become sacred signs. Thus, Dom Vonier attributed to the entire universe the capacity to be a sacrament of God. Dom Vonier concluded that spiritual realities, which belong to the economy of supernatural life, although they transcend time and space, can reveal themselves in the world of signs.[20]

The Abbot's capacity to place the Eucharist within the broad spectrum of the history of salvation comprises in his valuable contribution to sacramental theology. In the first half of the twentieth century, when there had been much controversy with regard to the nature of the Eucharistic sacrifice, Dom Vonier objectively presented the Mass as sacrament-sacrifice in order to facilitate dialogue among Catholics and Protestants.[21] In this sacrament, natural elements symbolize and contain the Body and the Blood of Jesus Christ, not in their natural or physical state of glory, but in their state as present in transformed bread and wine. The substantial change of natural food and drink into Christ's Body and Blood constitutes the possibility that the Church can offer with Christ a sacramental immolation. The Eucharist is, therefore, a sacramental sacrifice, for although the Victim is really sacrificed, the offering is not performed in its natural mode of existence, but in its sacramental one. The transubstantiated bread and wine, while truly re-presenting the Victim, Christ, retain their proper appearances, so that the participants in the Eucharist can eat and drink the Body and Blood of Christ in a manner which is not repugnant to them. While distinguishing the sacrifice of the altar from the once-and-for-all sacrifice of Jesus on the Cross, Dom Vonier also emphasizes their identity; they are one and the same sacrifice, offered, however, in a manner which is different.[22]

By such assimilation of Scholastic thought patterns, Dom Vonier was led to distance himself from two extreme positions held by the Post-Tridentine theologians. Against the teaching of those who advocated a mystical slaying of Christ in the sacrifice of the Mass, the Abbot stated that, in virtue of the words of consecration, not only is Christ rendered sacramentally present on the altar, but his salvific death on Calvary is likewise re-presented. Against the extreme realistic opinions of yet other theologians who held that a destruction of the substance of the bread and the wine took place at the consecration, the Abbot argued that they did not properly understand the power of sacramental signification. The sacrifice of the Mass is simply the sacramental re-presentation of the duration of time when Christ's Body was separated from his Blood. Since the risen Christ enjoys prefect impassibility and immutability in heaven, no actual separation of his Body from his Blood is brought about in the Eucharistic sacrifice.[23]

By means of his acquaintance with Thomistic theology, Dom Vonier was able to observe that many then contemporary theories were either insufficient or exaggerated, and thus failed to explain the true nature of the Eucharistic sacrifice. Grasping the meaning of a real symbol as an entity into which another being enters and reveals itself, exists and acts, Dom Vonier affirmed the nature of the mass as sacrament-sacrifice. Moreover, in the Eucharistic species the risen Christ continues to extend his salvific grace to Christians through the power of his Spirit in each age until he comes again. Thus by remaining faithful to the Scholastic tradition, Dom Vonier served modern theology by expounding the doctrine of the Eucharistic mystery in sacramental terms. In so doing, the Abbot forcefully restated the Church's authentic inheritance regarding the Eucharist, and did so in terms intelligible to his contemporaries. Since Dom Vonier was a theologian with clear perceptions concerning the mysteries of Christ, expressing these for others was one of his primary concerns. In this venture, it can be stated unambiguously, he was inspired by St. Paul, St. Benedict and St. Thomas.

2. The Spirit-Oriented Eucharistic Theology of Dom Anscar Vonier

As already noted, Dom Vonier understood the role and mission of the Holy Spirit as continually rendering the glorious life of Christ accessible and efficacious for Christians through the Eucharist. Here, further insights of Dom Vonier on the Holy Spirit as mediator, agent of unity and harbinger of moral action are depicted in relation to his Eucharistic theology. By stating that the Holy Spirit saved the life of Jesus Christ from remaining merely an historical event, Dom Vonier means that the Incarnate Word of God, who was raised from the dead to glory, now has in the divine Spirit a mediator between himself and his followers. When the Incarnate Word was on this earth, the Spirit could not yet fully reveal the majesty of the divinity that lay hidden in his humanity, whereas at and after the resurrection the Spirit confirms him as the universal Lord. In other words, in the glorification of the Word Incarnate by the Spirit, his full divinity was finally revealed so that all his words and deeds which could be grasped only with difficulty are understood through faith, hope and love.[24]

Dom Vonier attested that the Spirit is the divine mediator of the glorified Christ. The Spirit has the specific role of manifesting the mystery of the Incarnate Son to all peoples. Dom Vonier considered the symbolic universal manifestation of the Holy Spirit at Pentecost as the moment when the Church was born. From that point in time, the community of the elect became living witnesses to the redemption-in-person, Jesus Christ. The divine mediator, the Holy Spirit, who was active in the Incarnation, death and resurrection of Jesus Christ, presently reveals his hidden identity as the universal Lord of salvation through the symbolic actions of the Church, of which the Eucharist is the culmination.[25]

It follows for Dom Vonier that the Eucharist is realized in the Church by the Spirit of the glorified Christ. Animated by the divine Pneuma, the baptized celebrate the permanent *memoria* of their Lord so as through symbols to render present and effective his self-offering in the Cenacle and on Golgotha. Dom Vonier attributed the consecration of the elements not only to the *anamnesis* but also to the *epiclesis*, that is, to the invocation of the Spirit on the natural gifts of bread and wine so that they be changed into the Body and Blood of Jesus Christ. By articulating this theological stance concerning the epicletic action of the Spirit at the Eucharist, Dom Vonier emphasized that this sacrament entails the on-going process of human sanctification. The Holy Spirit is invoked to sanctify not only the natural elements of bread and wine, but also those who will receive the sacramental Body and Blood of Christ. In other words, through this dual epicletic role of the Holy Spirit, the glorified Christ is made available to the baptized as spiritual nourishment in the

Eucharistic species and in the grace they confer. By analysing the Eucharistic epiclesis, Dom Vonier attributed to the Holy Spirit the divine power of realizing this sacrament so as to extend the grace of the redemption-in-person Jesus Christ to many Christians throughout history.[26]

In order to understand the relevance of such views, Dom Vonier further explained the manner in which the Holy Spirit renders the *extra nos* of the salvific death and resurrection of Jesus Christ continually effective *in nobis* through the Eucharistic celebration of the Church. Besides, being the mediator between Christ and Christians, the Spirit is also the agent of unity among the members of the community. The superabundant grace of the Cross in extended by the Spirit of the risen Lord Jesus in such a way that the Redeemer and the redeemed form the *Totus Christus* through the liturgical actions of the Church. Dom Vonier understood that the essential nature of the Church consists in its oneness of life brought about by the divine sanctifier with the glorified Jesus. Dom Vonier thus attributed the unity of the Church to the Person and mission of the Holy Spirit. Sanctified by the Spirit, Christians experience their unity as the means to radiate the glory of the risen Christ, or to become, as the Abbot suggested the *Resurrection Church*. Because of the unitative role of the Holy Spirit at the Eucharist, it can be said that this sacrament constitutes the Church.[27]

Finally, Dom Vonier regarded the Holy Spirit as the harbinger of prophetic actions in society on the part of Christians who receive the Eucharist. The grace of this sacrament profoundly affects the character of Christians; it transforms their souls and enables them to view their social ambience in a different way. Thus, to show practical relevance of this sacrament for Christians, Dom Vonier designated them in the sense that their charitable works become concrete *Eucharistic beings*. In other words, the Eucharist stimulates Christians to create a symbolic world of their own signs of their spiritual union with Jesus Christ and with all people. The Abbot often affirmed that the distinctiveness of Christian charity is rooted in the values of Jesus Christ and the power of the Holy Spirit. At the celebration of the Eucharist, Christians learn from Christ and from the Spirit how to set up prophetic signs of love in society.[28]

By means of all these pneumatological reflections, Dom Vonier led one to perceive the Eucharist of the Church in relation to the process of Christian sanctification, the gift of the Holy Spirit. By re-enacting in the power of the Spirit the death and resurrection of Jesus Christ through the symbols instituted by him, the Church offers the reality of salvific grace to its members. Through active participation in the Eucharist, Christians continually renew their union with the risen Christ, with each other and with all people. Evidently, this unitative experience impels them to live a more holy life which is expressed in their practice of charity and mercy, peace and patience towards their fellow human beings. Such *Eucharistic acts*, which reflect those once performed by Jesus Christ, constitute concrete signs of the gradual growth of the Kingdom of God until the *eschaton* witnesses its completion.

3. Inherent Limits in Exposition

Bruno Fehrenbacher regrets that while Dom Vonier's writings deal mostly with contents of the faith, they were not developed into a systematic body of doctrine as such.[29] Obviously, while

Fehrenbacher appreciated Dom Vonier's profound theological intuitions, he admitted the lack of their orderly presentation. This applies as well to the Abbot's teachings on the Eucharist which are dispersed in almost all his writings; often his Eucharistic statements are inserted between philosophical principles, on the presupposition that his readers already possessed an academic training in theology. Dom Vonier's Eucharistic thoughts, if arranged more systematically with further reflections of a pneumatological, ecclesiological and eschatological character, would have had a greater impact on his readership.[30]

Furthermore, Dom Vonier's presentation of the Eucharist could have gained more influence had the author better delineated the meaning of such key words as *sign*, *symbol* and *sacrament*. By employing them as synonyms, he seemed to apply them to secular and sacred realities with equal emphasis.[31] This can be attributed to the fact the Abbot's primary purpose in writing theology was strictly a practical one, that is, he set out to instruct contemporary Christians concerning the wealth of divine revelation. Thus, he cared little for scholarly exactness of his thoughts. Nevertheless, *A Key to the Doctrine of the Eucharist* is more than what one Frenchman rated an *oeuvre de vulgarisation*.[32] This solid work is typical of the Abbot's manner of writing; he eschewed footnotes and quotations from writers known and obscure, which would have aided more discerning readers to be informed concerning the sources of his thought pattern. Admittedly, he preferred a large canvas and painted with bold strokes and vivid colours but did not concern himself for details.

Furthermore, Dom Vonier's dependence on St. Thomas is evident from the numerous texts cited from the *Summa Theologiae*; he took for granted his readership's intellectual capacity to grasp Thomistic philosophy on which the Abbot based his sacramental theology. For this reason, he did not see the need to explain the texts quoted. Besides, some of the full-length texts cited from the Pauline corpus as well as that of *Summa* seemed to constitute irrelevant digressions to the treatment of the subject under discussion. The use of those texts *tantum quantum*, to substantiate his arguments, would have, in fact, rendered his teaching on the Eucharist more effective.

For the main part, the attempt has been to collocate Dom Vonier's insights on the Eucharist which are dispersed in his separate articles and books on topics such as philosophical anthropology, Christology, pneumatology and ecclesiology. Although all of these were written independently of each other and provide forceful re-statements of the Church's teaching on diverse matters, the Eucharistic themes needed to be culled from here and there, and arranged in an orderly manner.[33] In the process of producing such an arranged presentation, it became evident that some complementary viewpoints were not included which were available to Dom Vonier, and which could have been profitably incorporated into his writings. For example, regarding the use of Scripture, the texts cited from St. Paul could have been complemented with the Eucharistic themes found in the Synoptic Gospels and in the Johannine corpus. They would have enhanced Dom Vonier's understanding of the social setting and of the prophetic character of Jesus' table-fellowship with sinners, and of the multiplication of loaves and fish. These texts would have enabled him to appreciate the communitarian significance of the Eucharistic meal which is shared by all participants, irrespective of their social and economic status.

Furthermore, the Gospel of John could have enriched Dom Vonier's treatment of the importance of Eucharistic orthopraxy. Jesus' washing of the feet of his disciples and encouragement of such action is the concrete sign of the realization of the Kingdom of God on earth would have further justified his stress on being *Eucharistic* persons. Likewise, the Pauline Eucharistic theology would have been substantiated, had Dom Vonier integrated into his works more detailed analysis of the Johannine discourse on the Bread of Life. For, by eating the Flesh of the Incarnate Word and drinking his Blood, Christians already are partakers of the Kingdom and are guaranteed their participation in the heavenly banquet. Similarly, the inclusion of the Johannine theme concerning Christ as the true Vine and Christians as his branches filled with the Holy Spirit would have afforded the Abbot a deeper awareness of St. Paul's understanding of the relationship between Christology and pneumatology in Eucharistic theology. Certainly, Dom Vonier would have been greatly enriched in his treatment of the Eucharist in human sanctification.

Motivated by his objective to place the Eucharist against the broad horizon of the economy of salvation, Dom Vonier employed patristic and medieval insights into this sacrament. In fact, St. Thomas Aquinas' approach to transubstantiation and to the presence of Christ in the Eucharist aided the Abbot in arriving at a clear comprehension of these matters. St.

Augustine's broad vision of the form of the Eucharistic change and the manner of Christ's presence would have inspired Vonier to come to more nuanced and pastoral explanations of the Eucharistic presence. For, in treating the presence on the altar both of Christ the head and the members of his mystical body, St. Augustine offers a more ecclesiological understanding of the Eucharist than does St. Thomas. Following the medieval desire for accuracy, St. Thomas maintained that in the Eucharist Christ is both signified and contained, whereas the Church is only symbolized. St. Augustine regarded the real presence in the Eucharist to be not only that of Christ the head but also that of the members of the Church his body. Such considerations would have motivated Dom Vonier to ground the sacramental encounter between Christ and Christians in the Eucharistic elements themselves as well as in the act of eating and drinking them at the rite of communion.[34]

Evidently, these themes were available to Dom Vonier because of his acquaintance with patristic writers who tend to integrate Christological, pneumatological and ecclesiological perspectives into their understanding of the sacred elements of bread and wine. In particular, he gained an awareness of the possibility of developing such themes during his formation in liturgical and Benedictine spirituality. However, since they were not accentuated in the early twentieth century, and have only recently come to the fore, Dom Vonier did not incorporate them into his comprehension of how the Eucharist confects the Church. [35]

Furthermore, it can be noted that, although Dom Vonier understood the end of the Eucharist to be everlasting life when

Christ comes in majesty, he did not sufficiently emphasize the *to-be-realized* eschatology found in Pauline theology as well as in the writings of Irenaeus. This would have supported him in his presentation of the prognostic significance of the Eucharist for the final realization of Christian life in glory. St. Paul stresses that the sanctity of Christians is rooted in the death, the resurrection and the final coming of Christ. In his Body, the Son of God assumed sin and death, and therefore was raised into heaven; in this way he promised his followers eternal happiness along with him the eschaton. Since they were sanctified by the death and resurrection of the Christ who will come in glory, Christians are already dead to sin with him and have risen with him. Nonetheless, the Spirit of the risen Christ continues the work of sanctification, for his epicletic role in confecting the sacramental Body and the Blood of Christ urges Christians to long for the final coming of the Lord hidden under the sacred signs. Further, use of St. Paul and St. Irenaeus in this regard would have enabled Dom Vonier to appreciate the Eucharist more fully as the joyful celebration of the Paschal mystery, and as the constant anticipation of eternal happiness at the table of the Lord in his Kingdom.[36]

These prognostic themes were well developed in the Eucharistic thought of Irenaeus who links this sacrament to the first creation, to the Incarnation as the new creation, to the Church as its focal point of the latter, and to the resurrection of the body as its final fulfilment. In the Cenacle, Jesus took natural bread and wine, the fruits of the earth, and gave thanks; he declared them to be his Body and Blood, and explained them to be the oblation of the New Testament. By identifying the natural elements with his Body and Blood and offering himself as a pure victim in and through them, Jesus Christ reconciled humanity with God, and also restored creation which had become alive to him. The Church receives this new oblation from Jesus through his Apostles and their successors and offers it with him to God. The Eucharist, thus, supplies Christians the first fruits of the new creation which is attested by the New Testament.[37]

For both St. Paul and St. Irenaeus, the eternal life of the believers is the necessary consequence of the glorious state of the risen Christ. The truth of the Paschal mystery guarantees forever that those who die in Christ will also rise in him. A share in eternity on the part of believers is the full memory of fellowship in Christ's resurrection (1 Thess.4: 13). Thus, St. Paul establishes the general truth, concerning the resurrection of the baptized from the fact that Christ is risen (1 Cor.15: 21-22). Insertion of such eschatological insights of Paul and Irenaeus would have supported Vonier more fully in his insistence that Eucharist is the pledge of future glory. Such themes would have enabled him to attain more perfectly his objective of setting the Eucharist against the wide spectrum of the economy of salvation.

Having appreciated Dom Vonier for his many contributions to the Eucharistic theology such as his reliance of Pauline, Benedictine and Thomistic insights, so as strongly maintain the authentic teaching of the Church, and making it relevant for contemporary Christians, as well as having openly stated some of the limits, complementary theological viewpoints are offered to Dom Vonier's Eucharistic theology.

Endnotes

[1] Aelred Graham, "The Work of Abbot Vonier," *The Tablet* (April 13, 1940), p. 353.

[2] Cf. Part Two, Ch. III, "The Middle Period: The Christological, Ecclesial and Liturgical Bases of Dom Vonier's Eucharistic Theology," pp. 116-17.

[3] *Ibid.*, sec.2, "The Eucharistic event as Effecting the unity of the Mystical Body," pp. 136-37.

[4] *Ibid.*, Ch. IV, sec. 3, "The Relevance of the Eucharist for the Personal and Public Life of Christians," pp. 192-93.

[5] Part Two, Ch. IV, "Introduction," p. 159.

[6] Bernard Cooke, "The Eucharistic Mystery," *The Bible Today* 14 (1964), pp. 938-39.

[7] Cf. Part II, Ch. II, sec. 1, "The Influence on Dom Vonier's understanding of Sacred Sings as a Universal Phenomenon," pp. 74 ff. Symbolism is "an expression of human person outside the limits of adequate intellectual formation; it seeks to convey a meaning, not through philosophical concepts, but through images which arise out of a complete human involvement with and re-enactment of the artist's inspiration; it reaches out toward truth and value but will not define them". William J. Rewak, *The Bible Today* 14 (1964), p. 931.

[8] Cf. Part Two, Ch. II, sec. 2, "The Reiteration and Enhancement of the Tridentine Notion of the Sacrificial Character of the Eucharist," pp 86 and 90.

[9] Cf. Part Two, Ch. IV, sec. 2, "The Eucharist as Conjoining the One Glorified Christ to the Many Christians in History," pp. 188-89. See also Part One, Ch. I, sec. 2, "The Preference for an Existential rather than Objectified Understanding of Sacramental Symbols," pp. 44, 45 and 49.

[10] Anscar Vonier, "The Monastic Ideal," *BACh*, V (September, 1935), pp. 160, 163); "Life in the Modern Monastery," *Chimes*, III (New Series, January-March 1929), p. 38; Ernest Graf, "The Monk and the Abbot," *A Study*, p. 119.

[11] A personal conversation with Dom Jerome Gladman, Dom Anscar Vonier's Confrere and contemporary (Buckfast Abbey, December 13, 1990).

[12] Cf. Part Two, Ch. IV, sec. 1, "The Spirit of the Glorified Christ Realizes the Eucharist," pp. 164-165.

[13] Cf. Part Two, Ch. IV, sec.2, "The Eucharist as Conjoining the One Glorified Christ to the many Christians in History," pp. 182-83.

[14] *Ibid.*, sec. 3, "The Relevance of the Eucharist for the Personal and Public Life of Christians," pp. 196 ff.

[15] Cf. Part One, Ch. I, sec. 2, "The Preference for an Existential rather

than Objectified Understanding of Sacramental Symbols," pp. 44 ff.

[16] A personal conversation with Dom Jerome Gladman and Dom Placid Hooper, contemporaries of late Dom Anscar Vonier (Buckfast Abbey, December 13, 1990).

[17] Anscar Vonier, *The New and Eternal Covenant*, pp. 77-89; *Coll. Works*, III, p. 213.

[18] A personal conversation with Dom Jerome Gladman, the contemporary of late Dom Anscar Vonier (Buckfast Abbey, December 13, 1990).

[19] Cf. Part Two, Ch. IV, sec. 3, "The Relevance of the Eucharist for the Personal and Public Life of Christians," pp. 201 ff.

[20] Part One, Ch. I, sec. 1, "The Economy of the Supernatural Life as the Setting for the Eucharist," pp. 27 ff.; see also sec. 2, "The Preference for an Existential rather than Objectified Understanding of Sacramental Symbols," pp. 44 ff.

[21] Ernest Graf, "The Writer," *Abbot of Buckfast: A Study of Anscar Vonier* (London: Burns and Oates, 1957), pp. 92-93.

[22] Cf. Part Two, Ch. II, sec. 2, "The Reiteration and Enhancement of the Tridentine Notion of the Sacrificial Character of the Eucharist," pp. 90 ff.

[23] *Ibid.*, sec. 3, "The Restricted Eucharist of Post-Tridentine Theology," p. 107.

[24] Cf. Part Two, Ch. IV, sec. 1, "The Spirit of the Glorified Christ Realizes the Eucharist," pp. 164-65.

[25] *Ibid.*, p. 165.

[26] Cf. Part Two, Ch. IV, sec. 2, "The Eucharist as Conjoining the One Glorified Christ to the Many Christians in History," pp. 184 ff.

[27] Cf. Part Two, sec. 1, "The Spirit of the Glorified Christ Realizes the Eucharist," pp. 173-74.

[28] Cf. Part One, Ch. 1, sec. 2, "The Preference for an Existential rather than Objectified Understanding of Sacramental Symbols," pp. 45 ff.

[29] Bruno Fehrenbacher, "Foreword," *The Collected Works of Abbot Vonier*, pp. ix-x.

[30] Cf. Part One, Ch. I, sec, 3, "Towards a Chronological and Systematic Presentation of Dom Vonier's Eucharistic Theology," p. 51.

[31] Part One, sec. 2, "The Preference for an Existential rather than Objectified understanding of Sacramental Symbols," p. 44; the following example culled from *A Key to the Doctrine of the Eucharist* illustrates how Dom Vonier employs sign, symbol and sacrament as synonyms: "The creative power of symbols, the productive efficacy of signs, the incredible resourcefulness of

simple things, nay to reproduce them in their historic setting, this is the sacramental world, and it is profoundly unlike any other world", pp. 35-36.

[32] Ernest Graf, "The Late Abbot Vonier," *The Tablet*, CLXXV (May 4, 1940), p. 429.

[33] Cf. Part One, Ch. I, sec. 3 "Towards a Chronological and Systematic Presentation of Dom Anscar Vonier's Eucharistic Theology," pp. 51 ff.

[34] Philip J. Rosato, "S. Agostino: i poveri e la communione con il corpo del signore," *La nuova alleanza* 5 (Ponteranica: Centro eucaristico, 1988), p. 219.

[35] Cf. Part Three, Ch. VI, sec. 2, "Failure to Consider the Augustinian View on the Mode of Union between Christ and Church in the Eucharist," p. 253.

[36] Cf. Part Two, Ch. III, sec. 3, "Temporal Aspects of Redemption as Symbolized in the Eucharist," pp. 149-50; see also Part Three, Ch. VI, sec. 3, "Irenaeus' Eschatological Explanation of the Eucharist as Complementary to that of Paul and Thomas," pp. 267 ff.

[37] Henry Bettenson, ed. and tr. *The Early Christian Fathers* (Oxford, New York: Oxford University Press, 1956), p. 95.

CHAPTER - 6

Complementary Theological Viewpoints

Without denying the solid Christological, ecclesiological and eschatological bases of Dom Vonier's Eucharistic theology, some complementary theological viewpoints are suggested by pointing out similar yet differently expressed motifs of New Testament as well as of patristic authors. These theological viewpoints clearly link the Christological to the practico-social dimensions of the Eucharist, the ecclesiological to the liturgical dimensions, and the eschatological to the pneumatological dimensions. If the critique of Dom Vonier's Eucharistic theology centres on his failure to make these links clear, because of his dependence on certain Pauline and Thomistic approaches, the complementary insights to be offered here greatly offset the critique and provide a means of rendering his contribution more acceptable to those familiar with the whole spectrum of the Eucharistic tradition.

1. The Practico-Social Dimension of the Eucharist as Conjoined to the Christology of the Synoptic, Paul and John

Dom Vonier's Eucharistic theology reflects the ecclesiological perspective of Pauline thought concerning participation in the Body and Blood of Christ (1 cor.10: 16-18). Inspired by this ecclesiological perspective Dom Vonier considered the Eucharist as possessing the sanctifying function of uniting all the members of the Church with Christ their head. Because of this spiritual unity between Christ and Christians, Dom Vonier perceived the Church as a new people of God. Yet, had Dom Vonier equally accentuated the practico-social effects of the Eucharistic communion which Paul described in 1 cor.11:17-19, he would have made his contemporaries more conscious of the moral import of the title *People of God*, that is, to become credible witnesses in their ambience to the redemption-in-person, Jesus Christ. By using the term *People of God*, Dom Vonier primarily sought to explicitate the spiritual wealth contained in it. Even though he did not perceive as clearly as Paul the practico-social character of ecclesial life, one must nevertheless recognize that he did view the Eucharist as the unitive force of the people of God. As Yves Congar has pointed out, "Dom Vonier was among the first to re-introduce the term, *People of God* in the twentieth century."[1]

What Dom Vonier failed to grasp is that Paul was aware of the disharmony between the rich and the poor within the Christian community at Corinth, and that he excoriated the former for not having shared their food with the latter.[2] Viewing the Lord's Supper as situated per force in a social context, Paul accentuated the fact that Jesus' command, "do this in remembrance of me" (1 Cor.11: 24-25), implies celebrating a fraternal meal by breaking the one bread and drinking of the one cup so that afterwards all possess a model by which to share their goods with each other.[3] It can be admitted that, since Dom Vonier was a theologian and not a Scripture scholar, he could not have been expected to enter into textual exegesis. However, no such expertise was necessary to comprehend Paul's stress on the moral and social dimensions of the Eucharist. Consideration of these dimensions would have strengthened Dom Vonier's argument in favour of the ecclesiological perspective of this sacrament which he based on 1 Cor.10: 16-18. Had Dom Vonier reiterated the social framework in which Paul placed the words spoken by Jesus to his disciples in the Cenacle, he would have been able to point out the inherently practical aspects of the Eucharist. This sacrament, which assumes the outward expression of a social gathering, produces in Christians what it symbolizes – their relationship with one another in Jesus Christ.[4]

At Corinth, Paul witnessed the opposite effect, and thus later described the Lord's Supper in order to enforce such Christian virtues as compassion, brotherhood and self-giving. For, to eat together even in the ecclesial context means to accept one another as equal members of the same family. It was self-evident for Paul that, by respecting one another, the socially privileged Christians at Corinth would share their resources with those less fortunate, and thus alleviate the acute embarrassment felt by the latter. Furthermore, the Pauline idea that acceptance of the social presence in the baptized should enable the entire assembly to practise the compassion of Jesus towards those who were the poor materially or spiritually. In other words, Christians who partake in the Eucharist are obliged to act on behalf of those who are in need. The inclusion of Pauline Eucharistic orthopraxy would have enhanced Dom Vonier's understanding of this sacrament as a countersign to unjust values and actions in any society.

Furthermore, had Dom Vonier sufficiently appreciated the attempt of the Synoptic Gospels to emphasize the table-fellowship of Jesus with sinners and tax collectors (Mt.9: 9-13; Mk.2: 13-17; Lk.5: 27-32; 7: 34; 15: 1-2), he could have enriched his presentation both of the practical and of the eschatological dimensions of the Eucharistic mystery. For, according to the Synoptic writers, Jesus associated with sinners at table to preach about the nearness of the kingdom of God by means of concrete acts of reconciliation, nourishment and unity. Aware of the various contexts in which the Eucharist was celebrated by Christians of their time, the Synoptic writers viewed the historical events of Jesus' life as fulfilling the eschatological promises of the Hebrew Scriptures (Deut.12: 4; Is.25: 6f; 55: 1f), according to which perfect harmony is to be established by the Messiah among the poor, and between them and God.[5]

By associating at table with sinners, Jesus reveals his messianic mission of breaking down the barriers that separate people from each other and from God. Furthermore, Jesus' acceptance of hospitality from the tax-collectors (Lk.19: 1-10) expresses his vehement protest against the self-righteousness of many Pharisees who seemed more eager to see people excluded from than admitted to the Kingdom of God. On the contrary, by fostering table-fellowship with sinners and publicans Jesus manifests the concrete dimension of charity (Lk.15: 1-2). In other words, Jesus' intentional association with the poor and the sinful is an object lesson for Christians who partake in the Eucharist; it is the basis for their conviction that faith in him as the Messiah, who re-establishes justice among all people, necessitates that they understand Eucharistic grace in terms of social commitment to the poor. These messianic and ethical themes found in the Synoptic could have deepened Dom Vonier's understanding of the charity which is produced by the Eucharist. As the memorial celebration of the death of the Messiah, the Eucharist entails adherence to the self-giving of Jesus which began at table with sinners, which culminated at the Last Supper and which led to the Cross. In fact, Jesus' Eucharistic behaviour was a concrete sign of his desire that his disciples do what he had done: give himself for the sake of the union of all people with God and with each other.[6]

The practico-social significance of the Eucharist could have been further enriched by Dom Vonier, had he treated at some length the texts recorded in the Synoptic Gospels concerning the multiplication of the bread and the fish (Mt.14: 13-21; 15: 32-38; Mk.6: 32-44; Lk.9: 10-17). The ortho-practical overtones of these Eucharistic passages could have provided Dom Vonier a means to encourage his contemporaries to view the breaking of bread on the altar as an existential call to imitate the compassion and charity of Jesus.[7] In other words, if Dom Vonier had sufficiently exposed these Eucharistic texts, he would have been able to show to what extent they shed light on the actions of Jesus in the Cenacle and on Calvary. For, in the multiplication accounts narrated by Mark the stress is not upon the miraculous nature of these events, but upon their revelatory nature.[8] Jesus who took bread, blessed it, broke and distributed the bread and fish reveals himself as full of compassion for the needy and ready to sacrifice himself for them. Jesus fed the hungry crowd in order to announce the in-breaking of the Messianic age in his person and actions. After the resurrection the Church would recognize in Jesus the long-awaited Messiah who continues to extend his loving care to the needy through the charity of his disciples. In this sense, Jesus is both the glorified as well as the self-giving Messiah; in his name Christians protract the celebration of the Eucharist into society by caring for the materially and spiritually hungry.

Furthermore, since the gestures adopted by Jesus in the multiplication accounts, such as taking loaves of bread, blessing and breaking them, and giving them to his disciples to be distributed, reflects his behaviour at the Last supper as described by St. Paul (1Cor.11: 23-24),[9] they deserved much greater attention on the part of Dom Vonier. Perhaps, the most obvious reason why he did not accentuate these Eucharistic themes of the Synoptic Gospels is that he deemed they would distract him from his primarily sacramental mode of thought. For, the Eucharistic themes employed by the evangelists in the accounts of the multiplication chiefly meant to bolster their Christological rather than sacramental concerns. Until the middle of the twentieth century, Catholic theologians considered the Eucharistic texts in the synoptic primarily as Christological statements; only now are theologians becoming aware of the practico-social dimension of the Eucharist which these texts underline. The universal charity to be manifested by all believers towards the poor is not separated from their faith in and reception of the Eucharist but flows from their liturgical actions and fulfils them.

Dom Vonier's insufficient emphasis on the socio-ethical significance of the Eucharist can also be attributed to his failure to consider yet another related theme of the Synoptic: Jesus' identification of the service done by Christians to others as hidden service of himself:

> The mysterious identification of the Son of Man with the hungry, the thirsty, the stranger, the naked, the sick, and the prisoner has long been the special focus of Christian exegetes. In what sense can it be understood that "as often as you did it for one of my least brothers, you did it for me" (Mt.25: 40)?[10]

By assuming flesh, the Word of God identified himself totally not only with the dignity but also with sin and suffering of humanity. In effect, Jesus associated himself with sinners and tax-collectors by offering table-fellowship to them and accepting it from them, and with the hungry crowd by showing compassionate love for them and so sharing in their suffering. Through such concrete acts of charity, Jesus also sets an example both for his disciples as well as for all who would believe in him through their witness. In other words, faith in Jesus entails more than knowledge of his words and actions; it consists in putting them into practice. In particular, Eucharistic faith entails becoming like Jesus in serving others, especially the poor and the sinners, who have been relegated to the fringe of society. Obviously, such Eucharistic service of the poor and the oppressed would imply not only sharing material and spiritual goods with them but also recognizing the presence of Jesus in them and serving him by respect for them and alleviation of their suffering and humiliation.

Thus, if Dom Vonier had placed greater emphasis on the Synoptic messages concerning compassion for the service of the poor, he would have been better able to explicitate the ethical as well as the sanctifying relevance of the Eucharist for his contemporaries. To serve the hungry, the sick and the imprisoned is not merely an obedient response to the call of Gospel; rather it is in itself an indirect personal service of the glorified Jesus (Mt.25: 35-36).[11] Such reflections would have certainly induced Dom Vonier to ground the moral obligations of Christians in the person of Jesus Christ whom they encounter in the Eucharistic elements. In the Pauline corpus, on which Dom Vonier generally relies for his insights, Eucharistic orthopraxy entails putting on the Lord Jesus Christ (Rom.13: 14), so as to join him in serving the least of the brethren and find him in the world by doing so.

It can be briefly mentioned here that Dom Vonier could have further deepened his understanding of Eucharistic orthopraxy, had he integrated into his thought the themes found in the Johannine discourse on the Bread of Life (Jn.6: 35-58) and in the account of the washing of the disciples' feet (13: 1-20). Dom Vonier would have been aided in demonstrating the practical implications of the Eucharist, had he pointed out that Jesus Christ, the Bread from heaven, nurtured his followers by humbly serving them. After satisfying the hungry crowd with miraculously produced loaves and fish, Jesus points to a greater form of satisfaction: if human beings partake of the life-giving food and drink which are his flesh and blood, they can have unending life (Jn.6: 55).[12] Yet, this eternal life, as it manifests itself within history, is not an escape from the call to meet the needs of the people with whom one lives and works. For this reason, the Eucharistic texts of John present Jesus, the Bread come down from heaven, as the humble servant who washes the feet of his followers and who thereby communicates to them – if I do not wash you, you have not part in me (Jn.13: 8)) – nothing less than himself. This self-communication means that he gives his disciples a share in his selfless death and in the glory promised to him. In a similar way, Christians who receive the Eucharistic Christ are to render themselves channels of his presence and self-giving to others through their service of their material and spiritual needs.

Dom Vonier could have incorporated these themes into his Eucharistic theology so as to support his interpretation of this sacrament as the privileged means by which the life of Christ becomes accessible to Christians. Since this sacrament symbolizes and contains the Body and Blood of Jesus Christ who lives forever, it bestows on communicants the initial phase of eternal life. Yet, John emphasizes that eternal life entails following the example of Jesus who demonstrated his identity as unending nourishment for humanity by assuming the role of servant of even the basic needs of his followers. Certainly, this theme could have been developed by Dom Vonier in order to substantiate the Pauline notion that the unity of all Christians springs from their being one Body with Christ as their head (1 Cor.10: 17), and is oriented toward building itself through love of others in his name (Eph.4: 15-16).[13] Thus, Dom Vonier's understanding of St. Paul's statements about the absolute reciprocity of life between Christ and Christians, which is grounded in the larger mystery of his indwelling presence, could have been concretized by referring to the

Johannine discourse on the Bread of life and account of the washing of the disciples' feet. Had Dom Vonier included in his Eucharistic theology the link found in the Synoptic and in John between the sanctifying and the practico-ethical dimensions of this sacrament, he would have been greatly aided in explicitating for his readers the ortho-practical way of life which is demanded of those who receive the Body and Blood of Christ. Yet, the Abbot's reliance on certain aspects of Pauline Eucharistic theology generally constrained him to limit the scope of his thought to the ecclesial and orthodox dimensions of the sacrament. Moreover, the need of Catholic theologians well into the twentieth century, to respond to the controversy with Protestants concerning the sacrificial nature of the Eucharist obliged Dom Vonier to be more apologetic and sound than innovative and prophetic in his explicitation of this sacrament.

2. Augustinian Notion of Union between Christ and Church

One of the principal contributions of Dom Anscar Vonier to Eucharistic theology lies in his intellectual capacity to restate for his generation the traditional teaching of the Church on the union of the head and members, which results from holy communion. Although the Abbot only rarely indicated that he was familiar with the Augustinian position that this union occurs in the sacred species themselves, he did not adhere to it, but based his teaching on union on that presented by Thomas Aquinas.[14] Had he more thoroughly investigated the motives which led Augustine to maintain the symbolic yet real presence and union of Christ and Christians in the consecrated elements, he would have more readily appreciated the Augustinian teaching on the totally unique efficacy of the Eucharist. For, the theological aim of Augustine was not simply to illumine the nature of the real presence of Jesus Christ in the Eucharist; rather he sought to explain the mystical and ecclesiological implications inherent in faith in the Eucharist. These implications would render this sacrament more credible to his interlocutors, as well as counterbalance the individualistic emphasis in the Eucharistic theology of the Donatists.[15]

Steeped in the Eucharistic theology of the New Testament, St. Augustine perceived the consecrated elements as constituting a sacramental symbol of the redemptive act of Christ on behalf of all humanity. In other words, the signs on the altar participate in the unrepeatable sacrifice of Christ, and conjoin to it the sacramental sacrifice of the entire Church and the personal sacrifice of each Christian.[16] In a most insightful manner he understood this sacrament as the liturgical act in which the Church actualizes itself; in re-presenting on the altar the death and resurrection of Jesus Christ, their head, Christians reaffirm their corporate existence as members of one Body united to him. Such reflection induced Augustine to identify the Eucharistic Body of Christ with his mystical Body, since at Holy Communion Christians receive what they are – the Body united to Christ – the reality already present in the consecrated elements.[17]

St Augustine clearly desired that Christians always understand more adequately their involvement in the mystery of Christ through the liturgy so as to recognize their presence in the consecrated elements together with that of Christ their head and to become, as he had done, bread broken and wine poured out for the world. Augustine considered the charity practised by Christians as the concrete evidence and expression of their valid reception of Eucharistic grace. Had Dom Vonier emphasized this theme, he would have better brought to light the Pauline teaching on the mystic-ecclesiological and the moral significance of the Eucharist. The reception of this sacrament creates the unity of the Church because the symbols antecedently indicate and contain this unity. In and through the sacramental symbols on the altar, Christ the head is really conjoined to his ecclesial Body and can act through it.[18] No doubt, greater emphasis on the Pauline and Augustinian understanding of the relationship between the glorious Body of Christ in heaven, the sacramental Body of Christ on the altar and the mystical Body of Christ in the assembly would have enabled Dom Vonier better to clarify the link between the union resulting from the celebration of the Eucharist and the socio-ethical commitment to be undertaken by communicants.[19]

The united existence of Christ and Christians, which is symbolized and contained in the consecrated bread and wine, impels communicants to give witness to Jesus' saving love not only as they stand around the altar but also as they move from it into their social ambience. Through their concrete acts of charity towards their neighbours, especially the poorer ones, they give witness to Jesus Christ who in the Cenacle, on Calvary and in the Eucharist offers himself fully for the salvation of the world. In fact, St. Augustine urges Christians to make an offering of themselves along with their material gifts to the poor, for in this manner such generosity will be more consciously associated with Eucharistic grace. Interpreting Mt. 5: 23-24 in a Eucharistic manner, St. Augustine exhorts Christians to approach the altar of God only after being reconciled with others so as to make a worthy offering of themselves together with their gifts. For, Christ is more interested in humanity whom he saved with his own Blood, than he is in their perishable sacrifice. Such existential self-giving and social commitment, which spring from Eucharistic grace, are modes of offering oneself to Christ as he gave himself to the Father, and thus of extending to many the universal effect of his unique sacrifice on the Cross.[20]

Thus, it is understandable that in the Johannine discourse on the Bread of Life, in which Jesus invites his followers to eat his flesh and drink his blood, St. Augustine perceives not a cannibalistic order but an existential call to the members of the Church to remain spiritually united to the unique benefits of the passion of Christ.[21] Such spiritual union is attained by Christians not only by means of their exterior acts of eating and drinking of the consecrated elements but also by means of their interior awareness of becoming self-giving persons as a result of their liturgical participation in the once-and-for-all sacrifice of Jesus on Golgotha. In this sense, the Eucharist represents the unique sacrifice of Jesus on the Cross, to which the spiritual sacrifices of communicants are constantly and objectively united. The bread and wine offered on the altar symbolize both dimensions of sacrifice: that of Jesus in the Body and the Blood, and that of Christians who render themselves living gifts to him. No doubt, this consideration of St. Augustine, which affirms that the Eucharist is a sacramental sacrifice would have aided Dom Vonier in providing a solid foundation for this treatment of the Eucharist as a sacrament-sacrifice, a concept which he borrowed chiefly from St. Thomas.

As one follows St. Augustine's logic regarding the Eucharist, one perceives yet another theme to which Dom Vonier could have dedicated more attention: the ecclesial realism resulting from the communion of Christians with Christ and among themselves. Christians who through the Eucharist form an organic whole with Christ do not exist *over against* him, but *within* him; together with Christ they are the *Totus Christus*. Thus, it can be said that in the signs of bread and wine on the altar, St. Augustine discovered the Church existing *within* Christ. Evidently, in this process of reflection, he adhered to faith in the unique presence of Christ in the consecrated elements. For, he explicitly states that, after the epicletic and the anamnetic words are pronounced by the ordained priest, the bread and the wine on the altar become the Body and the Blood of Christ.[22] Yet, Augustine could not imagine the presence of the head in the consecrated bread and wine apart from the presence of his members. In other words, the ecclesial realism of St. Augustine presupposes and guarantees the Eucharistic realism in which it is rooted and around which it centres.

The orthodoxy of St. Augustine's teaching on the mystic-ecclesiological dimension of the Eucharist cannot and should not be doubted. However, his attempt to state that the Eucharistic Body and the mystical Body of Christ are essentially co-ordinate realities led many early medieval sacramental theologians to consider his notion of the distinctive presence of Christ in the sacred species to be particularly weak and misleading. Therefore, instead of building on the patristic tradition that the Eucharist is a liturgical event, these theologians viewed this sacrament as a sacred object whose confection depended solely on the presiding minister and not on the active participation of the faithful joined to him in prayer. Moreover, in this period the concept *symbol* was interpreted to indicate an allegory rather than a reality. Thus, the external signs of bread and wine were said to hide rather than to reflect the Body and Blood of Christ. In reaction to Augustine some medieval theologians arrived at a Eucharistic ultra-realism, while others opposing them advocated a Eucharistic ultra-symbolism.[23]

As the synthetic resolution of these two extreme positions, St. Thomas developed the already extent teaching on transubstantiation by expressing it in ontological terms. He was able to propound, on the one hand, a solid realism without resorting to crude physicalism and on the other, a rich symbolism without embracing exaggerated allegorism. After the words of consecration, "the substance of the bread and the substance of the wine are not merely dissolved or disintegrated, either gradually or instantaneously; neither are these substances annihilated; they are changed into the Body and Blood of Christ".[24] Here, the change in the substance takes place on the metaphysical and spiritual plane and not on the chemical or physical one, while the accidents of bread and wine, such as size, shape, colour and taste, remain intact. These accidents serve as the symbolic or signifying reality which point to the invisible transformation of the essences of the bread and wine into essences of the Body and Blood of Christ, the signified reality. Thus, St. Thomas affirms that the teaching on transubstantiation guarantees that the essentially changed elements produce a true sacramental encounter with the Body and Blood of Christ. However, by concentrating chiefly on the change of the bread and wine on the altar, Thomas places the Eucharist within a Christological rather than ecclesiological context, and does not emphasize the reciprocity of the Eucharistic and the mystical forms of the Body of Christ.

Although Dom Vonier followed the Thomistic position, he did realize that throughout the patristic period, Eucharistic doctrine had been stated more in sacramental and ecclesiological rather than in Christological and metaphysical terms. The latter terms enabled theologians to defend the nature of the Eucharist as a true sacrifice without having to hold that it is a repetition of the unique self-offering of Jesus on Calvary. In other words, the Eucharist is the symbolic re-enactment of the passion and resurrection of Jesus Christ to render his salvific person and merits accessible to Christians, and provide them a guarantee of their promised definitive union with God. Very much aware that other theological means of illuminating the Eucharist were possible, Dom Vonier, nevertheless, adopted the prevalent Thomistic approach which the ecclesial magisterium favoured; yet in doing so, he sought to clarify it and to point out its often overlooked liturgical value. However, had Dom Vonier been able to show how the Eucharistic theology of St. Paul was furthered by St. Augustine, he would have supplemented the Thomistic concentration on the substantial change of the bread and the wine with reflections on how they produce in Christians ecclesial unity.

3. Irenaeus' Eschatological Explanation of the Eucharist as Complementary to that of Paul and Thomas

Dom Vonier's mode of explaining the eschatological dimension of the Eucharist would have been enriched by employing the pneumatological thought of Irenaeus. This would have enhanced the Abbot's understanding of the connection between the work of the Holy Spirit in all creation and his activity in the consecrated elements and in those who receive them. The *not yet fully realized* dimension of the Eucharist is touched upon in brief but significant passages in the writings of Paul and Thomas, the main sources of Dom Vonier's thought, were not sufficiently emphasized. Acquaintance with such a thinker as Irenaeus who articulates the future-oriented character of the Eucharist by placing this sacrament against the broad panorama, which is the work of the Holy Spirit in all dimensions of creation, would have enabled him to grasp the Pauline and Thomistic passages in their proper setting.

As has already been stated, Dom Vonier's Eucharistic theology has indeed been influenced by the eschatological insights of both Paul and Thomas. This is evident from the numerous references he makes while treating the eschatological dimension of this sacrament, to the Pauline corpus of the New Testament as well as to the *Summa Theologiae* of St. Thomas. By relating the Eucharist to the definitive events of the passion and resurrection of Jesus Christ and to the promise of his future coming, these authors treat this sacrament from the perspective of the specific grace it produces in Christians: actual membership in Christ and in his entire mystical Body and the pledge of unending union with him and each other. In other words, the efficacy of the paschal mystery in the Church at any historical moment points beyond itself to the future, when the Church will find its completion at the messianic banquet. In various ways, both Paul and Thomas are aware of the *still to be realized* fullness of the Eucharist in the glory of the Kingdom.[25]

It is of course true that, because of his Christocentric-soterio-mission to preach the living Christ, Paul placed greater emphasis on *realized* eschatology, that is, he viewed Christian existence as related to the definitive events of the death and resurrection of the Lord Jesus. The goal of Christian life is "to be found in Christ" (Phil. 3: 7-11; Gal. 2: 2-20), to share in Christ's Cross and resurrection, and to bring others to participate in this unique salvific reality. Furthermore, Paul's awareness that he may not love to see the Lord's coming led him to hope that he would be with the Lord immediately after his death (Phil. 1: 21-23). Moreover, in the *Epistle to the Romans*, Paul lays great emphasis on the sorrows and joys of actual life in Christ. Evidently, this Christ-experience influenced him to view the Lord's Supper as the memorial celebration in which the crucified and risen Jesus continues to be present within history through the liturgy of the Church. The Eucharistic meal, therefore, brings about the union of the head and the members of the Church since all partake of one bread and one cup (1 Cor.10: 17). Thus, for Paul this presently operative union is the *already realized* aspect of the Eucharist. By eating and drinking the Eucharistic elements, Christians now share in Christ's risen life through the indwelling of the Holy Spirit, and already "taste... the powers of the age to come" (Heb.6: 5).[26] Yet, for

Paul the Eucharist is also the prefiguration of the Kingdom which will be accorded to all humanity when Christ is fully revealed at the end-time, and for this reason Paul states that the Church announces the death of the Lord at the Eucharist "until he comes in glory" (1 Cor.11: 26). Therefore, St. Paul continues to expect that the Eucharist will be fulfilled at "the Parousia of Christ, the final judgement, the resurrection of the dead, and the establishment of the Kingdom of God (2 Cor.5: 10; Phil.1: 10-11; 3: 20-21; 4: 5; Rom.2: 3-10, 16; 5: 9-10; 13: 11; 14: 10-13)".[27]

Convinced that sacramental union with Christ is the essence of Eucharistic grace, St. Thomas states that "whosoever, then, receives the sacrament, signifies by that very fact that he is united to Christ and incorporated into his members".[28] Here, St. Thomas views the Eucharist as signifying and containing the effects of the death and resurrection of Jesus Christ, which provide Christians intimate union with him and with each other. In other words, the definitive salvation offered by Jesus Christ in person is rendered actual in Christians through the liturgical re-enactment of the sacrifice of this Body and Blood. Evidently, for St. Thomas this actuality is the *already realized* dimension of the Eucharist. Yet, he is also aware of the fact that the Eucharist points to the fulfilment of the Christian hope of final union with Christ in the eternal glory in heaven. The *not yet realized* aspect of the Eucharist is explained in the *Summa Theologiae* by referring to its nature as prefiguration of the resurrection of the body, immortal life and participation in the unending banquet of the Kingdom. St. Thomas affirms that it is characteristic of the Eucharist to cause the attaining of the eternal life. For, the spiritual satiety and the ecclesial unity which the sacred elements symbolize will be fully realized only in heaven. No doubt, the Eucharistic bread and wine do have their unitative effect, but only in an imperfect manner; they are fully to obtain their perfection as symbols in glory in heaven. For St. Thomas, therefore, the *sacramentum* will be totally conjoined to its *res* only in the eschaton. Thus, the Thomistic doctrine preserves the tension between the *already* and the *not yet realized* nature of the Eucharist: a certain satisfaction of the human desire for union with God and with others is accessible here and now, but the full satisfaction of this desire is reserved for the beatific vision when all will be united in God in the end-time. Viewed from this perspective, the eschatological aspect of the Eucharist renders it the prognostic sign of the messianic meal, the foretaste of the unending banquet.[29]

These eschatological insights, found in Pauline and Thomistic teaching, should have induced Dom Vonier to emphasize not only the *already realized* dimension of the Eucharist but also its complementary *not yet realized* dimension. Both these aspects would have made his Eucharistic theology more complete by conjoining it to the mysteries of the resurrection of the body, the immortality of human soul, the Parousia, the final judgement and the participation in the eternal banquet of the Kingdom. Yet, Dom Vonier was not able to articulate this integration of eschatological perspectives into his Eucharistic theology because he was not acquainted enough with the Fathers of the Church, who commented on Paul and prepared the way for Thomas. The most prominent Father of the Church who offers a well-developed eschatological perspective of the

Eucharist is Irenaeus of Lyons (c. 140 – 202). He explicitates the eschatological aspect of the Eucharist by linking the latter to the first creation, to the Incarnation as the new creation, to Easter as the initial glorification of all human flesh, and to the resurrection of the body as the full attainment of this glorification.

Irenaeus expounds two important aspects of Eucharistic theology: the essential role of the created things in the confection of the sacrament, and the resurrection of human flesh which already begins with its reception and will culminate at the end of time. These themes correspond to the two aspects lacking in the Eucharistic theology of the Gnostics. These heretical Christians admitted neither the goodness of creation nor its incorporation into the final resurrection in the eschaton. Instead, they held that all created things are corruptible, and hence must be denigrated and suppressed so that Christians can live a purely spiritual life; besides they affirmed that the Eucharist, as the sacramental Body and the Blood of Christ, is fundamentally a non-terrestrial reality which should not be linked in any manner to the corruptible flesh of the Christians and its eventual resurrection, but which is to be associated totally with their interior, spiritual perfection.[30]

Irenaeus defends the ecclesial position that salvation is realized by means of creation, and concretely through flesh. In other words, for Irenaeus the Incarnation of the Word reveals that divine salvation of humanity is effected through and not apart from the transformation of created realities and specifically of human flesh. Therefore, in order to counteract the Gnostic position, he shows the inseparable link between the creation, the Incarnation, the Paschal mystery, the Eucharist and the eschaton. This link then leads him to the formulation of his *incarnational principle* which underlines the fact that, both in the case of the Incarnate Word as well as in that of the Eucharistic bread and wine, the regeneration of humanity is realized in and through the transformation of created things which have been permeated by the divine power of the Holy Spirit:

> As we are his members, so too we are nourished by means of created things, he himself granting us the creation, causing his sun to rise and sending rain as he wishes, He has declared the cup, a part of creation, to be his own blood, from which he causes our blood to flow; and the bread, a part of creation, he has established as his own Body, from which he gives increase to our bodies.[31]

Irenaeus emphasizes the inherent goodness of every created thing. Even bread and wine are creatures which Jesus chose to identify respectively with his Body and Blood so that the corporal body and blood of individual Christians who receive the Eucharist might be nourished. Thus, by feeding Christians with his Body and Blood, which are affected by the transformation of created things, Jesus Christ communicates himself not only to the souls but also to the flesh and blood of his followers. This insight should have aided Dom Vonier's understanding of the Eucharist as having an effect both on the interiority of Christians as well as on their present and future corporal existence. The Abbot whose explicitation of the mutual influence of the soul on the body, and of the body on the soul for the full realization of the human person comprises a treatise in itself, did not apply this insight to the question of the nature of Eucharistic grace. Had he substantiated his own appreciation of Thomistic arguments regarding the close inter-connection of the human body and soul by means of the insights of Irenaeus, he would have been able more clearly to demonstrate the relationship in Christian life between the creation, the Eucharist and the resurrection of the body. In other words, Dom Vonier would have better explained that the consecrated elements symbolize and actualize the *already* of Christians' participation in the risen life of Christ as well as the *yet not* of their eternal bliss as souls and bodies in the Kingdom.

In the following well-known paragraph of the *Adversus Haereses*, Irenaeus attributes the Eucharist to the power of the divine Word, and insists that the body of the Christian begins to enter the process which will enable it one day to be raised to new life in Christ after the experience of death:

> When, therefore, the mixed cup and the baked bread receive the Word of God and become the Eucharist, the Body of Christ, and from these the substance of our flesh is increased and supported, how can they say that the flesh is not capable of receiving the gift of God, which is eternal life – flesh which is nourished by the Body and Blood of the Lord, and is in fact a member of him?... In the same way that the wood of the vine planted in the ground bears fruit in due season; or as a grain of wheat, falling on the ground, decomposes and rises up in manifold increase through the Spirit of God who contains all things; and then, through the Wisdom of God, comes to the service of men, and receiving the Word of God, becomes the Eucharist, which is the Body and Blood of Christ; so also our bodies, nourished by it, and deposited in the earth and decomposing therein, shall rise up in due season, the Word of God favouring them with resurrection in the glory of God the Father.[32]

In this text, Irenaeus explicitates how the creatures' bread and wine receive the Word of God and become the Body and Blood of Christ. By communicating the sacred species, Christians are nourished spiritually and corporeally by elements of creation which have been permeated by the Logos. Thus, the flesh as well as the soul of the baptized can receive the gift of God, the eternal life. Furthermore, Irenaeus mentions the vivifying work of the Holy Spirit in the process of the transformation of the body, when he states that the wood of the vine and the grain of wheat multiply through the Spirit of God who contains all things. For Irenaeus, the Logos and the Spirit are the "two hands of God the Father, with which He carries out His salvific design to save not only the human soul but also the human body: For with Him always are the Word and the Wisdom, the Son and the Spirit, through whom and in whom He made all things freely and spontaneously".[33]

It must be said in his favour that Dom Vonier did recognize the epicletic role of the holy Spirit in the transformation of the bread and wine into the Body and Blood of Christ. This understanding of the concerted mission of the Word and the Spirit was grasped by Dom Vonier through his study of Paul and Thomas, and he integrated it into his Eucharistic writings to a certain degree. This is true especially of his emphasis on the role of the Holy Spirit in the epiclesis, since until the second half of the twentieth century, the pneumatological dimension of the sacraments in general and Eucharist in particular was generally neglected by Catholic theologians, and only recently have they been attempting to integrate the mission of both the Word of God and the Holy Spirit into sacramental theology in a systematic manner.[34] Since the Spirit is the harbinger of the Kingdom, the eschatological aspect of the Eucharist as already sharing in the fullness of the end-time, but *not yet fully* has become more intelligible and meaningful to Christians in the West.

Yet, in order to have underlined more forcefully the pneumatological and eschatological dimensions of the Eucharist, Dom Vonier would have had to be informed about how Irenaeus conjoins the first creation of the human person as body and soul, the Eucharistic elements as granting the human body and soul a share in the risen Christ, and the resurrection of the human body to be conjoined with the soul in the new creation at the eschaton.[35] All three states of creation are inseparably linked in the Church's understanding of the sacramental life in general and of the Eucharist in particular. In effect, Dom Vonier did not grasp what can be called Irenaeus' *incarnational principle*. According to this principle, there is a parallel between the Spirit's activity of conjoining the Word of God to the flesh of Jesus of Nazareth and that of conjoining the Word of God to the Eucharistic bread and wine. At the annunciation of Mary, the Spirit of God descended upon her, so that the Word assumed flesh, and a real communication of the Word to the human race was made possible; similarly, at the Eucharistic epiclesis, the Holy Spirit descends upon the created elements of bread and wine in such a manner that the Logos is sacramentally incarnated in them. The aim of the Eucharistic transformation is to initiate in the body of Christians the mysterious process by which they are led towards the final incorruptibility of their flesh and its unity with their soul. This is possible only because in the Eucharist the Spirit has enabled the Word truly to communicate himself and the power of his resurrection to the created elements which Christians eat and drink, incorporate into themselves and confess to be the guarantee of the final resurrection of their bodies.

In Pauline theology, one finds a similar parallel between the resurrection of the dead body of Jesus Christ through the power of the Holy Spirit and the pneumatic transformation of food and drink at the Lord's supper. However, Irenaeus concentrates on the Incarnation rather than the resurrection of the Word because he wanted to reinforce a theological truth which the Gnostics would not accept: "That Word has at the end of time… united himself with his creation and become a mortal man… And by becoming man, he restored anew the lengthy series of man in himself and brought them under one head (recapitulavit), and in short has given us salvation".[36] This can be considered as a brief summary of Irenaeus' Christology and soteriology. He emphasizes that the Word assumed flesh by the power of the Holy Spirit in order to redirect the history of humanity towards its salvific goal of unity with God the Father. This soteriological theme logically pervades Irenaeus' Eucharistic teaching, and thus he shifts the accent from the resurrection to the Incarnation of the Logos. Thus, Irenaeus' incarnational principle led him to assert that the earthly bread receives the divine invocation and thereafter is no longer common bread, but the Eucharist compounded of two elements, one earthly and one heavenly.[37] Irenaeus affirmed that the earthly element is the bread, and that the heavenly one is the Body of Christ. To many Catholics in the period of Counter-Reformation, it seemed that Irenaeus could be viewed as the precursor of Luther who held the theory of impanation: the simultaneous presence of non-transformed bread and of the risen Body of Christ. However, Irenaeus' repeated insistence that the Eucharist is not ordinary bread but the Body of Christ indicates that his use of the words "compounded of" did not intend to describe the condition of the consecrated elements, but the two preceding factors – the bread and the word – which are to be conjoined to one another through the liturgical invocation. Therefore, what Irenaeus meant to affirm is that both the visible created elements and the invisible uncreated Logos are indispensable components of the confection of the Eucharist.

Had Dom Vonier integrated into his theological writings these pneumatological, soteriological and eschatological dimensions of the Eucharist as found in Irenaeus, he would have been able significantly to complement the major theses of Paul and Thomas on which he repeatedly depended. This judgement, similar to those made with regard to the failure of Dom Vonier to include themes from the Synoptic and John as well as from Augustine, is not meant to detract from the prophetic character of his Eucharistic theology, but to indicate its limits and offer perspectives which would have offset them. The irony which has been discovered in the process of discussion is that, by depending almost exclusively on Paul and Thomas, Dom Vonier arrived at a solid and multidimensional presentation of the Eucharist. Yet, by not being better acquainted with the whole New Testament and with the Patristic writers, his reading of Paul and Thomas narrowed his vision of the Eucharist, or at least prevented him from making such connections as those between the practico-social and the Christological dimensions of this sacrament, the ecclesiological and the liturgical, the pneumatological and the eschatological. The present attempt to rectify Dom Vonier's insights by adjoining Scriptural and Patristic approaches to the Eucharist has intended to highlight what greater prophetic force his theological contribution could have exerted.

Endnotes

[1] Yves Congar, "The Church: The People of God," *Concilium*, I, 9. It has gained an even greater significance because of the emphasis laid in the "Dogmatic Constitution of the Church": "All those, who in faith look towards Jesus, the author of salvation and the principle of unity and peace, God has gathered together and established as the Church, that it may be for each and every one the visible sacrament of this saving unity". "Lumen Gentium," *Vatican II*, p. 360, para. 9.

[2] Bruce W. Winter, "The Lord's Supper at Corinth," *Reformed Theological Review* 37 (1978), pp. 73-74.

[3] "Le Ceci" désigne donc non pas la substance du pain come telle, non pas le geste de rompre le pain, mais le repas fraternel inauguré par ce geste sur le pain," Xavier Léon Dufour, "Faites Ceci en Mémoire de Moi," *Christus* 24 (1974), p. 202.

[4] Joachim Jeremias admonishes the one trying to understand the words of Jesus at the Last Supper that he should not begin with the words of institution. "Rather he must first recall the framework within which they were spoken... the words of institution are not to be isolated." Such a mistake had disastrous consequences in the past; "they have been turned into a mysterious magic formula and their eschatological significance was lost". Joachim Jeremias, "This is My Body...," *The Expository Times* 83 (1972), p. 196.

[5] *Ibid.*

[6] John Navone, "The Parable of the Banquet," *The Bible Today* 14 (November 1964), pp. 926-27.

[7] Thomas Suriano, "Eucharist Reveals Jesus: The Multiplication of the Loaves," *The Bible Today* 58 (1972), pp 642-51.

[8] Pondering the possible rationale for Mark's insertion of the multiplication narratives in a particular context within his Gospel, Thomas Suriano remarks that the community's coming together and breaking of bread was a profound way of strengthening and refining some of their basic beliefs about the Lord. Thomas Suriano, "Eucharist Reveals Jesus: The Multiplication of the Loaves," *The Bible Today* 58 (1972), pp. 642-43.

[9] In his description of the Last Supper, Paul does not make reference to giving the bread to the disciples. For St. Paul "the context of Christian behaviour includes freedom, and love for Christ, for others, and for self"; this theme is related to the magnificent image of the Church as body in 1 Cor. 12. Richardson and Gooch, "Accommodation Ethics," *Tyndale Bulletin* 29 (1978), p. 111.

[10] Joseph A. Grassi, "I Was Hungry and You Gave Me to Eat (Mt.25: 35ff): The Divine Identification in Matthew," *Biblical Theology Bulletin* 11 (1981), p. 81.

[11] Interpreting Mt.25: 35 ff. Joseph A. Grassi observes that to serve the needy, the poor, hungry and downtrodden are in themselves a very direct personal service of Jesus himself, and likewise of God; this proves that Christians are obedient children of God, just as Jesus was. Such acts, in this sense, constitute a living tradition of obedience to God through Jesus as well as through his disciples. Joseph A. Grassi, p. 84.

[12] William E. Lynch, "The Eucharist: A Covenant Meal," *The Bible Today* 58 (March 1963), pp. 322-23. Describing the proper effects of the Eucharist, the author of this article logically concludes that, "since the Eucharist is a genuine meal, it strengthens the life of the partaker; but since the Eucharist is the Body and Blood of his who lives forever, it gives man the power to live forever. This perfect covenant meal will achieve the resurrection of the whole person, since the whole person is now part of the family of Christ".

[13] St. Paul's exhortation to the Christians at Corinth, to build up, to seek not their own interests but the interests of others while directly related to socio-ethical concerns, points to a greater mystery: union of the members of the Church as one Body of Christ. Richardson and Gooch, "Accommodation Ethics," *Tyndale Bulletin* 29 (1978), p. 110.

[14] *Summa Theologiae* III a, qq. 73-83.

[15] Donatism: A North African schismatic movement of the 4th century, which took its name from Donatus, the schismatic bishop of Carthage. Donatist teaching on the efficacy of sacraments led to a narrow concept of the Church. Their tendency was to exclude sinners, heretics or schismatics from the Church which, though, was here and now without spot or blemish. Hence, they insisted on re-baptizing all those heretics and *traditores* if they desired to be included in the true Church. Against such doctrine, Augustine taught the universal nature of the Church which contains both good and evil. Basing his arguments on the Scripture, he taught that the Church is the Body of Christ. "The advance in sacramental theology and ecclesiology made by Augustine in response to the Donatists was of great importance for the development of theology in the Middle Ages". D. Paul, "Donatism," *New Catholic Encyclopaedia* IV (1967), pp. 1001-3; Karl Rahner, Herbert Vorgrimler, *Concise Theological Dictionary*, sec. ed. (1983), p. 135; Pierre Guilloux, "Le Guetteur du Christ," *Lame de Saint Augustin* (Paris: Propriété de J. de Gigord, 1921), pp 231-40.

[16] Augustine, *De Doctrina Christiana.* III, 16, 24.

[17] *Lettera* 27, 2; see also Philip J. Rosato, "S. Agostino: I poveri e la comunione con il corpo del Signore," *La nuova alleanza* 5 (Ponteranica: centro eucaristico, 1988), p. 220.

[18] Interpreting St. Augustine, Jean-Marie Le Blond observes that the bishop of Hippo held the position that not only the reality of the historical Jesus but the total Christ is present in the sacramental elements; "Augustin ne sépare pas le chef de ses membres". Jean-Marie Le Blond, "Allegorie," *Les Conversions de Saint Augustin* (Paris: éditions Montaigne, 1950), p. 300.

[19] Philip J. Rosato, *La nuova alleanza* 5, p. 219.

[20] *Ibid.*, pp. 221-22.

[21] Augustine, *De Doctrina Christiana.* III, 16, 24.

[22] Augustine, *Epist.*, 6, 3.

[23] While Paschasius Radbertus (c. 785 – 860) held an ultra-realistic position, Berengarius of Tours (c. 1000 – 88) developed a theory of the Eucharist as mere sign and symbol. *New Catholic Encyclopaedia* Vol. II (1967), pp. 320-21; X (1967), p. 1050; *Encyclopédie Populaire sur L'Eucharistie* (Paris: Librairie Bloud et Gsy, 1934), pp. 981, 983, 984.

[24] *Summa Theologiae* III, q. lxxv, a. iii; see also Paul J. Glenn, "Transubstantiation," *A Tour of the Summa* (Rockford: Tan Books and Publishers, INC., 1978), p. 379.

[25] Paul looks with triumphant hope at the panorama of future history; now that this new element of resurrection has been introduced, the time will certainly come when the regime of death will be replaced by that of God. Edmund Flood, "Paul on the Resurrection," *Clergy Review* 69 (1984), p. 142.

[26] John N. D. Kelly, "The Christian Hope," *Early Christian Doctrines* (London: A & C Black, 1968), p. 459.

[27] Joseph Plevnik, "The Centre of Pauline Theology," *The Catholic Biblical Quarterly* 51 (1981), p. 468.

[28] *Summa Theologiae* III, q. lxxx, a. iv; see also Anscar Vonier, "The Eucharistic Banquet," *A Key to the Doctrine of the Eucharist*, p. 255.

[29] Hamish F. G. Swanston, "Liturgy as Paradise and as Parousia," *Scottish Journal of Theology* 36 (1983), p. 513.

[30] "Irénée enseigne la glorification du corps matériel"; Albert dufourcq, "La Doctrine de Saint Irénée," *Saint Irénée* (Paris: Librairie Bloud, 1905), p. 26; see also John N. D. Kelly, "The Gnostic Way," *Early Christian Doctrines* (London: Adam and Charles Black, 1968), pp. 22-28.

[31] *Adversus Haereses* V, 2, 2; see also William A. Jurgens, tr., "St. Irenaeus," *The Faith of the Early Fathers*, Vol. I (Collegeville, Minnesota: The Liturgical Press, 1970), p. 99.

[32] *Adv. Haer.* V, 2, 3; see also William A. Jurgens, *The Faith of the Early Fathers* Vol. 1 (Collegeville, Minnesota: The Liturgical Press, 1970), p. 99.

[33] *Adv. Haer.* IV, 20, 1; Cf. William A. Jurgens, "St. Irenaeus," *The Faith of the Early Fathers*, p. 96; Albert Dufourcq, "La doctrine de Saint Irénée," *Saint Irénée*, p. 12. Edward J. Kilmartin, "Twentieth Century Catholic Theology of the Sacraments," *Christian Liturgy*, p. 12.

[34] Edward J. Kilmartin, "Twentieth Century Catholic Theology of the Sacraments," *Christian Liturgy*, p. 12.

[35] *Adv. Haer.* IV, 18, 4; Cf. William A. Jurgens, "St Irenaeus," *The Faith of the Early Fathers* Vol. I (Collegeville, Minnesota: The Liturgical press, 1970), p. 95.

[36] *Adv. Haer.* III, 18, 1; see also Robert J. Daly, "Irenaeus of Lyons," *The Origins of the Christian Doctrine of Sacrifice*, p. 94.

[37] *Adv. Haer.* IV, 18, 5.

Conclusion

One of the main tasks of Catholic theology at the time of Dom Vonier was to conjoin the Christological, pneumatological and ecclesiological dimensions of the Eucharist, that is, to relate the person and the mission of both the Word and the Holy Spirit to the sacramental life of the Church. Because of his formation in Scriptural theology, in Thomistic thought and in Benedictine spirituality, Dom Vonier was able to link the Eucharist to the divine initiative whereby Jesus Christ, in the power of the Holy Spirit, nourishes and animates the existence of the mystical Body, the Church. By decidedly situating the Eucharist against the spectrum of the economy of salvation, the Abbot perceived that the Holy Spirit enables the *extra nos* of the redemptive death and resurrection of Jesus Christ continually to be rendered present *in nobis* through the ecclesial words and signs which constitute the Eucharist. In other words, the sacrament of the Eucharist is the answer of the triune God to the need of humanity to experience divine life from within.

By viewing the Eucharist against the horizon of the rituals practised by most world religions so as to relate this specific Christian sacrament to the universal search of humanity for intimate union with the divine, Dom Vonier appreciated the privileged role of symbols in the plan of God to offer salvation to all human beings. The New Covenant established once-and-for-all between God and humanity through the immolation of the Body and Blood of the Spirit-filled Jesus is perpetuated in time by means of specific and repeatable symbols. Because the consecrated elements of bread and wine not only symbolize the redemption-in-person, Jesus Christ, but actually contain him as well, Christians who eat and drink of them are mystically joined to their head, and thus form the visible sign of his presence in the world. It can thus be said that the Holy Spirit assures through the Eucharistic liturgy the continued presence of the redemption-in-person, Jesus Christ within history. The epicletic invocation both on the bread and wine and on the liturgical assembly renders the natural elements real symbols of Christ and transforms Christians into a community of charity. In other words, the Holy Spirit stimulates Christians who partake in the Eucharist to conform their entire behaviour to the practico-ethical values of justice and brotherhood as preached and exemplified by Jesus. Through the dedicated life of Christians in society, witness is given to the fact that the Eucharist anticipates the Kingdom of God promised to humanity once the Holy Spirit has oriented all things to the Son, and once the Son hands over the new creation to the Father.

Thus, Dom Vonier's approach to the Eucharistic mystery represents a fresh elucidation of the need to link Christology, pneumatology and ecclesiology to the very nature of this sacrament. Constantly nourished by the sacramental Body and Blood of Christ, which is brought about by the Spirit, members of the Church express their eschatological hope by adopting an ethical and prophetic style of life in society. In effect, Dom Vonier insisted that Christians must be taught that the Eucharistic liturgy is the locus where the Holy Spirit incorporates them into the mysteries of the Incarnation, the death and the resurrection of the Son of God so as to provide them a pledge of their definitive entry into eternal glory. Especially, by rediscovering the essential role of the Holy Spirit in confecting the Eucharist, Dom Vonier enriched Catholic thought concerning the way in which the Holy Spirit acts as the mediator between Christ and his followers, as the agent of ecclesial unity, and as the harbinger of the promised fulfilment of the prophetic actions of Christians in society. Dom Vonier's constant attempt to correlate Christological, pneumatological and ecclesiological themes in his Eucharistic theology truly prefigured major trends in the theology of the post-conciliar period.

Yet, once the achievement of Dom Vonier has been admitted, it must be observed that his intention to correlate the dimensions under discussion was not as successfully realized as it could have been both because of the sporadic way in which he articulated his insights and because of the restricted sources he employed. His dogmatic insights into the Christological, pneumatological and ecclesiological dimensions of the Eucharist were dispersed in various forms of theological writing, and needed to have been organized in a more systematic manner. Furthermore, his almost exclusive dependence on St. Paul and St. Thomas Aquinas, as dictated to a great extent by the ecclesial climate of his time, restricted his teaching on Eucharistic theology.

To highlight his understanding of the practico-social aspect of the Eucharist, Dom Vonier would have had to adopt certain Christological motifs found in the synoptic and in John. In these sources both the moral and the social implications of Jesus' table-fellowship with sinners as well as the feeding of the poor and the hungry are accentuated as preconditions of his behaviour in the Cenacle. For, by means of these prophetic acts at table or in deserted places, Jesus announced the in-breaking of the Kingdom especially to the needy and the oppressed in his social milieu. Furthermore, the Johannine discourse on the Bread of life and the account of the washing of the disciples' feet by Jesus should have been explicitated by Dom Vonier. Since the Eucharist symbolizes and contains the Bread descended from heaven, who compassionately nourishes the hungry masses, and humbly washes the feet of his disciples, the celebration of this sacrament by Christians necessitates that they too perform such acts of charity and service as a sign of authentic mystical union with him. In other words, through the Eucharistic encounter with the Bread come down from heaven, who as the humble servant gives his followers a share in his selfless death, Christians are to become in the world living witnesses of his continuing self-giving presence. They do this through the sharing of their material and spiritual goods in the name of the Eucharistic Christ. Thus, the correlation between the Christological and the practico-social dimensions of the Eucharist, as it is expressed in the synoptic and in John, would have enriched Dom Vonier's teaching on the ortho-practical way of life which is demanded of those who sincerely partake in the consecrated elements of bread and wine broken and poured out by Jesus for all.

Furthermore, Augustine's insight that this sacrament *per se* symbolizes and contains, from the moment of its liturgical confection, the *Totus Christus*, whereby the head and the members are joined together, would have, on the one hand, freed Dom Vonier from his exclusive reliance of the Thomistic position that such union results solely from reception of the sacred species, and on the other hand, would have enriched his understanding of the ecclesiological dimension of the Eucharist with the holistic view of Augustine that the sacramental Body and the mystical Body of Christ form one interrelated mystery.

Finally, Irenaeus' teaching concerning the relationship between the pneumatological and the eschatological dimensions of the Eucharist is proposed as complementary to Dom Vonier's thought. According to Irenaeus, the Holy Spirit causes the transformation of the natural elements of bread and wine into the sacramental Body and Blood of Christ so as to unite Christians in their head, and thus prefigure their definitive union with him at the resurrection of the body and the eternal banquet of the Kingdom.

Dom Vonier's Eucharistic Theology, conditioned as it was by his time, nonetheless offers a significant contribution to modern sacramental theology, since it strives to harmonize the dogmatic treatises on Christology, pneumatology and ecclesiology with what for a long period was the isolated tract on the sacraments. Dom Anscar Vonier was among the first Catholic theologians to rediscover and to restate the inherently dynamic nature of this sacrament as attested by Scripture and Tradition. Evidently, by comprehending the meaning of the Eucharist as a real symbol, Dom Vonier clearly related this sacrament to the redemption-in-person, Jesus Christ, to the sanctifying and transforming power of the Holy Spirit and to the very constitution of the mystical Body. Furthermore, by means of these perspectives, he rightly situated the Eucharist against the entire horizon of the economy of salvation so as to render it more relevant to the spiritual quest of all people as well as to that of Christians.

If Dom Vonier's thought did not sufficiently relate the Christological to the practico-ethical dimension of the Eucharist, the ecclesiological to the liturgical, and the pneumatological to the eschatological, this fact does not negate his achievement. By proposing some complementary viewpoints culled from Synoptic and Johannine theology as well as from St. Augustine and St. Irenaeus, this study has shown the potential inherent in Dom Vonier's contribution. He pointed out how the Catholic doctrine of the Eucharist is unexplainable apart from the gift of faith; it postulates a spiritual and intellectual outlook which very few people possess unless they are properly nurtured in a Catholic ambience. Faith in the triune God, and thus in the salvific design fashioned by the Father, accomplished in the person and mission of the Son, and brought to final fulfilment in the sanctifying work of the Holy Spirit. Aware of the then contemporary apologetics as well as controversial debates on the nature of the Eucharist, Dom Vonier explained this sacrament by rediscovering the psychological, spiritual, and moral force of symbols as indicated in the Scriptural and Scholastic sources. Such symbols are said to entail a profound harmony between the metaphysical and the physical world. In other words, Dom Vonier perceived that sacramental symbols, when properly explained and employed, can be effective in enabling Christians to enter into union with the triune God and to participate in the on-going mystery of human and cosmic salvation.

It may well be that this investigation of Dom Vonier's understanding of the Eucharistic symbols might stimulate Christian thinkers to develop the contribution which he made to a renewed theology of this sacrament. He was firmly convinced that all human beings are brothers who seek God through signs, and that Christians find in the sign who is Jesus Christ, and in the Eucharistic sign, a mystical union with God and with each other. For, the Eucharistic symbols are grounded in the Person of Jesus Christ who, in the power of the Holy Spirit, unites all mankind and all creation and directs them to the Father. In the recent past, a quarter of a century after the death of Anscar Vonier, Christians have exhibited their concern for more understanding and cordial relations with adherents of other religions. Today, if they are to fulfil the injunction of Jesus Christ, "Do this in remembrance of me", they have to proclaim the mystery of the Eucharist in categories which recognize the search of all mankind for God through the symbols of creation. Coming from a rich background of symbols and rituals, which are centuries old, one has found in Dom Anscar Vonier the courage to develop the full tradition of Eucharistic theology and, in so doing, to render it more relevant and appealing to those who do not yet know and confess Christ, but who through their use of symbols at worship acknowledge him and his Spirit implicitly and are united to his Church in an inchoate manner.

Bibliography

I. THE WORKS OF DOM ANSCAR VONIER

A. Books

The Human Soul: And Its Relations with Other Spirits. 1913. 3rd ed., Revised. London: Burns, Oates and Washbourne, 1914.

The Personality of Christ. London: Burns, Oates and Washbourne, 1914.

The Christian Mind. London: B. Herder, 1920.

The Divine Motherhood. London: B. Herder, 1921.

A Key to the Doctrine of the Eucharist. 1925. Westminster, Maryland: The Newman Press, 1960. French edition: *La Clef de la Doctrine Eucharistique*. Translated with a foreword by R. P. Roguet. Lyon: Les Éditions de l'Abeilie, 1942.

The Life of the World to Come. London: Burns, Oates and Washbourne, 1926.

The Angels. Vol. VIII of *The Treasury of the Faith Series*. Edited by George D. Smith. London: Burns, Oates and Washbourne, 1928.

The New and Eternal Covenant. London: Burns, Oates and Washbourne, 1930. French edition: *La Nouvelle et Éternelle Alliance: les Éléments Permanents du Catholicisme*. Translated with a foreword by Louis Lainé. Saint-Brieuc: A. Prvd. "Homme", 1932.

Death and Judgement. Vol. XXXI of *The Treasury of Faith Series*. Edited by George D. Smith. London: Burns, Oates and Washbourne, 1930.

Christ the King of Glory: *Tu Rex Gloriae Christe*. London: Burns, Oates and Washbourne, 1932.

Christianus. London: Burns, Oates and Washbourne, 1933.

The Victory of Christ. London: Burns, Oates and Washbourne, 1934.

Das Mysterium der Kirche. Salzburg: Verlag Anton Pustet, 1934.

The Spirit and the Bride. London: Burns, Oates and Washbourne, 1935. French edition: *L'Esprit et l'Épouse*. Translated with a foreword by D. B. Capelle. Paris: Les Éditions du Cerf, 1947.

The People of God. London: Burns, Oates and Washbourne, 1937.

Sketches and Studies in Theology. London: Burns, Oates and Washbourne, 1940.

The Collected Works of Abbot Vonier. Vol. I: *The Incarnation and Redemption*. Vol. II: *The Church and the Sacraments*. Vol III: *The Soul and the Spiritual Life*. London: Burns and Oates, 1952. Spanish edition: *Obras del Abad Vonier*. Vol. I: *La Encarnación y Redención*. Vol. II: *La Iglesia y los Sacramentos*. Vol. III: *El Alma y la Vida Espiritual*. Tr. Rdo, P. Beda Lazaro. Barcelona (II): Editorial Liturgica Española, S. A., 1962.

B. Articles (in chronological order)

"The Abbot of Buckfast as a Serbian Spy," *The Tablet*, CXXV (January 23, 1915), 113.

"Rex Pacificus," *Buckfast Parish Messenger*, I (July 1920), 4-7.

"On Church Union," *Buckfast Parish Messenger*, I (September 1920), 4-6.

"The Holy Angels," *Buckfast Parish Messenger*, I (October 1920), 3-4.

"Vita Venturi Saeculi," (Part I), *Chimes*, I (January 1921), 3-10.

"Vita Venturi Saeculi," (Part II), *Chimes*, I (April 1921), 63-73.

"Mabel Lady Clifford," *Chimes*, I (April 1921), 113-14.

"Vita Venturi Saeculi," (Part III), *Chimes*, I (July 1921), 121-28.

"Vita Venturi Saeculi," (Part IV), *Chimes*, I (October 1921), 181-88.

"Vita Venturi Saeculi," (Part V), *Chimes*, II (January 1922), 141-48.

"The Abbot's Christmas Wishes," *Chimes*, II (January 1922), 239-40.

"Vita Venturi Saeculi," (part VI), *Chimes*, II (April 1922), 303-8.

"Our Reward," *Chimes*, II (July 1922), 1.

"The Wreck of the *Sirio*," *Chimes*, II (July 1922), 31-35.

"Vita Venturi Saeculi," (Part VII), *Chimes*, III (January 1923), 3-9.

"The Resurrection of the Body," (Part I), *Chimes*, III (April 1923), 65-76.

"The Resurrection of the Body," (Part II), *Chimes*, III (July 1923), 143-54.

"Vita Venturi Saeculi (Part VIII), *Chimes*, III (October 1923), 211-15.

"Vita Venturi Saeculi," (Part IX), *Chimes*, IV (April 1924), 4-12.

"Vita Venturi Saeculi," (Part X), *Chimes* IV, (July 1924), 72-79.

"Vita Venturi Saeculi," (Part XI), *Chimes*, IV (October 1924), 162-67.

"Two Great Benedictine Abbots," *Chimes*, V (January 1925), 1-3.

"Smoking Flax," *Chimes*, V (January 1925), 4-11.

"The Personality of Christ," *Chimes*, V (April 1925, 66-77.

"The Main Stream," *Chimes*, V (July-September, 1925), 131-39.

"Sons of God," *Chimes*, V (October 1925), 199-206.

"The Psychological Import of the Catholic Faith in the Eucharist," *The Catholic Medical Guardian*, t. 3, 1925, 112-14.

"The Worth of the Supernatural," *Chimes*, VI (January-March 1926), 259-69.

"Christianus Orans," *Chimes*, VI (April-July 1926), 326-36.

"Vinculum Charitatis," *Chimes*, VI (October-December 1926), 426-32.

"Christianus Sacrificance: The Christian at Sacrifice," *Chimes* I (New Series, January-March 1927), 3-15.

"Eucharistic Theology," (Part I), *The Tablet*, CIL (April 30, 1927), 575-77.

"Eucharistic Theology," (Part II), *The Tablet*, CIL (May 7, 1927), 610-11.

"Spirit Tutelage," *Chimes*, I (New Series, July-September 1927), 119-25.

"Grimspound: A Dartmoor Laura," *Chimes*, II (New Series, January-March 1928), 3-15.

"The Good Samaritan," *Chimes*, II (New Series, July-September 1928), 136-41.

"Domus Spiritualis," *Chimes*, II (New Series, July-September), 1928), 102-9.

"Life in the Modern Monastery," *Chimes*, III (New Series, January-March), 1929), 37-40.

"Sacrificial Immolation," *The Tablet*, CLIII (May 25, 1929), 700.

"To Enter into the Kingdom," *Chimes*, III (New Series, April-June 1929), 84-89.

"Et Caetera," *The Tablet*, CLIV (November 16, 1929), 654-55.

"The Old and New in Eucharistic Worship," *Chimes*, IV (New Series, January-March 1930), 26-34.

"Our Friends," *Chimes*, IV (New Series, April-June 1930), 48-52.

"Our Three Easter Alleluias," *Chimes*, IV (New Series, April-June 1930), 53-56.

"The Christian Attitude Towards Death," *Chimes*, IV (New Series, July-September 1930), 94-99.

"The New and Eternal Covenant," *The Tablet*, CLVI (September 13, 1930), 340.

"Sacramental Stability," *The Tablet*, CLVI (September 13, 1930), 340-42.

"Conversion," *Chimes*, IV (New Series, October-December 1930), 136-41.

"The Pilgrimage to Aachen," *Chimes*, IV (New Series, October-December 1930), 158-61.

"The Meaning of the Human Soul," an article for Central Bureau Publications, special free leaflet No. 2, 1930, 1 - 8.

"Fireword," *BACh*, I (Spring, 1931), 1.

"Christianus Poenitens: The Christian in Repentance," *BACh*, I (Spring, 1931), 2-9.

"In the Light of God," *BACh*, I (Spring, 1931) 18-21.

"Calvary and the Mass," *The Tablet*, CLVII (May 23, 1931), 674-75.

"Christianus Gaudens: The Christian in Gladness," *BACh*, I (Summer, 1931), 67-73.

"The Benedictine Feast of the Eleventh of July," *BACh*, I (Summer, 1931), 79-81.

"The Final Act of the Council of Trent in the Matter of the Eucharistic Sacrifice," *The Tablet*, CLVIII (September 19, 1931), 362-64.

"Christianus Operans: The Christian at Work," (Part I), *BACh*, I (Autumn, 1931), 133-39.

"The Lesson of Ephesus," *The Tablet*, CLVIII (December 5, 1931), 721-24.

"Christianus Operans: The Christian at work," (Part II), *BACh*, I (Christmas, 1931), 202-8.

"Religious Community," *BACh*, I (Christmas, 1931), 234-5.

"Christianus Tentatus: The Christian in Temptation," *BACh*, II (Spring, 1932), 2-9.

"Mr. Henry Schiller," *BACh*, II (Spring, 1932), 19-21.

"Frederick A. Walters: The Architect of Buckfast Abbey," *BACh*, II (Spring, 1932), 38-44.

"Fifteenth Century of the Coming to Ireland of Saint Patrick," *BACh*, II (Spring, 1932), 10-17.

"The Exaltation of Christ," *The Tablet*, CLIX (April 23, 1932), 535-36.

"The Message," *BACh*, II (Summer, 1932), 67-68.

"Christianus Sanctificatus: The Hallowed Christian," *BACh*, II (Summer, 1932), 70-74.

"The High Altar Retable of Buckfast Abbey," *BACh*, II (Summer, 1932), 75-78.

"For Candlemas," *The Tablet*, CLXI (January 28, 1933), 109-10.

"Christianus Illuminatus: The Enlightened Christian," *BACh*, III (Spring, 1933), 5-10.

"The Passion of Christ and the Patience of the Monk," *BACh*, III (Spring, 1933), 11-12.

"The Catholic Church and Progress," *BACh*, III (Summer, 1933), 67-78.

"Saint Ignatius Loyola," *BACh*, III (Autumn, 1933), 133-39.

"De Senectute," *The Tablet*, CLXII (October 14, 1933), 509-10.

"The Quarterly Notes," *BACh*, III (Christmas, 1933), 202-8.

"A Ship's Company," *BACh*, IV (March 1934), 1-8.

"A Benedictine Almoner," *BACh*, IV (March 1934), 29-31.

"Christ's Sovereignty Over All Flesh," *BACh*, IV (June 1934), 73-80.

"A Sermon Delivered at Glastonbury by the Abbot of Buckfast, 16th June 1934," *BACh*, IV (September 1934), 141-44.

"Symbolism in Religion," *BACh*, IV (December 1934), 205-11.

"The Doctrinal Power of the Liturgy of the Catholic Church," *The Clergy Review*, IX (January 1935), 1-8.

"Homiletics," *The Clergy Review*, IX (March 1935), 222-30.

"The Roman Centurion," *BACh*, V (March 1935), 1-5.

"Francis Cardinal Bourne," *BACh*, V (March 1935), 13-15.

"The Monastic Ideal," *BACh*, V (September 1935), 153-64.

"Three Consecrations," *BACh*, V (December 1935), 229-38.

"A Message to America," *BACh*, VI (March 1936), 1-3.

"A Feast at St. Benoit-sur-Loire," *BACh*, VI (June 1936), 89-92.

"The Late Mr. G. K. Chesterton," *BACh*, VI (September 1936), 164-65.

"The Relationship Between Mass and Benediction," *The Clergy Review*, XII (September 1936), 73-89.

"The Man Who Sings a Hymn to God," *BACh*, VI (December 1936), 229-35.

"Abbot Benedict Gariador," *BACh*, VI (December 1936), 251-54.

"Prayers Before the Blessed Sacrament Exposed," *The Clergy Review*, VIII (January 1937), 1-10.

"La Promesse du Paraclet," *Irénikon*, XIV (mai – juin 1937), 217-27.

"Saint Philip Neri," *BACh*, VII (June 1937), 73-79.

"The Catholic Nurse," *BACh*, VII (September 1937), 141-47.

"Christmas Good Wish," *BACh*, VII (December 1937), 205-7.

"Le Sacrifice des Croyants," *La Vie Spirituelle*, t. 51 (1937), 113-28.

"St. Thomas of Canterbury," *The Tablet*, CLXXI (January 8, 1938), 62.

"Divine Preparations," *The Clergy Review*, XIV (January 1938), 25-40.

"Dom Edmond Boussard," *BACh*, VIII (March 1938), 5-7.

"The Salutation of Christendom," *BACh*, VIII (March 1938), 1-4.

"Sermon by the Abbot of Buckfast," *BACh*, VIII (March 1938), 7-9.

"The Glorification of Christ and the Eucharist," *BACh*, VIII (June 1938), 69 - 79.

"The Mother of the Risen Christ," *BACh*, VIII (September 1938), 137-42.

"The Late Miss G. Wills," *BACh*, (September 1938), 179-80.

"Greetings of the Season," *BACh*, VIII (December 1938), 200.

"St. Martin of Tours," *BACh*, VIII (December 1938), 201-10.

POSTHUMOUS PUBLICATIONS

"The Kingship of Christ," *BACh*, IX (March 1939), 39-46.

"The Religious Position in Germany," *BACh*, IX (Summer, 1939), 69-74.

"The Promise of the Spirit," *BACh*, IX (Winter, 1939), 188-97.

"The Christian Image of Man," *BACh*, X (Summer, 1940), 55-63.

"A Great Mystery for Little People," *BACh*, X (Autumn, 1940), 114-16.

"Knowing Christ," *BACh*, XI (Spring, 1941), 1-3.

"The Grace of Repentance," *BACh*, XII (Spring, 1942), 2-3.

"The Catholic Layman and the Sacrifice of the Mass," *BACh*, XII (Summer, 1942), 41-45.

"A Victory of Faith," *BACh*, XII (Autumn, 1942), 77-80.

"Witness to the Resurrection," *BACh*, XIII (Spring, 1943), 1-7.

"St. Gregory the Great and St. Augustine of Canterbury," *BACh* XVII (Spring, 1947), 21-28.

"Bona Mors," *BACh*, XIX (Spring, 1949), 28.

II. UNPUBLISHED WORKS OF DOM ANSCAR VONIER

"De Infinito," Doctoral Thesis in the Faculty of Philosophy, Rome: P. U. Anselmiana, 1900.

Sermon preached at Buckfast Abbey, Sunday, July 11, 1910. "The People of God," "The Brethren of Jesus," "The Mother of God," "The flock of Peter," The Body of Christ," "The Salt of the Earth," Series of Sermons preached at Westminster Cathedral, Lent, 1920.

"God in the Midst of Men," Unfinished Article begun at Buckfast Abbey, April 6, 1921, 1-34.

"The Holy Spirit," Retreat preached at Grayshott, May 9-13, 1921.

"The Passion of Our Lord," Sermon preached at Buckfast Abbey, January 1923.

"Invention of the Holy Cross," Sermon preached at Buckfast Abbey, May 3, 1925.

"The Element of Honour in Christianity," Sermon preached at Buckfast Abbey, February 17, 1938.

"The Spiritual Principle in Man," Lecture to the Catholic Students of London University, (not dated).

"Instaurare Omnia in Christo," Series of Conferences at St. Scholastica's Abbey, Teignmouth (not dated).

"The Christian Pasch," Sermon for Easter, Buckfast Abbey (not dated).

"The Dignity of Christian Thinking," "The Christian Position," Series of Conferences (Place and date not marked).

"The Gifts of the Holy Ghost," Series of Sermons preached at Buckfast Abbey (not dated).

"The Struggle round the Honour of the Son of God," Sermon preached at Buckfast Abbey, February 28 (year not indicated).

"The Glory of the Passion," Sermon preached (place and date not marked).

"Christ's Glorification from the Father," Sermon preached (place and date not marked).

"Doxa," Sermon preached (place and date not marked).

"St. Leo the Great," Conference (place and date not marked).

"The Salutation of Christendom," Sermon preached at Buckfast Abbey on the Feast of the Annunciation, March 25 (year not marked).

"1 Cor.4: 1;" Sermon preached on the occasion of a Priestly Ordination, Buckfast Abbey (not dated).

III.   THE WORKS ON DOM ANSCAR VONIER

A. Books

Froehle, Ch. *The Idea of Sacred Sign According to Abbot Anscar Vonier.* Rome: Catholic Book Agency, 1968.

Graf, E. *Abbot of Buckfast: A Study of Anscar Vonier.* London: Burns and Oates, 1963.

Stephan, J. *Buckfast Abbey Guide.* Revised edition. Devon: Buckfast Abbey, 1965.

In Memoriam Abbot Vonier, 1875-1938. Bristol: Buckfast Abbey Publications by the Burleigh Press, 1939.

B. Articles

Conway, B. L. Review of *A Key to the Doctrine of the Eucharist*, by Anscar Vonier, Catholic World, CXXII (January 1926), 560-61.

Diekmann, G. Review of *The People of God*, by Anscar Vonier, *Orate Fratres*, XII (June 1938), 380-81.

______________. Review of *The Sketches and Studies in Theology*, by Anscar Vonier, *Orate Fratres*, XV (December 1940), 92-93.

Fehrenbacher, B. "The Works of Abbot Vonier: A Spiritual Edifice," *BACh*, VI (September 1936), 157-63.

Graf, E. "Abbot Anscar Vonier," *BACh*, IX (March 1939), 22-30.

______________. "Abbot Vonier as a Spiritual Writer," *BACh*, XXXII (Spring, 1962), 37-46.

__________. "The Late Abbot of Buckfast, *The Tablet*, CLXXV (May 4, 1940), 429-30.

Graham, A. "The Work of Abbot Vonier," *The Tablet*, CLXXV (April 13, 1940), 353-54.

__________. "The Work of Abbot Vonier," *The Tablet*, CLXXV (May 11, 1940), 453.

James, S. B. "Dom Anscar Vonier: A Man of the People," *Orate Fratres* XIII (April 1939), 264-69.

Parker, S. Review of Vols. I and II of *The Collected Works of Abbot Vonier*, by Anscar Vonier, *Blackfriars*, XXXIII (December 1952), 524-25.

Upson, W. "Abbot Anscar Vonier," *BACh*, IX (March 1939), 1-7.

__________. "Anscar Vonier," *The Dublin Review*, CCIV (April 1939), 236-46.

__________. "The Essential Vonier: A Vision of the Whole," *The Tablet*, CCIII (January 9, 1954), 35-36.

__________. "Abbot Anscar Vonier," *In Memoriam Abbot Vonier*, Sermon preached at the funeral of the Abbot of Buckfast, Devon: The Buckfast Abbey Publication, 1938, 1-7.

"The Victory of Christ," A review of *The Victory of Christ*, by Anscar Vonier, *The Ecclesiastical Review*, XCII (April 1935), 438-39.

R. S. (cryptic abbreviation of author's name) Review of *The Human Soul*, by Anscar Vonier, O. S. B., *BACh*, IX (March 1939), 115-16.

IV. OTHER REFERENCE WORKS

A. Books

Alfaro, J. "Eucaristia e impegno Cristiano per la trasformazione del mondo," in *Cristologia e Antropologia*. Assisi: Cittadella Editrice, 1979.

Aquinas, Th. *De Veritate*. 9th edition revised. Vol. I of *Quaestiones Disputatae*. Torino: Marietti, 1953.

__________. *Summa Contra Gentiles*. 2 Vols., Editio Leonina. Roma: Riccardi Garrone, 1918-26.

__________. *Summa Theologiae*. 5 Vols., Mariti: Biblioteca De Autores Christianos, 1952.

Baker, R. J. *Symbol in the Thought of Schubert M. Ogden*. Rome: P. U. G., 1977.

Balasuriya, T. *The Eucharist and Human Liberation*. New York: Orbis Books, 1979.

Baudrillard, J. *L'Échange Symbolique et la Mort*. Paris: Galimard, 1976.

Benoit, P. "L'istituzione dell-Eucaristia: Testi e Prospettive Teologiche," in *Enciclopedia Eucaristica* (A cura di Innos BIFFI). Milano: Ed. Paoline, 1964, 15-45.

Bettenson, H. ed. & tr. *The Early Christian Fathers*. Oxford, New York: Oxford University Press, 1956.

Betz, J. *Die Eucharistie in der Zeit der Griechischen Väter*. Band I/1: Die Aktualprasenz der Person und des Heilswerkes Jesu im Abendmahl nach der Vorephesischen Griechischen Patristik. Freiburg: Verlag Herder, 1955. Band II/1" Die realprasenz des Liebes und Blutes Jesu im Abendmahl nach dem Neuen Testament. Freiburgh: Verlag Herder, 1964.

——————————. "Eucharist," in *Sacramentum Mundi*. Ed. Karl Rahner, Vol. I, London: Burns & Oates, 1969, 1214-33.

Bouyer, L. *Eucharist*. London: Notre Dame Press, 1968.

——————————. *Eucharist, Theology and Spirituality of the Eucharistic Prayer*. Tr. Ch. Underhill Quinn, London: University of Notre Dame Press, 1969.

Boyer, Ch. *Essais sur la Doctrine de Saint Augustin*. Paris: Beauchesne et ses fils, 1932.

Cabie, R. *The Eucharist*. Collegeville, Minnesota: The Liturgical Press, 1986.

Carena, O. *Cena pasquale ebraica per comunità cristiane: Haggadah*. Torino: Marietti, 1980.

Chenderlin, F. *"Do This As My Memorial"*. Rome: Biblical Institute Press, 1982.

Clark, F. *Eucharistic Sacrifice and the Reformation*. London: Darton, Longman & Todd, 1960.

Coupe, Ch. *Lectures on the Holy Eucharist*. London: R. and T. Washbourne, Ltd., 1906.

Daly, R. J. *The Origins of the Christian Doctrine of Sacrifice*. London: Darton, Longman & Todd Ltd., 1978.

De Vaux, R. *Ancient Israel: Its Life and Institutions*. London: Darton, Longman & Todd Ltd., 1961.

Dix, M. *The Sacramental System*. London: Longman, Green & Co., 1893.

Dufourcq, A. *Saint Irénée*. Paris: Librairie Bloud, 1905.

Durrwell, F. X. *L'Eucaristia: Sacramento del Mistero Pasquale*. Trans. Elena de Rosa, Roma: Editrice Paoline, 1983.

Eliade, M. *Traite d'Histoire des Religions*. Paris: Payot, 1949.

Emminghaus, J. M. *The Eucharist: Essence, Form, Celebration*. Collegeville, Minnesota: The Liturgical Press, 1978.

Evans, M. *Is Jesus Really Present in the Eucharist?* London: Catholic Truth Society, 1986.

Fairweather, E. R. ed. *The Oxford Movement*. New York: Oxford University Press, 1964.

Filograssi, I. *De Sanctissima Eucharistia: Questiones Dogmaticae Selectae*. Roma: P. U. G., 1968.

Flannery, A. gen. ed. *Vatican Council II: The Conciliar and Post Conciliar Documents*. Dublin: Dominican Publications, 1981.

Galbiati, E. "Riti, simboli e temi che preparano l'Eucaristia," in *L'Eucaristia nella Bibbia*. Milano: Jaca Book, 1968, 15-105.

Ganoczy, A. *An Introduction to Catholic Sacramental Theology*. New York, Ramsey: Paulist Press, 1984.

Gerken, A. *Teologia dell'Eucaristia*. Milano: Edizione Pauline, 1986.

Girard, R. *La Violence et le Sacré*. Paris: Grasset, 1972.

_____________. *The Cross and the Altar*. New York: Joseph F. Wagner INC., 1937.

Glenn, P. J. *A Tour of the Summa*. Rockford: Tan Books and Publishers, INC., 1978.

Goosens, W. *Les Origines de l'Eucharistie, Sacrament et Sacrifice*. Paris: Beauchesne, 1931.

Guilloux, P. *L'ame de Saint Augustin*. Paris: Propriété de J. de Gidord, 1921.

Guzie, T. *Jesus and the Eucharist*. New York: Paulist Press, 1974.

Hamer, J. *L'Église est une Communion*. Paris: Les Éditions du Cerf, 1962. English edition: *The Church is a Communion*. Trans. Ronald Matthew. London: Geoffery Chapman, 1964.

Hardlin, A. *The Tractarian Understanding of the Eucharist*. Uppsala: Almquist and Wiksells, 1965.

Häring, B. *Grazia e compito dei sacramenti*. Roma: Edizioni Paoline, 1965.

Hedley, J. C. *The Holy Eucharist*. London: Longman, Green & Co., 1907.

Hengel, M. *The Atonement: A Study of the Origins of the Doctrine in the New Testament*. London: SCM Press, 1981.

—————————. *La Crucifixion dans l'Antiquité et la Folie du Message de la Croix*. Paris: Le Cerf, 1981.

Houssiau, A. *La Christologie de Saint Irénée*. Louvain: Publications Universitaires de Louvain, 1955.

Iserloh, E. *Der Kampf um die Messe in den ersten Jahren der Auseinandersetzung mit Luther*. Münster: Aschendorff, 1952.

Jeremias, J. *Eucharistic Words of Jesus*. Trans. Norman Perrin, London: SCM Press., 1982.

John Paul II. *The Bread of life*. Athlone, Ireland: St. Paul Publications, 1982.

Jungmann, J. A. *The Mass*. Collegeville: Minnesota: The Liturgical Press, 1976.

Jurgens, W. A. *The Faith of the Early Fathers*. 3 Vols., Collegeville, Minnesota: The Liturgical Press, 1970-1979.

Kearney, J. *The Meaning of the Mass*. London & Dublin: Burns, Oates and Washbourne, 1936.

Kelly, J. N. D. *Early Christian Doctrines*. London: A & C Black Ltd., 1977.

Kilmartin, E. J. *Christian Liturgy*. Kansas City: Sheed & Ward, 1988.

Lafont, G. *Dieu le Temps et L'Être*. Paris: Les Éditions du Cerf, 1986.

Lattey, C. *Catholic Faith in the Holy Eucharist*. Cambridge: W. Heffer and Sons Ltd., 1924.

Leeming, B. *Principles of Sacramental theology*. 2nd ed., Westminster, Maryland: The Newman Press, 1960.

Le Blond, J. M. *Les Conversions de Saint Augustin*. Paris: Éditions Montaigne, 1947.

Léon Dufour, X. *Le Partage du Pain Eucharistique selon le Nouveau Testament*. Paris: Ed. Du Seuil, 1982.

Lepin, M. *L'Idée du Sacrifice de la Messe d'après les theologiens depuis l'origine jusqu'à nos Jours*. Lyon: Gabriel Beauchesne, 1926.

Ligier, L. *Il Sacramento dell'Eucaristia* (uso degli studenti). Roma: P. U. G. 1977.

Miller, B. V. *The Eucharistic Sacrifice*. London: Burns, Oates and Washbourne, 1930.

Neuner, J. and Dupuis, J. eds. *The Christian Faith*. London: Collins Liturgical publications, 1983.

Nicolas, M. J. *What is the Eucharist?* London: Burns and Oates, 1960.

O'Neill, C. *New Approaches to the Eucharist*. Dublin & Sydney: Gill and Son, 1967.

O'Neill, A. M. *The Mystery of the Eucharist*. Dublin: M. H. Gill and Son Ltd., 1933.

Perrin, J. M. *L'Eucharistie: De l'Évangile a Vatican II*. Doctrine pour le Peuple de Dieu, no. 8, Paris: Beauchesne, 1971.

Power, D. N. *The Sacrifice We Offer: The Tridentine Dogma and Its Reinterpretation*. Edinburgh: T. & T. Clark Ltd., 1987.

Powers, J. M. *Eucharistic Theology*. London: Burns and Oates, 1967.

Quinn, J. *Theology Today: The Theology of the Eucharist*. Cork and Dublin: The Mercier Press, 1973.

Rahner, K. and Hausling, A. *The Celebration of the Eucharist*. London: Burns and Oates, Herder and Herder, 1966-68.

__________. *Le Sacrifice Unique et la fréquence des Messes*. Traduit de l'allemand par Charles Müller. Tradition revue par Daniel Olivier. Paris: Desclée de Brouwer, 1972.

Rahner, K. *Kirche und Sakramente*. Freiburg: Verlag Herder, 1958. English edition: *The Church and the Sacraments*. Trans. W. J. O'Hara. London: Burns and Oates, 1963.

__________. *Encyclopedia of Theology: A Concise Sacramentum Mundi*. London: Burns and Oates, 1975.

__________. *L'Eucaristia in Chiesa e Sacramenti*. Brescia: Queriniana, 1969.

__________. *Sull'Eucaristia: meditazione teologiche*. Brescia: Queriniana, 1969, 31-32.

Renward, L. and Johanny, R. *Eucaristia: aspetti e problemi dopo il Vaticano II*. Assisi: Cittadella, 1968.

Righetti, M. *I sacramenti – I sacramentali*. 2nd ed. Revised. Vol. IV of Manuale di storia liturgica. Milano: Ancora, 1959.

Rocchetta, C. *I sacramenti della fede*. Bologna: Edizione Dehoniane, 1985.

Roquet, A. M. *Les Sacrements: Signes de Vie*. Paris: Les Éditions du Cerf, 1952. English edition: *Christ Acts Through the Sacraments*. Trans. Carlsbrooke Dominicans. Collegeville, Minnesota: The Liturgical Press, 1954.

——————————. *La cena del signore: la messa oggi*. Milano: Ed. OR, 1970.

Rordorf, W. *The Eucharist of the Early Christians*. Trans. M. J. O'Connell. New York: Pueblo Publishing Co., 1978.

Rosato, Ph. J. *De Eucaristia et de Sacerdotio: Schemi Elaborati*. Roma: P. U. G., 1983.

Rossi, L. G. *L'Eucaristia, Mistero di fede, cuore della Chiesa*. Genova: Stringa Ed., 1970.

Sartore, D., Triacca, A. M. *Nuovo dizionario di liturgia*. Roma: Edizione Pauline, 1984.

Schmaus, M. *Dogma 5: The Church as Sacrament*. London: Sheed & ward, 1975.

Segundo, J. L. *Il messaggio Cristiano oggi, IV: I sacramenti oggi*. Brescia: Morcelliana, 1974.

Sheerin, D. J. *The Eucharist: Message of the Fathers of the Church 7*. Delaware: west Fourth Street, 1986.

Smith, G. D. *The Sacrament of the Eucharist*. London: Burns, Oates and Washbourne, 1930.

Sobrino, J. "Jesus in the Service of God's Kingdom," *Christology at the Crossroad*. London: SCM Press, 1978, 41-79.

Tillard, J. *L'Eucaristia: Pasqua della Chiesa*. Roma: Edizioni Paoline, 1965.

Wainwright, G. *Eucharist and Eschatology*. London: Epworth Press, 1971.

Watteville, J. *Le Sacrifice dans les Textes Eucharistiques des Premiers Siècles*. Neuchatel: Delachaux et Niestle, 1966.

Winklhofer, A. *L'Eucaristia come celebrazione pasquale*. Brescia. Morcellina, 1969.

Young, F. *Sacrifice and the Death of Christ*. London: SCM Press, 1983.

——————————. *The Use of Sacrificial Ideas in Greek Christian Writers from the New Testament to John Chrysostom*. Philadelphia: The Philadelphia Patristic Foundation, 1979.

240   Bibliography

B. Articles

Adamo, D. T. "The Lord's Supper in 1 Corinthians 10: 14-22, 11: 17-34," *Africa Theological Journal*, 18 (1989), 36-48.

Amphaoux, C. B. "Le Dernier Repas de Jesus. Lc. 22: 15-20, par," in Études *Théologique et Religieuses*, 56 (1981), 449-54.

Bandstra, A. J. "Interpretation in 1 Corinthians 10: 1-11," *Calvin Theological Journal*, 6 (1971), 5-21.

Benoit, P. "Le Récit de la Cène dans Lc. XXII: 15-20," *Revue Biblique*, 48 (1939).

Betz, J. "Sacrifice and Thanksgiving," *Theology Digest*, 17 (1967), 16.

Bonnard, P. "Mattieu 25: 31-46: Questions de lecture et d'interprétation," *Foi et Vie*, (1977), 81 - 87.

Box, G. H. "The Jewish Antecedents of the Eucharist," *The Journal of Theological Studies*, 3 (1902), 357-69.

Braaten, C. E., "The Christian Doctrine of Salvation," *Interpretation*, 35 (1981), 117-31.

Brosnan, J. B. "Thomist Metaphysics and the Sacrament-sacrifice," *Irish Eccl. Record*, t. 6, (1946), 289-97.

Burkitt, F. C. "The Last Supper and the Paschal Meal," *The Journal of Theological Studies*, 9 (1908), 569-71.

Byrom, J. K. "Eucharistic Theology Today," *Theology*, 77 (1974), 124-27.

Catchpole, D. R. "The Poor on Earth and the Son of Man in Heaven: A Re-appraisal of Matthew 25: 31-46," *Bulletin of the John Rylands Library*, 61 (1979), 355-97.

Chadwick, H. "Luke 22: 15-20," *Harvard Theological Review*, 1 (1957), 249-59.

Coffey, D. "A Christological Note on the Memorial-Saying of Jesus," *Faith and Culture*, 13 (1987), 35-44.

Collela, P. "L'ultima Cena una cena pasquale?" *Lateranum*, 2 (1984), 330-43.

Cook, W. R. "Eschatology in John's Gospel," *Criswell Theological Review*, 3 (1988), 79-99.

Cooke, B. "The Eucharistic Mystery," *The Bible Today*, 14 (1964), 336-41.

Coppens, J. "Les Origines de l'Eucharistie d'après les Livres de NT.," *Ephemerides Theologicae Lovanienses*, 2 (1934), 54-62.

__________. "Les Soit-disant Analogies Juives de l'Eucharistie," *Ephemerides Theologicae Lovanienses*, 8 (1931), 238-48.

__________. "L'Eucharistie des Temps Apostoliques," *Ephemerides Theologicae Lovanienses*, 53(1977), 192-201.

__________. "La Celebration Eucharistique: Ses Origines et son Adaption," *Ephemerides Theologicae Lovanienses*, 50 (1974), 263-69.

__________. "L'Evolution des Rites Eucharistique du NT. Au IV Siècle," *Ephemerides Thologicae Lovanienses*, 50 (1974), 269-72.

Coventry, J. "Eucharistic Presence," *One in Christ*, 4 (1968), 267.

Delorme, J. "La Cène et la Pàque dans le NT." *Lumen Vitae*, 31 (1957), 9-41.

De Vogel, C. J. "The Eucharist Today," *Theology Today*, 25 (1977), 24-31.

Didier, J. Ch. "L'Eucharistie: Problèmes du Temps Présent," *Esprit et Vie*, 80 (1970), 49-59, 129-39, 441-50.

Dobbs, F. "The Church: The Body of Christ, *Search*, 11 (1988), 82-86.

Feuillet, A. "Le Caractère Universel du Jugement et la Charité sans Frontières an Mt. 25: 31-46," *Nouvelle Revue Théologique*, 102 (1980), 179-96.

Flood, E. "Paul on the Resurrection," *Clergy Review*, 69 (1984), 140-44.

Garlatti, G. J. "La eucaristia como memoria y proclamación de la muerte del Señor," *Revista Biblica*, 47 (1985), 1-25.

Gisel, P. "Du Sacrifice: L'Avènement de la Personne face à la Peur de la Vie et la Fascination de la Mort," *Foi et Vie*, 83 (1984), 1-45.

Gourgues, M. "Section Christologique et Section Eucharistique en Jean VI: Une Proposition," *Revue Biblique*, 88 (1981), 515-31.

Grassi, A. J. "The Eucharist in the Gospel of Mark," *The American Ecclesial Review*, (1974), 133-38.

__________. "I was Hungry and You Gave Me to Eat, (Matt. 25: 35 ff.): The Divine Identification in Matthew," *Biblical Theological Bulletin*, 11 (1981), 81-84

Guzie, T. "The Church as a Eucharistic Community," *Chicago Studies*, 22 (1983), 283-96.

Hahn, F. "Herrengedächtnis und Herrenmahl bei Paulus," *Liturgisches Jahrbuck*, 32 (1982), 166-77.

Hall, B. "Our Sacrifice," *Bellarmine Commentary*, 1 (1956), 48-53.

Hellwig, M. K. "The Christian Eucharist in Relation to Jewish Worship," *Journal of Ecumenical Studies*, 13 (1976) 322-30.

Hickling, C. "The Eucharist and Time," *Theology*, 80 (1977) 197-203.

Hiers, R. H. and Kennedy, C. A. "The Bread and Fish Eucharist in the Gospels and Early Christian Art," *Perspectives in Religious Studies*, 3 (1976), 20-47.

Higgins, J. B. "The Origin of the Eucharist," *New Testament Studies*, (1954-1955), 200-9.

Hook, N. "The Dominical Cup Saying," *Theology*, 77 (1974), 624-30.

Hughes, J. J. "Eucharistic Sacrifice Transcending the Reformation Deadlock," *Worship*, 43 (1969), 532-44.

Inch, M. A. "Matthew and the House-Churches," *Evangelical Quarterly*, 43 (1971), 196-202.

Jamoulle, E. "Le Sacrifice Eucharistique au Concile de Trente," *N. R. T.*, t. 67 (1945), 1121-39.

Jeremias, J. "This is My Body…," *The Expository Times*, 83 (1972), 196-203.

Jones, P. R. "1 Corinthians 15: 8: Paul the Last Apostle," *Tyndale Bulletin*, 36 (1985), 3-34.

Kilmartin, E. J. "Current Theology: Sacramental Theology. The Eucharist in Recent Literature," *Theological Studies*, 32 (1971), 233-77.

——————————. "Eucharist as Sacrifice," *New Catholic Encyclopedia*, Vol. 5 (1967), 609-15.

——————————. "The Eucharistic Cup in the Primitive Liturgy," *The Catholic Biblical Quarterly*, 24 (1962), 32-43.

Klauck, H. J. "Der Gottesdienst in der Gemeinde von Korinth," *Pastoralblatt*, 39 (1984), 11-20.

Knockaert, A. "A Fresh Look at the Eschatological Discourse (Mt. 24-25)," *Lumen Vitae*, 40 (1985), 167-79.

Lapoorta, J. "'…Whatever you did for one of the least of these… you did for me' (matt. 25: 31-46)," *Journal of Theology for Southern Africa*, 68 (1989), 103-9.

LaVerdiere, E. "The Breaking of Bread," *Emmanuel*, 95 (1989), 554-60, 577.

Léon Dufour, X. "Do This in Memory of Me," *Theology Digest*, 26, 1 (1978), 36-42.

——————————. "'Faites Cèci en Mémoire de Moi.' Lc 22: 19 – 1

Corinthiens 11, 25," *Christus*, 24 (1977), 200-8.

Linskens, J. "The Eucharist in the Synoptic Gospels," *Teaching All Nations* (East Asian Pastoral Institute), 2 (1978), 83-90.

Luke, K. "The Night in Which He was Delivered up," (1 Cor. 11: 23)," *Biblebhashyam*, 10 (1984), 261-79.

Lussier, E. "Some Reflections on the Narratives of the Institution of the Eucharist. Scripture Survey," *Chicago Studies*, 8 (1969), 249-59.

_______________. "The Eucharistic Bread and Wine," *Emmanuel*, 79, 2 (1973), 64-71.

Madeja, S. "Analisi del concetto di concelebrazione eucaristica nel Concilio Vaticano II, e nella riforma liturgica postconciliare," *Ephemerides Liturgicae*, 96 (1982), 3-56.

Manns, F. "Le Lavement des pieds: Essai sur la Structure et la Signification de Jean 13," *Revue des Sciences Religieuses*, 55 (1981), 149-69.

Mattam, J. "The Sacrament of our Redemption: Eucharist," *Vidyajyoti*, 41 (1977), 161-70.

Moloney, F. J. "John 6 and the Celebration of the Eucharist," *Downside Review*, 93 (1975), 243-51.

Moloney, R. "The Early Eucharist: An Hypothesis of Development," *The Irish Theological Quarterly*, 45 (1978), 167-76.

_______________. "The Early Eucharist: The Jewish Background," *The Irish Theological Quarterly*, 47 (1980), 34-42.

Monsarrat, V. "Mattieu 24-25: Du Temple aux démunis," *Foi et Vie*, 76 (1977), 67-80.

Morris, A. E. "Jesus and the Eucharist," *Theology*, 26 (1973), 242-63.

Murphy-O'Connor, J. "House Churches and the Eucharist," *The Bible Today*, 22 (1984), 32-38.

Navone, J. "The Parable of the Banquet," *The Bible Today*, 14 (1964), 923-29.

Nereparampil, L. "A New Commandment I Give You: Johannine Understanding of Love," *Jeevadhara*, 13 (1983), 104-14.

Osborne, K. B. "Contemporary Understanding of the Eucharist: Survey of Catholic Thinking," *Journal of Ecumenical Studies*, 13 (1989), 192-213.

Pack, F. "The Holy Spirit in the Fourth Gospel," *Restoration Quarterly*, 31 (1989), 139-48.

Plevnik, J. "The Centre of Pauline Theology," *Catholic Biblical Quarterly*, 51 (1989), 461-78.

Porter, C. L. "An Interpretation of Paul's Lord's Supper Texts: 1 Corinthians 10: 14-22 and 11: 17-34," *Encounter*, 50 (1989), 29-45.

Prout, A. "One Loaf... One Body," *Restoration Quarterly*, 1982), 78-81.

Ratzinger, J. "Form and Content in the Eucharist," *Theology Digest*, 26, 2 (1978), 117-21.

Rewak, W. J. "Symbolism and the Eschatological Discourses," *The Bible Today*, 14 (1964), 931-35.

Richardson, P. and Gooch, P. W. "Accommodation Ethics," *Tyndale Bulletin*, 29 (1978), 89-142.

Rosato, Ph. J. "S. Agostino: I poveri e la comunione con il corpo del Signore," *La nuova alleanza*, 5 (1988), 219-224.

Roullard, P. H. "From Human Meal to Christian Eucharist," *Worship*, 52 (1978), 425-39, 53 (1979), 40-56.

Sage, A. "En Marge du Sacrifice de la Messe: Le Role du Pain et du Vin," *L'Année Théol.*, t. 6 (1945), 75-95.

Schurman, H. "Jesus' Words in the Light of His Actions at the Last Supper," *Concilium*, 2 (1968), 61-67.

Schussler, F. E. "Partecipazione all mensa e celebrazione dell'Eucaristia," *Concilium*, 2 (1982), 15-32, 171-88.

Sesboue, B. "Esquisses Critique d'une Théologie de la Rédemption," *Nouvelle Revue Thélogique*, 106 (1984), 801-16 et 107 (1985), 68-86.

Sloyan, G. "Primitive and Pauline Concepts of the Eucharist," *The Catholic Biblical Quarterly*, 23 (1961), 1-13.

Stegner, W. R. "Lucan Priority in the Feeding of the Five Thousand," *Biblical Research*, 21 (1976), 19-28.

Suriano, T. "Eucharist reveals Jesus: The Multiplication of the Loaves," *The Bible Today*, 58 (1972), 642-51.

Swanston, H. F. G. "Liturgy as Paradise and as Parousia," *Scottish Journal of Theology*, 36 (1983), 505-19.

Synge, F. C. "Common Bread: The Craftsmanship of a Theologian," *Theology*, 75 (1972), 131-35.

Taft, R. "La frequenza dell'Eucaristia nella storia," *Concilium*, 2 (1982), 33-53.

Talley, Th. J. "From Berakah to Eucharistia: A Reopening Question," *Worship*, 50 (March, 1976), 115-36.

Van Cangh, J. M. "Le Thème des Poissons dans les Récits Évangélique de la Multiplication des Pains," *Revue Biblique*, 78 (1971), 71-83.

Vollert, C. "The Eucharist: Quests for Insights from Scripture," *Theological Studies*, 21 (1960), 404-43.

Walvoord, J. F. "Christ's Olivet Discourse on the End of the Age," *Bible Society Record*, 129 (1972), 307-15.

Werner, E. "The Eucharist in Hebrew Literature during the Apostolic and Post-Apostolic Epoch," *Journal of Ecumenical Studies*, 13 (1976), 316-22.

Winter, B. W. "The Lord's Supper at Corinth: An Alternative Reconstruction," *Reformed Theological Review*, 37 (1978), 73-82.

Index

C

Humanity 14, 18, 21-22, 25, 29, 36, 42, 57, 81, 90, 92-100, 102-105, 108-110, 120, 132-133, 139, 142, 145, 152, 169, 175, 184, 194, 196, 198, 200, 206, 208, 213, 219

Humiliation 77-79, 98, 101, 167, 194

Hungry 193-195, 222

Hypocritical 27

I

Icon 29

Identity 54, 64, 68, 104, 105, 111, 121, 126, 128, 132, 146, 157, 174, 176, 196

Immolation 26, 29, 41-42, 54, 64, 70, 74-76, 78-80, 82-83, 94-95, 120, 165, 173, 220

Immutability 55, 174

Impassibility 55, 174

Incarnate 19-20, 23, 27, 90, 92-94, 100, 103, 120, 125-126, 129, 175-176, 181

Incarnation 14, 20, 23, 35, 39, 60, 92, 93, 96, 127, 130, 133, 138-139, 170, 176, 183, 208, 213, 221, 227

Inchoate 225

Infidel 109

Inheritance 13, 16, 19, 25, 98-100, 102, 106, 175

Inheritors 16, 99

In mysterio 76

In nobis 14, 166, 177, 219

In sacramento 76

Insights 13, 15, 42, 51, 63, 84, 130, 133, 148, 163-164, 166, 168, 175, 180-181, 184, 188, 195, 204, 207, 210, 214, 221

Institution 22-23, 36, 147, 151

Intellectual 15, 17, 34, 39, 57, 163, 180, 197, 224

Invisible 21, 32, 61-62, 76, 114, 118, 138, 143, 202, 214

Irenaeus 167, 183-184, 204, 208-210, 212-214, 223-224

Iserloh 237

Israel 16, 60, 235

J

Jerusalem 17, 141

Jesus 14, 16, 20-22, 24-26, 28-30, 32-33, 35-40, 42-43, 53-54, 56-58, 60, 62-68, 70, 72-79, 82, 90-95, 97-104, 107-108, 111, 115-121, 126-127, 129-132, 134-135, 137-138, 142-143, 148, 150-152, 164-169, 171-173, 175-178, 180-181, 183, 189-196, 198-200, 203, 204-206, 209, 212-213, 219-220, 222, 224-225, 232, 236-237, 239-240, 243-244

Jews 16

Johannine 180-181, 195, 197, 200, 222, 224, 243

John 74, 166, 181, 189, 196, 214, 222, 237, 239-240, 243

Jubilee 34

Z